THE SCARY WORLD OF NUCLEAR WEAPONS

AGENDA FOR ELIMINATION

Gar Pardy

Agora Books™
Ottawa, Canada

The Scary World of Nuclear Weapons. Agenda for Elimination

Copyright © 2023 by Gar Pardy

All Rights Reserved. No part of this book may be reproduced, stored in a retrieval system, or transmitted, in any form or by any means, electronic, mechanical, photocopying, recording or otherwise, without the expressed written consent of Agora Books.

The views, opinions and perceptions of the author of the book herein expressed in this text are intended to support civil and creative social discussion in Canada and internationally.

Care has been taken to trace the ownership/source of any references made in this text. The publisher welcomes any information that will enable a rectification in subsequent edition(s) of any incorrect or omitted reference or credit.

Agora Books
B.P. 24191
300 Eagleson Rd.
Kanata, Ontario K2M 2C3 CANADA

Agora Books is a trade mark of The Agora Cosmopolitan which is a not-for-profit corporation.

ISBN 978-1-77838-036-5

The author acknowledges the use of a variety of sources for the information used in this document and especially with appreciation to the publications of the American Federation of Science, the International Atomic Energy Agency, The Stockholm International Peace Research Institute (SIPRI), Wikipedia, the Carnegie Endowment for International Peace, the Nuclear Suppliers Group, the American Arms Control Association and the UN Office for Disarmament Affairs.

Other Writings by Gar Pardy

Consular and Diplomatic Protection in an Age of Terrorism, The Human Rights of Anti-Terrorism, Eds. Nicole Laviolette & Craig Forcese, Irwin Law, Toronto, 2008.

Shared Vison or Myopia: The Politics of Perimeter Security and Economic Competitiveness, Rideau Institute, 2011.

The Long Way Home: The Saga of Omar Khadr, Omar Khadr Oh Canada, Ed. Janice Williamson, McGill-Queen's University Press, Montreal, 2012.

Afterwords From a Foreign Service Odyssey, Friesen Press, Victoria, 2015.

Canadians Abroad: A Policy and Legislative Agenda, Rideau Institute & Canadian Centre for Policy Alternatives, 2016.

Kidnapped Canadians: The Need for Policy Change, Rideau Institute, 2017.

China in a Changing World, Agora Books, Ottawa, 2020.

For Laurel, Julian, and Michael and Kari and Rowan and Shania
Close Companions on the Odyssey of Life

Contents

Preface 9

Introduction 14

2. The Scary World 18

3. The Countries of the Scary Nuclear World. 34

4. Nuclear Weapons and Their Science 82

5. The Manhattan Project 90

6. Nuclear Weapons and Hiroshima and Nagasaki 111

7. Control and Management of the Scary World 143

8. Soviet/Russian and American Agreements on Nuclear Weapons . 152

9. Elimination of Nuclear Weapons 157

10. Nuclear Weapons, Testing and Delivery 161

11. Peaceful Uses of Nuclear Energy 172

12. Agenda and Measures for The Elimination of Nuclear Weapons . 179

13. Canadian Involvement in the Scary World 194

Annexures 200
    A. Terms Associated with Nuclear Weapons 201
    B. International Agreements on the Non-Proliferation,
    Testing and Elimination of Nuclear Weapons 206

Index 265

Biographical Note 274

Preface

The scary face of nuclear weapons has been hidden for some time; now it is being revealed once more, uglier than ever. The errant, wobbly Ukrainian missile missed the incoming Russian one and landed in Poland, killing two people. Tweets from mischievous calamitists push the world into World War III, using NATO's collective policy of "one for all, and all for one." Meanwhile, President Putin, who has lost more generals than the British have lost Prime Ministers, remains confident that his threats of nuclear weapons will salvage his reputation and that of the Russian military after a year marked by the carnage of a war he started. In Asia, the snarling wolf of Asian diplomacy, President Kim of North Korea, lobs his seemingly endless supply of nuclear capable missile towards California and beyond. In the meantime, China increases its own stockpile of nuclear weapons. And in the Middle East, the bully of Israeli politics is back as Prime Minister Netanyahu, having walked past the prison gates, will soon threaten once more that "Iran will never have nuclear weapons." Meanwhile, the quivering voice of American power says "never, never, never" to the Russian nuclear threats, yet cannot find the off switch for Iranian centrifuges inexorably spinning toward the production of weapons-grade uranium. Sleep will not knit up this "raveled sleave of care." The night threatens as we sit in the twilight of nuclear weapons while the adults of global politics sleep on.

1959 was a year that loomed large in the world of nuclear weapons. It had been less than fifteen years since the destruction of Hiroshima and Nagasaki, and now the Americans and the Chinese were quarrelling over Taiwan. There were suggestions there might be need for the United States to resort to the big ones once again. That episode passed with Quemoy and Matsu remaining part of the small island that occupied the seat for China on the Security Council. As the year began, Tom Lehrer was on the radio sardonically crooning that "We will all go together when we go . . . For the bomb that drops on you/ Gets your friends and neighbours too . . . Universal bereavement/ An inspiring achievement." This was an anthem for the Atomic Age.

I was working in Goose Bay at the time as part of a team providing weather services to the Strategic Air Command (SAC) of the United States Air Force. Early in the spring, we were all commanded to move to the edges of the runways. We were given shovels and axes to create a firebreak against an approaching forest fire. Our work quickened when we were told about the atomic bombs stored in nearby bunkers. A fortunate rain storm put a quick end to the threat of the fire, and we happily retreated to the nearest mess hall to became less sobered by the thoughts of atomic bombs.

We hummed Tom Lehrer as we worked with little understanding of the air becoming "uranious" and all of us going "simultaneous." The song was a little-understood backdrop to the delivery of an exciting new aircraft: the B-47. The bomber was still the dominant deliverer of the new weapons world-wide, a short-term interim between the B-29 that dropped the bombs on Japan and the B-52 that was to become emblematic of the nuclear age. Peter Sellers made the B-52 almost the main character in 1964's *Dr Strangelove*. But in the meantime, imbuing meaning into our work was another film that arrived at the base in 1959, Nevil Shute's dystopian *On the Beach*. There was almost quiet audience disapproval as Gregory Peck left Australia on his fictional nuclear-powered submarine to take his crew back to America to die at home in the slowly spreading nuclear winter.

The B-52 was a rarity at Goose Bay in the late fifties as it flew overhead northward, providing daily assurance that Soviet bombers were not on their way south. It lived up to its nickname as BUFF or BUFFY, the big, ugly, flying fella (the more polite rendering). We were more familiar with the B-47. It was the epitome of an airborne avenging angel striking vengeance upon the evildoers of world conflicts. As one pilot reported, the Stratojet was reluctant to leave the ground, needing the added power of 18 small rockets during take-off. At night it resembled an elementary force surrounded by fire, clawing its way into the heavens. It was even reluctant when returning to the earth, requiring a drag chute to slow down before the runway disappeared.

Late in 1959, I followed the B-52s north to Frobisher Bay, now Iqaluit and the capital of Nunavut. In 1959, it was a town of migrants rapidly expanding to support the construction of the Distant Early Warning radar sites. These were designed to provide the southern population with a few additional minutes to prepare should the Soviet Union send its bombers with nuclear weapons over the North Pole. Even the Inuit were migrants, having moved to the area as the World War II-era runway was being built. The newest migrants were part of a squadron of KC-97 aircraft, stationed there to rise up and refuel B-52s. They were "kerosene carriers," airborne gas stations that could fly into the skies and provide the B-52s loaded with atomic bombs enough fuel to reach the Soviet Union. A few years later, *Dr Strangelove* provided the less-than-fictional ending of a B-52 somewhere over the Soviet Union, with Major T. J. King Kong (Slim Pickens) strapping an atomic bomb between his legs and dropping with it into the wilds of the Soviet Union. Sex and war were never closer.

This was the dramatic era of the atomic bomb and we were its enablers. In Ottawa, the government was ineptly struggling with the issues of nuclear weapons in Canada and whether a new American defensive missile (the Bomarc) system should be based in Canada along with its nuclear armament. Over time, the intercontinental ballistic missile made this system obsolete.

My stay in the north was interrupted in the summer of 1961 with a vacation to Japan. The trip was prompted by the condition known as "bushed," or being in the north too long. Soon I was wandering the gentle land of the blossom. Throughout my years of travelling the world, there was no greater contrast than austere treeless northern

Canada and the soft gentleness of both land and people in what we then called the Far East. As an antidote for the austerity of the north, it was both magic and practical. The trip was also prompted by my reading John Hersey's *Hiroshima* fifteen or so years after its publication in 1946. It was and remains the most memorable of all reporting on the use of atomic weapons. As I had been working among wielders of nuclear weapons in 1961, I was curious to see the land where the weapons were used for the first and only time.

Surprisingly, there was little evidence of their use. Japan was now a land adapting admirably to post-war conditions. At the time, the rice farmers were complaining over the price for their crop and the alienation of their land by an industrial explosion that was on pace to make Japan one the most important players in the economy of the world. While Hiroshima now had a museum and a Peace Park memorializing its dramatic ending in 1945, the rest of the country had moved on with more confidence than most in providing a good life for its millions.

The only protesters were those objecting to the visit of the Soviet Foreign Minister, Andrei Gromyko, for the lack of progress in the return of several small Japanese northern islands after the war ended. The Soviets declared war on Japan on August 8, 1945, and it was only a week later on August 15 that the emperor announced Japan's unconditional surrender, having little to do with the Soviet declaration. The protest was a short one, ending in the midst of a small afternoon shower. The captured Japanese islands have never been returned and remain a minor irritant in Japan's relationship with today's Russia.

My travels throughout Japan in the summer of 1961 provided a needed balm before my return to the Canadian north. It also inspired me toward further education; within a year I was resident in another bucolic place, the Annapolis Valley of Nova Scotia. Acadia University became both my home and the beginning of a lifelong adventure in an understanding of a world that has had more change, and in its own way, good change, than was evident in the millennia before 1945. My entry into Canada's foreign service in 1967 provided the opportunity for that adventure to continue on a global basis.

Part of that adventure entailed efforts to deal with the legacy of the atomic bombs dropped on Japan in 1945, and this has never been far from my daily preoccupations. The slow expansion of nuclear capabilities beyond the United States continues into the years of my retirement. This book will hopefully provide some help in ensuring the end of the proliferation, and, more importantly, the elimination of the bomb from the daily machinations of intercontinental turmoil. My concerns are the same as those that existed in 1959, the same that inspired the chilling and irreverent visions of John Hersey, Tom Lehrer, Nevil Shute, and Peter Sellers; they are about the fear of where we may be heading, but more so, the hope for a better world.

Introduction

"Gentlemen, you can't fight in here! This is a war room."

Peter Sellers as American President Merkin Mulley in the 1964 Stanley Kubrick's film, ***Dr Strangelove or: How I learned to Stop Worrying and Love the Bomb***

In 2045, the world will recognize three significant and historic centenaries. The first will celebrate the end of the Second World War and the beginning of one of the most peaceful periods in human history. Associated with this has been the end of colonialism with the associated emancipation and freedom achieved by the peoples of the world through the exercise of self-determination. The second celebrated centenary will be the creation of the United Nations and its associated agencies, which support political, economic, and social changes through global cooperation, security, and peace. In 1945, 52 countries attended the first meeting of the General Assembly of the United Nations; today, 193 nations attend.

The third centenary of 2045 will not be a celebration, but rather the anniversary of the first nuclear explosion and the first and only use of nuclear weapons in war. This was the dawn of the Atomic Age. While nuclear weapons have not been deployed since they destroyed the cities of Hiroshima and Nagasaki in Japan on August 6 and 9, 1945, they loom as a dark and threatening factor of international politics. Today, there are nine nuclear weapons states instead of the original one, the United States. In 1945, the United States had an inventory of three weapons. Today, the global inventory is thousands of times greater.

Today the nine nuclear weapons states – the United State, Soviet Union/Russian, the United Kingdom, China, France, Israel, India, Pakistan, and North Korea – individually and collectively represent a grave and continuing danger to our security and well-being. While there is a global understanding of this danger, only one nation, South Africa, has ever had nuclear weapons and voluntarily dismantled and destroyed them. By contrast, there is a chance that Iran is actively working to develop a nuclear arsenal in the foreseeable future.

In the seventy-seven years since nuclear weapons were invented, there have been ongoing international efforts to contain this danger and ultimately eliminate nuclear weapons. These efforts are driven by the world-threatening dangers these weapons represent; that threat is magnified by the number of existing nuclear warheads and the possibility of further proliferation as some nations continue to engage in nuclear testing. The number of nuclear weapons peaked in 1986 when there were more than 64,000 owned by six countries – the Soviet Union, with over 40 thousand; the United States, with over 23 thousand; France, with 355; the United Kingdom, with 350; China, with 224; and Israel with over 40. Since then, India, Pakistan and North Korea have become nuclear weapons states, with each now possessing fewer than 100 weapons.

The early international efforts toward non-proliferation succeeded, partially, with the Nuclear Non-Proliferation Treaty (NPT) in 1970. Today there are 193 signatories to the Treaty. These include the five permanent members of the UN Security Council: the United States, the Soviet Union/Russia, China, France and the United Kingdom, which had their nuclear weapons programs legitimized if not legalized by the Treaty. At the time, the five made a treaty commitment to initiate actions for the elimination of nuclear weapons. In the aftermath of the Treaty, the United States and the Soviet Union commenced bilateral discussions resulting in their inventories being reduced to 5500 and 6000 respectively.

Today, the Russian-American bilateral discussions have come to an end, except for minor exchanges of information at the working level as required by the 2010 Strategic Arms Reduction Treaty (START). Now, Russia, in the midst of a war with Ukraine, is threatening the use of nuclear weapons should the interventions of Ukraine's allies create dangers for Moscow. As well, the nuclear weapons of China, India, Pakistan, and North Korea have become a backdrop to security in Asia. China has modernized its nuclear forces, and while estimates are inconclusive, there is evidence it is increasing its inventory. Equally dangerous are the inconclusive efforts to contain Iran's nuclear weapons activities. Both Israel and the United States have stated Iran will not be permitted to have nuclear weapons and threaten the use of their militaries. The tragic irony is that the United States and Israel carry significant responsibility for the breakdown in the efforts associated with the P5+2 process, which offered some expectation Iran would remain as a non-nuclear weapons state.

These increasing dangers relating to the possible use of nuclear weapons are occurring at a time when international efforts for their containment have faltered. Today, there are no efforts similar to the ones that attended the negotiations resulting in the NPT of 1970, the Comprehensive Ban on Nuclear Testing of 1998 (not yet in force), the 2021 Treaty on the Prohibition of Nuclear Weapons, nor the extensive American-Soviet/Russia bilateral discussions and agreements on their inventories of nuclear weapons and associated delivery systems.

It is in this abyss that there is urgent need for renewed collective international actions to see the elimination of nuclear weapons. This was the goal of the 1970 Non-Proliferation Treaty, yet it remains unfulfilled and often ignored. There is urgent need for Canada and other like-minded states to initiate and increase collective efforts for the elimination of nuclear weapons before the 2045 centenary of their first use. The mechanisms are already in place with the various existing non proliferation and testing treaties, the Soviet/Russia-United States weapons reduction agreements, and the 2019 Stockholm Initiative on Nuclear Disarmament in which Canada is a full participant.

Canada has standing and experience, more than most, for this work. This unique status comes from a few sources: Canada's partnership with the United States and the United Kingdom in the development of nuclear weapons during the Manhattan Project of the Second World War; its early export of nuclear technology to India, Pakistan, China, South Kores, Romania, Argentina and Taiwan; and its own efforts to promote and use nuclear energy for peaceful purposes. Canada's efforts over the last fifty years have emphasized the non-proliferation, non-testing, and elimination of nuclear weapons. In support of its policies, Canada has been a member of the 1971 Zangger Committee and the 1975 Nuclear Suppliers Group

2021 saw the enforcement of a new agreement – the Treaty on the Prohibition of Nuclear Weapons (TPNW). Most nations have signed the Treaty, but the nuclear weapons states have refused. Canada, accompanied by its NATO partners, has also refused. In doing so, Canada has broken with its longstanding support for the elimination of nuclear weapons. This is a significant and tragic mistake.

Not so many years ago, Canada initiated efforts internationally for the elimination of another class of weapons, landmines, and participated in work for the elimination of chemical, biological, and cluster munitions weapons. These weapons had established a firm presence in the arsenal of militaries around the world, but the dangers they represented provided the international community with the confidence needed for their elimination. During the same period, Canadian talents were engaged in the creation of the International Criminal Court, which, in its own way, made a significant contribution for a better and more secure world.

These initiatives were of a different order than the issues involved with nuclear weapons. However, past successes in disarmament, along with the urgency of eliminating nuclear weapons, provide encouragement for renewed action by Canada and other like-minded countries. Nothing could give greater historical legacy to Canada and the role it has played in the world since 1939 than if, on the 2045 centenary of the Second World War, it heralded in a new legacy in the elimination of nuclear weapons.

Ottawa, November 30, 2022

2. The Scary World

And we will all go together when we go
What a comforting fact that is to know
Universal bereavement –
An inspiring achievement!
Yes, we all will go together when we go.

—***Tom Lehrer** 1959*

July 16, 2022 was the seventy-seventh anniversary of the arrival of nuclear weapons. It is little celebrated, but on that day in 1945, the United States tested the world's first nuclear weapon near the conclusion of World War II. The Trinity atomic device was exploded near Alamogordo in the deserts of New Mexico. Three weeks later, the United States dropped nuclear bombs – *Little Boy*, with 15,000 equivalent tons of TNT using enriched uranium, and *Fat Man*, with 21,000 equivalent tons of TNT using plutonium – on the Japanese cities of Hiroshima and Nagasaki. There were over 200,000 casualties, and the use of nuclear weapons contributed significantly to the unconditional surrender of Japan nine days later. The associated technologies of uranium enrichment and plutonium used in these first two bombs remain the basis for all nuclear explosions. The nuclear genie or, to reflect the origins of the word, the nuclear djinn, was out of the bottle: from the minds of scientists and into the hands of political and military leaders.

The Scary World of Nuclear Weapons

The Atomic Age, or rather the Nuclear Age to use its modern iteration, began with the July 16, 1945 nuclear explosion and was the collective work of the United States, Canada, and the United Kingdom. In large measure, that explosion also resulted from pre-war efforts involving Albert Einstein and other scientists who had introduced American political leaders to the concept of nuclear energy and its close associate, the atomic bomb. Einstein was living in the United States after leaving Germany once the Nazis came to power in 1933, just prior to the start of the Second World War. He agreed to sign a letter to President Franklin Roosevelt on August 2, 1939, warning of the possibility Germany had initiated work to build such a bomb.

In the letter, written by fellow scientists Enrico Fermi and Leo Szilard, refugees from Italy and Hungary, Einstein reported, "In the course of the last four months it has been made probable . . . that it may become possible to set up a nuclear chain reaction in a large mass of uranium, by which vast amounts of power and large qualities of new radium-like elements would be generated. Now it appears almost certain that this could be achieved in the immediate future. This new phenomenon would also lead to the construction of bombs, and it is conceivable – though much less certain – that extremely powerful bombs of a new type may thus be constructed." The letter went on to mention that Canada could be a source of uranium ore for use in the construction of such bombs.

Six years later, Einstein, in realization of what he had helped to do after the bombings of Hiroshima and Nagasaki, commented that his letter to President Roosevelt was "one great mistake" after he learned Germany's atomic bomb efforts were far from credible. Subsequently, Einstein suggested he did not "consider myself the father of the release of atomic energy." His part in it was quite indirect. Nevertheless, he felt that it was prudent, along with Fermi and Szilard, to warn the President of the dangers involved. Roosevelt, with the war underway in Europe and the possibility of war in the Pacific, was sufficiently concerned to initiate governmental arrangements leading to the establishment of the Manhattan Project and the first atomic bombs five years later.

Within a year of the war's end, the United States began a series of nuclear tests – atmospheric, on the ground, and underwater – on Bikini Atoll in the Marshall Islands of Micronesia. There were twenty-three such nuclear test explosions between 1946 and 1958, including the first hydrogen bomb in 1952. The islanders, under false pretenses, were removed to neighbouring islands, but not from the effects of the radiation. Their descendants are still victims of those explosions. In a report from the congressional legislature of Micronesia, which became independent in 1979, it is stated "No other group of people . . . has been exposed to the same amounts and differing kinds of radioactivity, and no other group in the world has been so carefully studied for the results of such effects."

It was from these studies of Micronesians that the long-term effects of iodine 131, strontium 90, and cesium 137 on the human body were learned. But it was not until 2013, during the Obama Administration, that the affected islanders were reimbursed for their medical treatment. These cataclysmic events in the South Pacific were trivialized when a Paris designer named his new two-piece swim suit the bikini after the first Bikini explosion on July 1, 1946.

Discussions of nuclear issues in the post-war period involving Canada, the United Kingdom, and the United States were frequent and involved the heads of all three governments. The role of Canada on nuclear matters, and that of the emerging United Nations, began in earnest once the war in the Pacific came to an end. The British were especially concerned with their own nuclear weapons program, code named "Tube Alloys," and future cooperation with the United States. The bulk of the British nuclear research effort had been moved to Canada in late 1942, and in the following three years, it grew to include some 300 or so persons at McGill University, coordinated through the National Research Council. In 1943, this Canadian-British effort was incorporated into the American Manhattan Project under the control of the American military. A combined policy committee of senior American, British, and Canadian officials (C. D. Howe was the Canadian representative) provided overall coordination between the three governments.

A variety of policy issues arose as the American and British programs used different technologies for the production of fissile material necessary for the production of nuclear weapons. The British's "Tube Alloys" weapons program and the earlier RAF MAUD program had been subsumed within the Manhattan Project, with the research of the British and Canadian team providing a jump start for the Americans. While the two technologies – enriched uranium vs plutonium – were both used as the source of fissile material in each of the two bombs used in Japan, the British research was preferable. Ironically, the end of the war immediately made nuclear secrecy a priority for the Americans. The Gouzenko affair and evidence of other Soviet espionage activities convinced the Americans that allied arrangements had the potential for leaks, so the trilateral cooperation with Canada and the United Kingdom was an early casualty. In 1946, the United States legislated its Atomic Energy Act, eliminating international cooperation; it was not until 1958 that the United States and the United Kingdom re-established their special relationship on nuclear matters.

For Canada, there was uncertainty as to the role it would play in the postwar nuclear world. In an October 29, 1945 memorandum to the Clerk of the President of the Privy Council, the Acting President of the National Research Council offered the following comments.

On the source of uranium: the NRC head reported that while the Canadian supply was significant, he wrote that the Americans "might have carried out their immediate plans without our material."

On research: while the Canadian effort was tied to that of the United Kingdom, from the "standpoint of results obtained by our contribution, I think, was much greater than the ratio of money spent."

"Canada's development work was not a major factor in the production of the atomic bombs dropped on Japan, but may have a very great effect on future plans. The development work in Canada using heavy water was not duplicated anywhere else and was one of the several alternative methods tried."

Looking to the future the NRC Acting President of the NRC wrote that he thought "Canada's present situation as a source of raw material is much stronger than the total amount of ore in sight, as our geographical position as far as the United States is concerned is of very great importance.

Canada has no advantage in knowledge of relevant scientific technical and industrial "know how" over the United States or Great Britain but definitely has over the rest of the countries of the world . . . As the owner and operator of the only plant [Chalk River] in the British Empire, I think we, at the moment, a rather strong position as far as everyone else excepting the United States is concerned.

As for the United States, largely I think owing to an honest fear of security leakages, they feel, as they do in the matter of military defence, that they are quite competent to look after themselves."

As to proliferation: the comments of the Acting President were particularly prescient: "I do not think that the control of the raw materials in Canada, the United Kingdom and the United States would prevent, for any great length of time, developments [nuclear weapons] in other countries."

As for time period: "the more theoretical scientists are apt to put a lower limit of three to five years on it. The more experienced engineer industrialists, who in my opinion know more of the actual difficulties to overcome place a minimum of five with a probable ten years as the time that it would take countries like Russia, Germany or Japan to it if they were working under pre-war conditions. 'He suggested it would take the United Kingdom five to seven years to make an atomic bomb.'" The Soviets took four years, exploding their first device on August 29, 1949, and the British seven years, with its first explosion on October 3, 1952.

As to the destructiveness of future bombs: the Acting President wrote, "It is certain that the destructiveness of the atomic bomb can be increased but figures of the magnitude of a thousand times are not talked about by those who know most about it. [. . .] There is always available the simple expedient of increased destructiveness by dropping more and more bombs at the same time, i.e., "sticks of bombs."

President Truman met with Prime Minister Clement Attlee of the United Kingdom and Canadian Prime Minister Mackenzie King in Washington on November 11, 1945, "in an effort to effect agreement on the conditions under which cooperation might replace rivalry in the field of atomic power." Attlee had been elected Prime Minister three months earlier in a landslide victory for the first majority Labour Party government on July 5, 1945.

Lester Pearson, the Canadian ambassador in Washington, detailed the meeting for Ottawa and reported that before the November 1 lunch, "the President and the two Prime Ministers discussed between themselves the problem that had brought them together in Washington, the use of atomic energy for destructive purposes, and found that they were in general agreement on the main principles which should govern national and international action in this matter." After lunch, "there was complete agreement on the fundamental and far-reaching nature of the problem, on the necessity of an international approach to its solution, on the importance which the world attached to these discussions, and the desirability of issuing a combined statement embodying the agreement reached, as quickly as possible."

The only point requiring further discussion and refinement was over the idea of having the new United Nations appoint a special commission "to prepare recommendations for submission to the organization" to prevent the use of atomic energy for destructive purposes and to promote its use for peaceful and humanitarian ends. The issue was whether the Soviet Government would be in agreement with the proposal, and, especially, that it would be a commission appointed by the General Assembly and not the Security Council, on which the Soviet Union would have the power of veto.

In any event, on January 24, 1946, the General Assembly met for the first time and passed a resolution, promoted by Canada and the United Kingdom "to deal with the problems raised by the discovery of atomic energy." The Commission was asked to make specific proposals: (a) for extending between all nations the exchange of basic scientific information for peaceful ends; (b) for control of atomic energy to the extent necessary to ensure its use only for peaceful purposes; (c) for the elimination from national armaments of atomic weapons and of all other major weapons adaptable to mass destruction; (d) for effective safeguards by way of inspection and other means to protect complying States against the hazards of violations and evasions.

This was the first resolution passed by the new organization.

The Commission was duly appointed as the United Nations Atomic Energy Commission. But from the outset they had trouble meeting a consensus on the issues involved, and this was largely due to Soviet opposition. Several reports were issued but without agreement on content. While it only became clear after the fact, the Soviet Union's tactic was to delay any recommendations by the Commission until such time as it exploded its first nuclear device. This happened on August 29, 1949, by which time the Commission was non-functional. Less than five weeks later, the Communist Party of China won its 25-year civil war and formed a new government on October 1, with Mao Zedong as head of state and Chou en Lai as the Prime Minister. Nine months later, June 25, 1950, North Korea invaded South Korea with Soviet support. Any suggestion that the new United Nations would unite the world on nuclear security, let alone any other major issue, disappeared for a few decades. The United States in particular turned inwards, and the Cold War dominated international relations for the next forty years. The UN Atomic Energy Commission officially folded its tent in 1952.

In the 77 years since those first nuclear explosions, there have been two remarkable facts associated with nuclear weapons. The first is that they have never been used again in war, despite conflicts in which possible use was discussed and considered. These conflicts, while not numerous, were of considerable international concern. The first was the 1950 war in Korea. The early successful intervention by the United States and associated countries under United Nations authority and their move into North Korea prompted the overwhelming military intervention by China. American troops came under significant pressure, leading to serious consideration by American leaders of using nuclear force. When asked at a press conference about the use of the atomic bomb, President Truman replied, "There has always been active consideration of its use."

And that was not the end of the issue. After Korea, there were the two crises in the Taiwan Strait. The first, in 1954-55, was occasioned by China shelling the Taiwanese islands of Kinmen (Quemoy) and Matsu, killing two American military advisers. The U.S. Joint Chiefs of Staff recommended the use of nuclear weapons to President Eisenhower, while British Prime Minister Churchill, now back in power, recommended against doing so. Secretary of State, John Foster Dulles, stated publicly that the United States was seriously considering a nuclear strike.

Eisenhower decided against doing so, but he was faced with the same recommendation from the Joint Chiefs of Staff three years later during the second crisis in the Taiwan Strait in late 1958. The Americans sent conventional military support to Taiwan, and following discussions with the Soviet Union, announced a ceasefire. A few years later, in 1964, China had its first nuclear test explosion. Five years after that, China had its border war with the Soviet Union.

In the aftermath of these wars and the associated threats of the use of nuclear weapons by the United States, Tom Lehrer wrote his anthem to the atomic age, "We Will All Go Together When We Go." On January 1, 1959, Lehrer first sang this to his nervous audiences:

> No more ashes, no more sackcloth
> And an armband made of black cloth
> Will some day never more adorn a sleeve
> For if the bomb that drops on you
> Gets your friends and neighbours too
> There'll be nobody left behind to grieve

> And we will all go together when we go
> What a comforting fact that is to know
> Universal bereavement
> An inspiring achievement
> Yes we all will go together when we go.

A decade or so later, the American military was again under considerable pressure, this time from North Vietnam and an insurgency in South Vietnam by the Viet Cong. This came in the aftermath of the defeat of France and the collapse of its Indo-China empire in 1954. The sound of falling dominoes resounded in the American administrations of Kennedy, Johnson, and Nixon. The debates at that time have been carried down into the present, centering on the effectiveness of nuclear weapons versus what might be accomplished by conventional weapons associated with large interventions of troops. All three administrations decided against the use nuclear weapons, with the reasoning largely centered on three elements: "First, fear of inadvertent escalation, rooted in calculation about the risk of uncontrolled escalation, plus the potential for an infinitely catastrophic outcome. . . second, preserving the tradition of non-use . . . and finally, a taboo, a normative belief that using nuclear weapons would be wrong." [For a full discussion of these considerations see Nina Tannenwald, *The Nuclear Taboo: The United States and the Non-use of Nuclear Weapons Since 1945*, Cambridge University Press, 2003.]

From the information available, it does not seem that the Soviet and American wars in Afghanistan resulted in discussions on the possible use of nuclear weapons. The wars tested the abilities of both militaries, and, while an extensive range of weapons were used, the fundamental issues of geography and the durability of insurgencies with support from Pakistan neutralized Moscow's and Washington's abilities to dominate either the battlefields or Afghan obduracy against change promoted by outsiders. There have been occasional reports that the United States did use near-nuclear weapons, but these were not central to the conduct of the wars. Instead, both the Soviet Union in 1989 and the United States in 2021 came to the conclusion that more troops and more time would not lead to an acceptable ending. These decisions were politically catastrophic for both countries. The disintegration of the Soviet Union accompanied the Soviet departure from Afghanistan. For the United States, the effects of the military defeat continue to resound in the cultural and political consciousness.

In 1962, the Cuban Missile Crisis represented the closest that any state got to launching nuclear weapons since the Second World War. The Soviet Union, at the request of Cuba, installed nuclear missiles as a deterrence to future American invasions in the wake of the 1961 Bay of Pigs fiasco. The public disclosure of the missiles during the American 1962 congressional elections led President Kennedy to declare a naval quarantine of Cuba in October. This was intended to prevent further missiles deliveries to Cuba; Kennedy also demanded the removal of existing Soviet missiles on the island.

Several weeks of discussion, along with a naval standoff in the Atlantic, resulted in a resolution in which the Soviet Union agreed to remove all missiles, while the United States would similarly remove any missiles deployed before the crisis in Turkey and Italy. The United States also committed not to invade Cuba again. Significantly, the agreement also produced an agreement for the establishment of a telephone "hot-line" between the two countries so that both could consult immediately in the event of future nuclear crises. Ultimately, the crisis exposed the need for bilateral discussions and catalyzed agreements on the role, use, and numbers of nuclear weapons.

The second unique feature of the age of nuclear weapons is that the associated technology has been replicated by only nine countries. The Soviet Union was the first, in 1949. Today, Russia and the United States maintain 90% of the world's nuclear weapons. China has approximately 250 weapons. The American Department of Defence in its 2021 report to Congress predicted that China could have approximately 1000 nuclear weapons by 2030. One of the early nuclear weapons countries, South Africa, became the world's only country to destroy its inventory of nuclear weapons. All seven were dismantled in the midst of the country's dramatic domestic political changes in the 1989-91 period.

Today, six other states – the United Kingdom, France, Israel, India, Pakistan, and North Korea – possess all of the remaining nuclear weapons. All have operational inventories and have active nuclear weapons programs keeping their inventories current, along with appropriate delivery systems. Today, there is only one country, Iran, with an active nuclear development program capable of obtaining sufficient fissile material. Iran asserts that its nuclear activities are for peaceful purposes only. But the nature of those activities, even if for peaceful purposes, provides infrastructure for the manufacture of nuclear weapons. Iran nevertheless remains a signatory to the NPT.

The nuclear weapons of India, Pakistan, and China are interrelated, and any change by one would create changes for the other two. The development of nuclear weapons by China was largely driven by the accumulation of nuclear weapons by the Soviet Union and the United States. This remains the motivation for China's nuclear armament, which in turn impinges on the Indian and Pakistani arsenal.

The Israeli and North Korean programs are largely consequential for their geopolitical isolation. Israel, from its creation in 1948, faced serious and ongoing threats from its neighbours. Its early leadership, fearful of invasion and annihilation, decided that nuclear weapons offered significant leverage against invasion and embarked on a development program in the early 1950s. France assisted in the construction of a nuclear research station at Dimona, fittingly located near the Dead Sea. Within a decade or so, Israel had a small inventory of nuclear weapons that has never been openly acknowledged.

North Korea has been a pariah state since its inception in 1949. Its borders, stalemated since the ceasefire associated with its 1950 invasion of South Korea, and its successive totalitarian regimes dominated by the family Kim, have fought for survival in self-imposed isolation. North Korea faces political and economic sanctions promoted by the United States and others. Though these sanctions receive only circumspect support from neighbouring China and Russia, North

Korea remains a garrison state. There was little surprise when it exploded its first nuclear device in 2006, and there have been five others, all underground, since. Various estimates suggest North Korea has more than 20 nuclear weapons. Alongside its nuclear weapons development, North Korea has produced missiles capable of delivering nuclear weapons to neighbouring countries and possibly to the mainland United States.

Beyond these countries known to possess nuclear capabilities, Taiwan, Iraq, Syria, Libya, and possibly Argentina and Brazil, have actively engaged in activities that over time could have resulted in the manufacture of nuclear weapons. All such activities have now ended, with those of Iraq and Syria destroyed by direct military attacks by Israel. For the others, domestic decisions and outside pressure contained and eliminated potential nuclear weapons development.

The United States, in the aftermath of the Second World War, made nuclear weapons an essential component of the security policy for the nation. It also sought to control the technology and to limit its spread to and use by other countries. There were also initiatives promoting peaceful uses of nuclear energy, as in President Eisenhower's 1953 *Atoms for Peace* speech at the United Nations. In those early years, the United States regularly considered the use of nuclear weapons. Conflicts with Korea/China, China/Taiwan, Soviet Union/Cuba, and Vietnam/China prompted discussions and recommendations to the President for the use of nuclear weapons. While they have yet to be deployed since the Second World War, United States policy on the use of nuclear weapons is highly situational; thus, any significant conflict could motivate the use of nuclear force.

The outlines of an American nuclear doctrine emerged during the Cold War and was largely in place from 1948 to 1989. The doctrine, mostly unwritten, provided that nuclear weapons would be used as the major deterrence in protecting the United States and its allies in the event of threat or coercion from other countries. As well, the doctrine permitted the United States and allies in NATO to use nuclear weapons as a last resort, but also permitted their first use if necessary to deal with non-nuclear attacks. Clearly, this approach was not effective in enforcing non-proliferation.

Since the disintegration of the Soviet Union in 1991, there has been ongoing debate in the United States on the importance of nuclear weapons for international policy. In some measure, this debate was sidelined by the terrorist attacks in New York and the Pentagon in northern Virginia in 2001, but it has not disappeared. There were internal reviews, but these were episodic. Eventually, Congress imposed a statutory requirement, following the election of a new President, for the submission of a confidential report to Congress providing a review of American nuclear posture.

The first of the post-Cold War nuclear posture reviews was attempted in 1994 during the Clinton administration. As one non-military participant commented afterwards, "The military officials knew the lay of the land, we didn't. Ash Carter [Secretary of Defence] set us up for disaster." The issue at stake was the proposal by the Secretary of Defence "to have a military that doesn't need to use [nuclear, biological and chemical] weapons. We can use conventional forces to prevent anywhere in the world." Inherent in this approach would have been the elimination of two of the three pillars of the American nuclear systems: the ICBMs and the bombers. This attempt at disarmament failed as ICBMs and the bombers are still part of the American nuclear triad.

A second review was attempted early in the new century and a report was prepared and partially released in 2002 in the aftermath of the 2001 attacks. The report supported nuclear weapons all the way. The Pentagon was to draft "contingency plans for the use of nuclear weapons against at least seven countries, naming not only Russia and the 'axis of evil' – Iraq, Iran, and North Korea – but also China, Libya and Syria." According to the introduction to the review written by the Secretary of Defence Donald Rumsfield, there were also proposals for a new US nuclear triad based on offensive strike systems, defenses, and a revitalized defense structure that would call for new types of nuclear weapons.

Amid this culture of retention of nuclear weapons, President Obama submitted the first statutory review to Congress in 2010. During the previous year, the Council on Foreign Relations issued a report, co-chaired by the former Secretary of Defense, William Perry, and Brent Scowcroft, a former national security adviser. They noted that "the geopolitical conditions that would permit the global elimination of nuclear weapons do not currently exist," but provided an agenda that is still of value today. They suggested nuclear weapons should be reduced to the lowest possible level consistent with retaining a credible deterrent, but with the "imperative before the Obama administration . . . to use all available tools to prevent the use and further acquisition of nuclear weapons."

Perry and Scowcroft itemized a specific agenda:

- Bolstering the global non-proliferation regime is the best way to contain the threat of proliferation posed not only by Iran, but also by other potential nuclear states.
- State clearly that it is a U.S. goal to prevent nuclear weapons from ever being used . . . and that the sole purpose of U.S. nuclear weapons is providing deterrence for itself and its allies.
- Reaffirm nuclear security assurances to allies.
- Continue to reduce reliance on nuclear weapons . . . and take the international lead in reducing the salience of nuclear weapons in security policy.
- Seek further reductions in nuclear forces, beginning with a bilateral strategic arms control agreement with Russia.
- Seek to ratify the 1996 Comprehensive Test Ban Treaty (CTBT).
- Call for a moratorium on the production of fissile material for weapons purposes.
- Strengthen the International Atomic Energy Agency's vital role of containing proliferation.
- Work cooperatively to ensure that every state with nuclear weapons or weapons-usable materials – even those remaining

outside the Non-proliferation Treaty like India and Pakistan – implement best nuclear security practices.
- There is an opportunity to make deeper cuts in American and Russian nuclear arsenals.
- While China is a "nuclear-armed rival," to the United States, the time may not be right for a formal nuclear arms control agreement because of the significant asymmetry in their respective arsenals. Nevertheless, there should be renewed military-to-military discussions to encourage transparency.

President Obama reflected much of this thinking in an earlier speech in Prague when he outlined a "vision of a world without nuclear weapons." His Posture Review to Congress renounced development of any new nuclear weapons, such as the bunker-busters proposed by the Bush administration, and for the first time ruled out a nuclear attack against non-nuclear weapons states that are in compliance with the 1970 Non-Nuclear Proliferation Treaty, although the rule excluded Iran. A year after the Review, a senior American official reported that the United States would develop proposals for potential further reductions in its nuclear stockpile.

In releasing his Review, Obama noted that he was taking "specific and concrete steps to reduce the role of nuclear weapons" and that "for the first time, preventing nuclear proliferation and nuclear terrorism is now at the top of America's nuclear agenda." American nuclear weapons will be used to sustain deterrence for the "narrower range of contingencies in which these weapons may still play a role."

Needless to say, the 2018 Nuclear Posture Review (NPR) by the Trump administration significantly altered Obama's nuclear weapons policy agenda. It suggested a need to close the gap in the American nuclear arsenal for low-yield nuclear weapons, suggesting the United States would consider using nuclear weapons, if necessary, in regional conflicts. Also, the Trump review noted a need for sea-launched cruise missiles and confirmed the United States would not ratify the

Comprehensive Test Ban Treaty. The review also rejected the idea of a treaty prohibiting nuclear weapons.

According to press reports in July, the Biden 2022 Nuclear Posture Review has been written and shared with Congress but has not been released. One press report suggests there is a dispute with the pending cancellation of the program to develop a nuclear armed submarine-launched cruise missile. Such a missile was part of President Trump's NPR of 2018. The delay by Biden may last some time as there is also the suggestion that his NPR will await the completion of its National Security Review. That review has itself been delayed with the Russian invasion of Ukraine and increased military activity by China over Taiwan and the South China Sea.

3. The Countries of the Scary Nuclear World

"Now we are all sons of bitches."

Harvard Professor of Physics, Kenneth Banbridge, *speaking to Robert Oppenheimer, after observing the July 16, 1945 nuclear test explosion.*

To reduce the inherent threat of nuclear weapons and ultimately eliminate them involves the policies and programs of several specific countries. These include the nine countries owning weapons, along with several other countries directly affected. The political relationships between these countries provide the essential rationale for the maintenance of nuclear weapons. Any success in their elimination must start with an understanding of those relationships and the reasons for both the development of the weapons and the belief in the need for their maintenance and continuation. These relationships require review and examination for an understanding of the scary world of nuclear weapons.

The Soviet Union/Russia

On August 29, 1949, three years before the 1952 British nuclear weapons test, the Soviet Union exploded its first nuclear device, *First Lightning*, at the Semipalatinsk Test Range in the northeastern area of the Kazakh Soviet Socialist Republic. It was a plutonium implosion device, similar to the first American device, *Trinity*, exploded in New Mexico, and the *Fat Man* bomb dropped at Nagasaki. It had the equivalent of 20,000 tons of TNT. The nuclear arms race was underway.

The Soviet explosion surprised many, most of all for how it demonstrated the country's rapid recovery after the Second World War. The nuclear test demonstrated the significance, depth, and strength of the Soviet scientific and engineering communities. There remains controversy over how much critical information was obtained through espionage from the United States, but the story of Soviet ingenuity remains a significant element of lingering propaganda efforts among both countries. Building on this technological momentum, the Soviet Union launched the world's first artificial orbiting satellite, *Sputnik*, on Oct 4, 1957.

After 1917, Russian and Soviet scientists, along with their colleagues in western Europe, were directly involved in the examination of radioactivity. Soviet scientists Georgi Gamov and Pyotr Kapitsa studied with Ernest Rutherford at the Cavendish Laboratory at Cambridge University. The public reporting of the splitting of the atom by the German scientist Otto Hahn in 1939 created the same understanding in the Soviet Union as in the United Kingdom and the United States of the possible military uses. Following up on the same concerns Einstein expressed in his letter to the President, the Soviet Union also established a commission to research possible military applications.

Publication of nuclear research in the United States and the United Kingdom ended suddenly around 1939/40, creating strong suspicion among the Soviets that serious nuclear weapons research was underway. The Premier of the Soviet Union, Joseph Stalin, was informed of these developments. In 1942, he established a dedicated nuclear weapons program within the Soviet Army headed by nuclear physicist Igor V. Kurchatov. Given the presence of German troops well within Soviet borders at this time, research was limited. But the nuclear explosions in Hiroshima and Nagasaki in August 1945, the first public demonstration of the success of American efforts to produce nuclear weapons, energized Soviet nuclear weapons efforts. The first Soviet test explosion, four years later, was based on American designs. But the success probably owes as much to the pressure put on scientists as it does to the fruits of espionage. The successful test demonstrated one of the basic understandings of science – once an experiment is done, replication by others will follow.

The quality of Soviet science of the time was reflected in the work of Andrei Sakharov, who worked with Kurchatov and others within the Soviet nuclear program and was known as the designer of Soviet fusion-based thermonuclear weapons, more commonly known as hydrogen bombs. His work overlapped with that of the Americans Edward Teller and Stanislaw Ulam in the development of such weapons. This involved the concept of "radiation implosion" and led to the production of the most powerful nuclear device ever detonated, the fifty-megaton *Tsar Bomba* in October, 1961.

Sakharov's nuclear work led to his status as one of the world's best known nuclear physicists. In 1950, he developed the idea for a "controlled nuclear fusion reactor, the tokamak," which remains a safer and more practical choice over the more common fusion reactors. Tokamak reactors perhaps offer the most promising peaceful use of nuclear energy available. Sakharov joined with other nuclear physicist around the world in promoting an understanding of the dangers of nuclear weapons. He sympathized with Robert Oppenheimer and Edward Teller of the United States in a concern with the general public's limited understanding of nuclear weapons.

For this work in support of the peaceful use of nuclear energy, Sakharov was attacked by his own government in 1972, awarded the Nobel Peace Prize in 1975, and internally exiled within the Soviet Union for the last years of his life. He was not allowed to leave the Soviet Union to accept his Nobel Prize, but his wife, Yelena Bonner, was able to do so. In presenting the award, the Nobel committee wrote, "In a convincing manner Sakharov has emphasized that Man's inviolable rights provide the only safe foundation for genuine and enduring international cooperation." In fact, Sakharov provided groundwork for thinking about how to eliminate nuclear weapons that can guide us today. In a 2008 publication, he was quoted as saying:

After more than forty years, we have had no third world war, and the balance of nuclear terror . . . may have helped to prevent one. But I am not at all sure of this; back then, in those long-gone years, the question didn't even arise. What most troubles me now is the instability of the balance, the extreme peril of the current situation, the appalling waste of the arms race . . . Each of us has a responsibility to think about this in global terms, with tolerance, trust, and candor, free from ideological dogmatism, parochial interests, or national egotism.

In the intervening years, the Soviet Union and its successor, Russia, have been partners with the United States in efforts to prevent the proliferation of nuclear weapons and their testing. The numerous agreements arising from the period of the 1962 Cuba crisis and the period of détente were fundamental to the situation today. Russia remains a signatory to the NPT and the CNTBT (not yet in force). Russia, in its military doctrine issued by presidential decree on June 25, 2010, stated that its nuclear weapons could be used "in response to the use of nuclear and other types of weapons of mass destruction against it or its allies, and also in case of aggression against Russia with the use of conventional weapons when the very existence of the state is threatened." The decree was updated in 2014, but the changes did not affect the use of nuclear weapons.

In June 2020, President Putin issued a new decree specific to nuclear deterrence titled *Basic Principles of the Russian Federation's State Policy in the Domain of Nuclear Deterrence*. It specified two conditions under which Russia would use nuclear weapons. The first condition essentially copied that of the 2010 Degree but added that nuclear weapons could be used "Also in the case of aggression against the Russian Federation with the use of conventional weapons, when the very existence of the state is put under threat." At the onset of the Russian invasion of Ukraine on February 24, 2022, President Putin used this language as he regarded developments in Ukraine as "anti-Russian." Such language moves into the direction of "first use" of nuclear weapons; it runs counter to the policy of China, and possibly that of the United States, where "no first use" is contemplated.

United Kingdom and France

The United Kingdom's first nuclear test explosion in 1952 on an island of Western Australia was followed by France in 1960 with a test in central Algeria. The British explosion followed from the country's exclusion from the American program following the 1946 USA Atomic Energy Act. Both Canada and the United Kingdom had been nuclear partners with the United States following the 1943 Quebec Agreement driven by need for collaboration during the war. But with the successful conclusion of the Manhattan Project, the United States decided nuclear secrets could no longer be shared with foreign countries, so the wartime collaboration ended abruptly. While efforts were made in 1945 by the Prime Ministers of Canada and the United Kingdom to continue the three-way wartime cooperation, they could not overcome American paranoia of spies under all beds.

The British nuclear weapons program had no difficulty re-establishing operations at home. The rich scientific pool had gained experience in the American program and was available. In 1947, Prime Minister Attlee authorized "research and development work on atomic weapons." The initial work included the construction of nuclear plants to produce usable plutonium and enriched uranium. The first bomb design was based on the one used by the Americans in the bombing of Hiroshima in that it was a plutonium implosion device. The plutonium came from their own production along with plutonium from the Chalk River reactor in Ontario. Anti-communist paranoia in the United States intensified following the Soviet 1949 test explosion, and a series of spy scandals involving British scientists and others intensified the Americans' unwillingness for foreign sharing. The Americans, even after the return of Churchill to office, refused further cooperation, even denying an agreement for the testing of the first British device in Nevada. Instead, the British obtained an agreement with Australia, and its first nuclear device was exploded in the Monte Bello Islands, Western Australia.

The British nuclear program included thermonuclear weapons along with appropriate delivery systems. After 1958, cooperation with the United States resumed, and this included the sharing of fissile material and delivery systems. Today, the British nuclear program is again dependent on the United States for delivery systems, including the American Polaris missiles and nuclear submarines. These use four nuclear powered submarines, armed with sixteen Trident II missiles, each carrying warheads with up to eight multiple independently targetable re-entry vehicles.

In the 1946 Cabinet discussions on the re-establishment of the program, there was opposition until the Foreign Secretary, Ernest Bevin, intervened following unsuccessful discussions with the United States in an effort to resume wartime cooperation. Bevin's intervention ensured Cabinet support. He is quoted as saying, "We've got to have this thing. I don't mind it for myself, but I don't want any other Foreign Secretary of this country to be talked at or to by the Secretary of State of the United States as I have been in my discussion with Mr. Byrnes. We've got to have this thing over here, whatever it costs . . . We've got to have the bloody Union Jack flying on top of it."

Mr. Bevin's concerns, while realistic in the postwar period, were largely illusory as decolonization eliminated Britain's pre-war global position. Today, the British nuclear weapons program is a footnote to the American program. It lives on without military significance, but dismantling Britain's nuclear arsenal might be useful as an opening gambit in the process for the elimination of nuclear weapons.

France was the fourth country with nuclear weapons. The first French nuclear test explosion in 1964 in central Algeria reflected France's determination to follow a made-in-France foreign policy. The explosion, along with the development of its *Force de Frappe*, were elements in support of France's global status following the creation of the Fifth Republic in 1958. This resolve also reflected France's disastrous defeat in Indochina, the fiasco of working with the United Kingdom and Israel in the 1956 invasion of Suez, its ongoing nasty colonial war in Algeria, and the failure of its postwar Fourth Constitutions. At the same time, Paris decided in 1954 to develop nuclear energy for electrical power generation and today is the world's largest user of nuclear-generated power. The present government, however, has announced plans to reduce reliance on nuclear power, largely due to the cost of replacing aging reactors.

The French were motivated to produce nuclear weapons for much the same reasons as the British, for the promotion and maintenance of France's international reputation as a major world power. Given the security conditions of the time, the decision had very little to do with national defence. Nevertheless, France's nuclear weapons program developed quickly and is today the third largest in the world after the United States and Russia. There was early cooperation with Israel in the development of that country's nuclear weapons program and with the United Kingdom.

Historically, the French program reflected the pioneering nuclear research of Marie Curie and her husband Pierre. It was furthered by their daughter, Irène Joliot-Curie and her husband Frédéric Joliot-Curie. All four were Nobel Prize winners. The Joliet-Curies remained in France during the war, and in its aftermath promoted the use of nuclear energy for peaceful purposes. Frédéric wrote in August 1945, "It is ... true that the immense reserves of energy contained in the uranium devices can be liberated slowly enough to be used practically for the benefit of mankind. I am personally convinced that ... [atomic energy] will be of inestimable service to mankind in peacetime." The acceptance of his views perhaps accounts for France unmatched enthusiasm for nuclear-generated electrical power.

In the post-war period, the French nuclear weapons program was promoted and funded and became one of the most successful in the world. It started in October 1945 with the creation of the Commission on Atomic Energy, with Joliet-Curie in charge of all scientific and technical research. The Commission promoted "scientific and technical research" with the expectation of "using atomic energy in the various domains of science, industry and national defence." Three of the associated scientists, Lew Kowalski, Jules Guéron, and Bertrand Goldschmidt, had worked on nuclear issues at the Chalk River laboratories in Ontario during the war, largely as part of the Anglo-Canadian Tube Alloys nuclear weapons development project, which became part of the Manhattan Project in 1943. All three scientists returned to France after the war. By 1948, their research resulted in the construction of France's first atomic pile, which used uranium and heavy water owing to the materials available at Chalk River.

Joliet-Curie resisted pressure from the Commission to begin development of nuclear weapons and was dismissed as a result in 1950. By the late 1950s, the Commission was engaged in the construction of three nuclear reactors designed for the production of electricity. A by-product of these reactors was the production of large amounts of plutonium. With high costs for producing heavy water, graphite was chosen as the moderating agent, and this has remained an essential feature of French nuclear power reactors.

Through this postwar period, France's geopolitical position worsened as a result of the establishment of NATO and the membership of Germany, over the objections of France, in 1955. The disaster in Suez the following year made matters worse and influenced the French decision to move forward with the nuclear weapons program as part of the new *Force de Frappe*, France's defensive or deterrence strike force. By 1958, Charles de Gaulle was back in office as President of the Fifth French Republic, triggering a renewed sense of national unity; his ten years in office represented the dawn of a modern France.

By 1960, the first French nuclear device, *Gerboise Bleu,* was available for testing, and it was exploded on February 13 near the town of Reggane in central Algeria. The official French document on the explosion reported, "For the explosion at low altitude, the earth, the water, and varied debris [. . .] formed a vertical column between the sun and the sphere of gas heat which had the appearance of snow." There was considerable radioactive contamination and there was need to establish a protective zone as "certain regions nearby to the test received a significant dose of radioactivity." There were additional nuclear tests in Algeria until 1966, and radioactive materials were buried in the Sahara until control was ceded to the Algerians in 1967. Between 1961 and 1966, France conducted thirteen underground tests in Algeria. A news item from 2015 in Al Jazeera reported that Saharan winds made investigation of lingering radioactivity impossible.

After leaving Algeria, France moved its nuclear testing program to French Polynesia in the southern reaches of the Pacific. The island of Mururoa was the principal site as it was considered sufficiently distant from the main populated island of Tahiti. Nearly 200 additional nuclear tests were carried out near the Mururoa and Fangataufa atolls, 46 of them atmospheric and largely without appropriate safeguards to protect the populated neighbouring islands. Tahiti, some 1500 kms away from the test sites, received 500 times the maximum allowed dose of radiation exposure following a 1974 test. Recent medical studies in the region conducted by the French organization INSERM have concluded that the nuclear testing in the region, especially the atmospheric tests, accounts for the high rate of cancers, especially thyroid, among the population. Before the testing, the islands were often referred to as an earthly paradise.

Opposition to French nuclear testing in the South Pacific became world-wide in the intervening years, but the testing did not come to an end until 1996. New Zealand-based groups led the opposition, and, in 1985, France retaliated by sinking the Greenpeace protest vessel, *Rainbow Warrior*, in the harbour of Auckland, killing one protestor. The French agents were arrested and convicted by the New Zealand authorities, but following sentencing were repatriated to France. It was not until 2009 that the French Parliament enacted legislation acknowledging the impact of the nuclear testing and provided compensation for only some of the French troops affected by the testing. There is no suggestion of compensation for the residents of Polynesia.

France today has the world's third-largest inventory of nuclear weapons, with approximately 300 operational. They are deployed using four nuclear powered submarines, one of which is always operational in the Atlantic. The Dassault Mirage IV supersonic strategic bomber was also capable of delivering nuclear weapons. In 2006, amidst numerous terrorist attacks, then-President Jacques Chirac declared that France's nuclear weapons could be used against states sponsoring terrorist activity: "The leaders of states who would use terrorist means against us, as well as those who would envision using . . . weapons of mass destruction, must understand that they would lay themselves open to a firm and fitting response on our part." In 1998, France signed the Comprehensive Nuclear Test Ban Treaty (CTBT), the only nuclear weapons state to have done so.

Since the bellicose statements of the President in 2006, France has taken a number of positive steps to reduce and contain its nuclear weapons program. It has established 300 weapons as the upper limits of its inventory, reduced aircraft deliverable weapons to about 30, and eliminated its inventory of land-based weapons associated with missile delivery. Importantly, it has reduced its budgeting for nuclear weapons by over fifty percent. By signing the 1998 CNTBT, it has provided evidence that its existing inventory of weapons will not change dramatically in the coming years.

Today, the nuclear weapons of the United Kingdom and France have minor relevance in global affairs. Their programs are legacies from a time when London and Paris were clinging to a power that was on the wane. Today, both countries stumble at the edges of world affairs and their ownership of nuclear weapons is a lingering, expensive legacy of a long-disappeared world. Both nations are part of NATO's nuclear umbrella shield, but they are not significant with respect to the dangers of proliferation. They are, however, two countries that could play a much larger role in the efforts to see the elimination of nuclear weapons. An offer by one or both countries to eliminate their nuclear weapons could provide a significant impetus in the efforts for the elimination and banning of nuclear weapons globally.

China

In 1964, at Lop Nur in the southeastern corner of the far western province of Xinjiang, China became the fifth nuclear weapons state. It exploded its first device on October 16 using uranium 235 in an implosion design. It had a yield of 20 kilotons equivalent of TNT. This design was followed by an explosion using plutonium, and by 1996, China conducted 23 atmospheric and 22 underground tests. In 1967, it tested its first fusion device with a yield of three megatons using lithium-6 deuteride.

The Chinese nuclear weapons program evolved quickly after the 1949 revolution and the war with the United States in Korea. The urgency for the weapons was increased with the two crises over Taiwan in the 1950s when the United States backed its miliary-countering actions with nuclear weapons. China's program was initially dependent on support from the Soviet Union, but after their break in relations in 1960 over issues associated with the Kremlin's efforts for a better relationship with the United States and the border conflict in 1969, the program became completely indigenous. It represented China's determination not to be intimidated by the nuclear weapons of either the United States or the Soviet Union.

China engaged with the world on nuclear matters in 1984 when it became a member of the International Atomic Energy Agency and has since participated in various international discussions on non-proliferation and disarmament. It signed the 1970 NPT in 1993 and the 1998 Test Ban Treaty. It has signed nuclear power agreements with Pakistan with appropriate safeguards against dual-use technologies in the development of nuclear weapons.

China regularly publishes papers on its defence strategy and profile. These have emphasized its no first use policy and emphasizes that its nuclear weapons are part of its strategic deterrence system in its relation to other nuclear weapon states. Reports stress that China's nuclear weapons would also be used in response to attacks involving nuclear weapons. As well, China has declared it will not use nuclear weapons in response to conventional attacks. A Chinese representative stated to the United Nations in 1995, "China undertakes not to use or threaten to use nuclear weapons against non-nuclear weapons states or nuclear-weapons-free zones at any time or under and circumstances."

There are no reliable figures on the size of China's nuclear arsenal. Estimates range from approximately 260 to the low three-hundreds. There are suggestions, mainly unreliable ones from Washington, that the inventory of Chinese nuclear weapons is increasing. The American Department of Defense annual report to Congress in November 2021 suggested that China could have 1000 nuclear weapons by the year 2030.

China has been relatively static in its inventory of nuclear weapons delivery systems but has been improving its early warning systems, along with sea-based nuclear deterrent facilities and technology. In its last detailed inventory of Chinese delivery systems, the International Institute of Strategic Studies' *Military Balance 2010* estimated that China had approximately 90 intercontinental ballistic missiles, with 20 having a range of over 10,000kms. It also has over 30 Submarine Launched Ballistic Missiles (SLBM), but there is ambiguity as to the number of its operational nuclear-powered submarines. China still uses its versions of Soviet aircraft as part of its nuclear bomber force, and while old, they are not as old as the American B-52 Stratofortress, still in active service. It has also developed the Xian JH-7 Flying Leopard fighter-bomber capable of delivering nuclear weapons. More recently, it has purchased more than a hundred Su-30s from Russia, which have a tactical nuclear weapons capacity.

The Chinese nuclear weapons program remains minimal in comparison to the United States and Russia, but with sufficient capabilities for deterrence. There have been few incidents of it threatening to use nuclear force for any reason. It has been a reasonably responsible nuclear weapon state, and, with the exception of aiding Pakistan four decades or so ago, China has not contributed to nuclear weapons proliferation. It participated with the United States and Russia in the P5+2 process to contain the Iranian nuclear weapons program and the earlier process involving North Korea. China thus remains an important and available resource in the ongoing efforts to contain and possibly eliminate nuclear weapons.

East Asia

A year after China's first nuclear test in 1965, Taiwan began its own nuclear weapons program using a nuclear research reactor provided by Canada. The program was terminated under pressure from Washington in the late '80s, and its fissile material inventory was transferred to the United States. However, Taiwan retains significant expertise in nuclear research and has three nuclear power reactors in use.

Despite a hopeful period of economic cooperation and quiescence in the political rhetoric between China and Taiwan, there has been a significant deterioration in the relationship over the last three years. The rhetoric has returned to historic levels of conflict, with almost daily iterations from Beijing that Taiwan remains a part of today's China and, with time, will be reintegrated.

The rhetoric has been accompanied by a significant increase in military activity from China in the air and waters around Taiwan. In response, the United States has sought to re-establish its dominant military position in the region with support from Canada and other allies. The opportunities for conflict have dramatically increased. Nuclear weapons have not been emphasized by either country in these efforts for dominance, but there can be little confidence the situation will remain static. The situation remains dangerous until such time as the future of the international status of Taiwan is established.

There are also nuclear weapons issues in East Asia involving China, with its increasing efforts for dominance in the East and South China Seas. The verbal iteration of those claims has moderated slightly, but ongoing demonstrations of China's military competence around Taiwan and in the South China Sea continue. For China's neighbours and the rest of the world, the nuclear weapons threat represented by China today creates a complex sense of insecurity for the region. The threat of nuclear weapons reinforces China's ground, air, and naval forces. As well, a lessening of American military posture in the region makes an invasion of Taiwan increasingly attractive to Beijing.

Adding to the worries of China's neighbours, especially for South Korea, Japan, and Taiwan, was the recent Trumpian diplomatic dalliance with the leader of North Korea, Kim Jong-un. This was short-lived, but its idiosyncrasy drew into question the soundness of the American nuclear umbrella under which the three countries have prospered. The continuing disruptive and destabilizing presence of Trump and his uncertainty in the American political universe does not provide comfort to those who can already see Chinese military activity from their own shores.

The September 2022 statements by President Biden do not necessarily instil full confidence in American security guarantees for the region. In a September 18 interview, Biden responded "yes" to the question of whether or not "U.S. forces, U.S. men and women, would defend Taiwan in the event of a Chinese invasion." This was the most direct statement on the issue by any recent President. It is a useful statement, but only reflects a temporary guarantee since it would likely be reversed should a Republican be elected president. For the countries of East Asia with a longer-term perspective on the future, the inherent uncertainty of American politics, and its uncertainty specifically on international security issues, creates a need for the careful examination of their future security needs. This uncertainty, combined with the uncertainty in Chinese policy on the issues involved, creates a degree of frisson not singularly caused by nuclear fission or fusion.

North Korea

North Korea, the most recent state to develop nuclear weapons, exploded its first device in 2006 in Hamgyong Province in the northeast of the country. The program is ongoing and is largely designed to offset military pressure from the United States and to ensure the security of its rogue regime. Associated with its nuclear weapons program is an extensive missile delivery system that periodically provides suggestions of its ability to reach continental United States. At this time, there is no expectation that these programs will be curtailed or ended in the coming years. North Korea remains of value to both China and Russia in their regional efforts for influence and ascendency. As such, without a concerted effort involving Beijing and Russia, North Korea will remain as an outlier in the universe of nuclear weapon states.

The United States retains a significant military force in South Korea and in recent months has increased its effectiveness, or, in the view from the North, its threat. In early July 2022, the Americans surged F-35 Lightning II multi-role strike aircraft into the Korean peninsula for ten-days of joint maneuvers with the South Korean Air Force. The Air Force noted that the flights "will enhance the interoperability of the two Air Forces to perform and operate on and around the Korean Peninsula." The F-35 will have a nuclear weapons capability in 2024.

In June, the Biden administration threatened North Korea with a "swift and forceful response" if Pyongyang conducts another nuclear test. The words reflect expectation North Korea will soon carry out another nuclear weapons explosion at Punggyeri, its known nuclear test site. In the past few months, North Korea has also tested a number of ballistic missiles, including intercontinental, hypersonic, and short-range, reflecting its ability for the delivery of its nuclear weapons.

North Korea was a signatory to the 1970 NPT but withdrew in 2003. It has had nuclear weapons ambitions for some time and exploded its first device in 2006. With its withdrawal from the NPT, five countries, China, Russia, United States, Japan, and South Korea began discussions with the North in an effort to curtail its nuclear weapons program and, more broadly, the elimination of all nuclear weapons from the Korean Peninsula. The discussions were called the Six Party Talks on North Korea's Nuclear Program and involved numerous multilateral and bilateral discussions between 2003 and 2009. There was relative cohesion in the five countries, but despite some suggestions of progress in 2005-06 period, ultimately there was no success, and North Korea withdrew from the process in 2009.

There have been occasional efforts to see the talks resumed, but so far little has been accomplished. In one of President Donald Trump's more erratic and unpredictable policy initiatives, he met with President Kim Jong-un of North Korea on two occasions to promote the elimination of nuclear weapons. The meetings in Singapore on June 12, 2018 and Hanoi on February 27-28, 2019 were abject failures and, if anything, accentuated North Korea's determination for the intensification of its nuclear weapon activities.

Throughout the period of the talks, North Korea continued its nuclear weapons activities with the explosion of its first device in 2006 along with the expansion of its missile delivery systems. Today, nuclear weapons status has been included in its constitution and has become an essential element in its "modernization and prosperity." It now suggests the elimination of its nuclear weapons will only occur as part of their world-wide elimination.

To emphasize its belligerence, North Korea ritualistically launches missiles whenever there is a prominent political visitor to the South. The launches in late September 2022 maintained the ritual when US Vice President Kamala Harris visited the Demilitarized Zone; such visits were ritualistically protested with the launch of missiles towards Japan. American officials simply reiterated the visit signaled American commitments to defending South Korea: "The key messaging that she's talking about on this trip is how our defense commitments are ironclad. We know there's been a lot of discussions with the Koreans about extended deterrence commitments. And to really put those words into action, we believe it's [the visit] a powerful signal of that." After the visit, there have been more ritualistic expressions that North Korea will conduct its seventh nuclear test.

The International Crisis Group in its report *North Korea: Beyond the Six-Party Talks* (Asia Report 269, June 16, 2015) summarized the situation: "The deadlock creates considerable finger-pointing. Dissatisfied Americans often blame China for not sufficiently pressuring Pyongyang; dissatisfied Chinese often blame the U. S. for not alleviating DPRK insecurity so as to create a more conducive environment. In the ROK, the right blames the left for coddling Pyongyang, while the left blames the right for policies that exacerbate its insecurity. All these views are flawed. Historical issues aside, the North's nuclear motivations are now driven by militant *son'gun* ideology [military first] that prescribes acquisition of a nuclear arsenal regardless of approaches in Beijing, Seoul, or Washington."

India and Pakistan

In 1974, India exploded its cheekily-named *Smiling Buddha* nuclear test device in western Rajasthan. Gautama was not amused as it could be heard from under his eternal Bodhi at Bodh Gaya in the not so far away state of Bihar. This test came ten years after China's first nuclear weapons test and was spurred by India's dramatic defeat in the traumatic 1962 war with China. The test device used plutonium produced by the Canadian financed CIRUS research reactor near Mumbai using heavy water provided by the United States.

India's nuclear research capabilities began with independence in 1947. Homi Bhabha, an Indian physicist, convinced Prime Minister Jawaharlal Nehru of the need to establish the Indian Atomic Energy Commission. After Dr. Bhabha's death, the Bhabha Atomic Research Centre at Trombay was founded in 1966. Nehru emphasized the peaceful uses of Indian nuclear research at the time, but he was also quoted as remarking, "Of course, if we are compelled as a nation to use it for other purposes, possibly no pious sentiments of any of us will stop the nation from using it that way." Nehru's daughter, Prime Minister Indira Gandhi, gave reality to these words with her agreement for the "peaceful" *Smiling Buddha* nuclear test in 1974.

Pakistan's nuclear weapons program was initiated by Prime Minister Zulfiqar Ali Bhutto following the country's defeat in the 1971 war largely initiated by India and which gave way to the emergence of East Pakistan as Bangladesh. Pakistan's weapons program paralleled the Indian program, especially after the Indian nuclear test explosion in 1974. The program was made possible with the return to Pakistan of Dr. Abdul Qadeer Khan, a physicist and metallurgist trained in Europe with knowledge and experience of gas centrifuge technology obtained during his work with a uranium enrichment facility in the Netherlands. He was instrumental in the establishment of the nuclear research facility at Kahuta, later called the Khan Research Laboratories (KRL).

In the aftermath of the Indian test series in early May of 1998, Pakistan had sufficient fissile material for its own nuclear test series on May 28 and May 30, 1998. The Pakistani tests were initially assessed through American monitoring as using low levels of weapons grade plutonium. Others have disputed this, suggesting the use of enriched uranium. The Pakistani official announcement of the tests reported 40 to 45 kilotons for the May 28 tests and 15 to 18 kilotons for the May 30 tests. Outside monitors suggested that the May 28 tests were 9 to 12 kilotons and 4 to 6 kilotons for those on May 30. Pakistan has also developed nuclear weapons including ballistic and cruise missiles with an arsenal likely matching India in its nuclear weapons capability

Since 1998, there is evidence Dr. Khan shared (or sold) aspects of Pakistani nuclear technology to North Korea, Syria, and Libya. There is also evidence that this was done with the knowledge of the Pakistani government; while Dr. Khan was put under house arrest in 2004, that decision was overturned by the High Court. Dr. Khan died in 2021, and many aspects of his proliferation activities have never been completely explained.

One aspect of Dr. Khan's work was close cooperation with China, as revealed in letters to his wife. Before China signed the 1970 Nuclear Non-Proliferation Treaty in 1992, it provided Pakistan with information on uranium enrichment, along with enriched uranium and design information for compact nuclear weapons. In return, Pakistan provided China with information via Khan on the Dutch enrichment technology and helped create a centrifuge facility for enriching uranium in China. The products from the facility were shared with

Pakistan along with tons of natural and slightly enriched uranium. In turn, Chinese scientists assisted Pakistan in the construction of its own facilities, including a production facility for plutonium.

Canada was involved in the Indian and Pakistani nuclear weapons programs from their early years. In 1955, it provided India a research reactor (Canada India Reactor Utility Services – CIRUS) similar to the one subsequently provided to Taiwan. India used plutonium from CIRUS for its '74 test. Hundreds of engineers, scientists, and technical personnel were trained in Canada during this period and contributed to the development of nuclear weapons.

In 1963, Canada signed an agreement with India to supply a 200MW CANDU power reactor based on the design used at Douglas Point in Ontario. Three years later, in 1966, Canada and India signed another agreement for the supply of a second reactor, again based on Douglas Point. Both reactors were for the Rajasthan Atomic Power Project and were designated as RAPP-1 and -2. RAPP-1 became operational in 1972, but assistance by Canada for RAPP-2 and cooperation on nuclear energy ended in 1974 following the test explosion, also in the state of Rajasthan. Since then, India has constructed 17 additional nuclear power stations using technology similar to that used at RAPP.

In 1966, Canada signed an agreement with Pakistan for the construction of a CANDU type nuclear power reactor at Karachi. It was smaller than the RAPP reactors, rated at less than 150mw. Originally named Karachi Nuclear Power Plant (KANUPP) and later K-1, it became operational in 1972 and was covered by IAEA monitoring and safeguards. It was decommissioned in 2021 after 50 years of reasonably assured power production. Two new nuclear power reactors have been built at the same site using assistance from China. The first was commissioned in 2021, and the second is expected to be finished in the next few months. Both of these power reactors are covered by IAEA safeguards and monitoring.

Israel and the Middle East

Secrets abound on most matters relating to national security, but there is exceptional security surrounding nuclear weapons. Nuclear weapons states have elaborate and detailed security arrangements preventing others from obtaining knowledge and understanding that could be used defensively and/or aggressively. Despite this level of security, there is much that is known, especially as to the development of nuclear weapons, their capacity, and their use in deterrence. Eight of the nuclear weapons states share information on their nuclear weapons for this purpose, emphasizing their effectiveness and giving credence to their availability. Russia is the most recent in doing so, reminding or warning the world of the availability of its nuclear weapons should its invasion and annexations of Ukraine continue to meet opposition.

The one exception in the use of information as an aspect of its possession of nuclear weapons is Israel. It has maintained a long-standing policy of ambiguity based on security for its nuclear weapons, including their numbers, size, and delivery systems. That policy continues even though ambiguity has largely disappeared in the knowledge and understanding available to others who observe events in the Middle East. Nevertheless, there are few, if any, indications future governments of Israel will change its nuclear weapons policy as it offers a significant deterrence against future wars with its surrounding enemies.

Equally, its nuclear weapons are weapons of last resort for the survival of the country. This was reflected in the apocryphal stories of the two nuclear devices, rapidly assembled, for possible use in the 1967 War and the labelling of its first two nuclear weapons as *Never Again*. Since Israel's war for independence in 1948, there have been numerous conflicts with its neighbours that emphasize the dangers to its survival. These ongoing conflicts reinforce a sense of identity built around the idea of Israel as a refuge state, an escape from the Holocaust and the continuing dangers from a still-hostile world. All this provided rationale for the early development of nuclear weapons as a singularly important element for national security. The ongoing efforts by Palestinians to maintain a permanent position in the conflicted land, the Suez war of 1956, the Six Day War of 1967, and the successive War of Attrition, followed by the Yom Kippur War of 1973, wars involving Lebanon in 1982 and 1985, and, more recently, weeks long conflicts in Gaza, have all provided strong domestic support for Israel's nuclear weapons.

Despite Israel's commitment to secrecy, there has been one notable source of information from inside the Israeli program. That detailed information came from an Israeli nuclear technician, Mordechai Vanunu, who worked at the main research facility at Dimona from 1976 to 1986. The rarity and specificity of the information attracted global interest and attention. In part, the attention was generated by the harshness of Israel's reaction to the leak as it was to the information itself. After his public disclosures through detailed articles in the London *Sunday Times* in 1986, Mr. Vanunu was eventually kidnapped by Israeli agents in Rome, returned to Israel, tried, convicted and sentenced to a lengthy prison term. He was released in 2004, but strenuous parole conditions and travel restrictions have led to his re-arrest on several occasion. He has been lauded internationally for his disclosures, with Daniel Ellsberg of Pentagon Papers fame describing him as "the preeminent hero of the nuclear era."

The *Sunday Times* had also published the *Hitler Diaries*, which were revealed to be fake. So, they did not take any chances with the Vanunu papers. The paper hired Theodore Taylor, an American nuclear weapons physicist who had worked at the Los Alamos Nuclear Laboratory in New Mexico, along with a British weapons expert to examine the Vanunu papers. Taylor, while working at Los Alamos, designed and developed the smallest, most powerful, and most efficient fission weapon ever made by the United States. Nicknamed the "Davy Crockett," the bomb weighed only fifty pounds, was 12-inches in diameter, yet could produce 10 to 20 tons of TNT equivalent. Taylor specialized in fission bombs and designed one that produced 500 kilotons of TNT equivalent.

Taylor and the British nuclear expert, after their examination of the Vanunu papers, assured the *Sunday Times* of the accuracy. With that, the papers were published. Taylor concluded that Israel's thermonuclear or H-Bomb weapons designs were "less complex than those of other nations," and as of 1986, "not capable of producing yields in the megaton or higher range." There was evidence that Israel could boost the yield of such devices, so Taylor concluded that Israel had "unequivocally" tested a miniaturized nuclear device. The Institute for Defense Analyses (IDA), a private American non-profit organization, also reviewed the Vanunu papers and concluded that Israel's nuclear weapons development was similar to that of the United States' ten years earlier. Israel's plutonium processing, according to Vanunu, produced about 30 kg per year and used approximately four kilograms for each weapon. It was from this information that Israel's nuclear weapons inventory was estimated of up to 150 weapons.

Israel began activities leading to the development of nuclear weapons within weeks of its independence in 1948. In those early years of unrestrained and uncontained nuclear weapons proliferation, Israel established a policy framework for the development of nuclear weapons; it also had the scientific and technical talents among the millions who migrated in the aftermath of the Second World War. There was considerable support internationally for its efforts. France was the most supportive, especially in the development of the Negev Nuclear Research Centre at Dimona in the desert area of southern Israel. By the end of the 1950s, the Centre had a research reactor and a reprocessing plant for plutonium. Israel was also able to obtain from the United Kingdom associated fissile material for use at the Negev Centre, including uranium-235, plutonium, enriched lithium-6, and heavy water. Norway also provided heavy water. This support was important, but the Israeli nuclear program was essentially a domestic effort, and its sophistication today reflects its long history.

At the latest, Israel became the world's sixth nuclear weapons state by 1968 immediately after its Six Day War the previous year. A report from the American Council of Foreign Relations stated that on the eve of the War, Prime Minister, Levi Eshkol, "ordered scientists to assemble two crude nuclear devices. . . One [Israeli] official said the operation was referred to as Spider because the nuclear devices were inelegant contraptions with appendages sticking out. The crude atomic bombs were readied for deployment on trucks that could race to the Egyptian border for detonation in the event Arab forces overwhelmed Israeli defenses." In 1969, Henry Kissinger reported that President Nixon asked Israeli Prime Minister Golda Meir to "make no visible introduction of nuclear weapons or undertake a nuclear test program."

The Nixon request to Meir reflected an end to the earlier American efforts, largely during the Kennedy Administration, to contain, if not end, Israel's nuclear weapons efforts. Kennedy sought agreement for regular American inspection of Israel's nuclear research facilities, but these were delayed by Israeli procrastinations and fabrications. In 1960, there was a flurry of press stories on the Israeli program, including official confirmation from the chair of the American Atomic Energy Commission, that Israel had built a nuclear research reactor with France providing assistance.

The speculation was sufficiently intense at the time for Israeli Prime Minister Ben-Gurion to speak publicly about the program. In the Knesset, the Prime Minister confirmed that it was building a 24MW reactor, "which will serve the needs of industry, agriculture, health, and science . . . designed exclusively for peaceful purposes." The long-term chair of the Israeli Atomic Energy Commission was more truthful when he spoke, saying "There is no distinction between nuclear energy for peaceful purposes or warlike ones" and that "we shall never again be led as lambs to the slaughter."

It has been reported for some time that Israel and Apartheid-era South Africa cooperated closely on the development of nuclear weapons. One unverified report suggested Israel was able to test an early nuclear device at the South African Vastrap testing site in the Kalahari. There has been ongoing speculation as well that the nuclear explosion in the far southern regions of the Indian Ocean on September 22, 1979 was a joint effort involving Israel and South Africa. The explosion was detected between the Crozet Islands, a French possession, and the Prince Edward Islands, belonging to

South Africa, approximately halfway between southern Africa and Antarctica. This was known as the Vela Incident as it was detected by sensors on an American Vela satellite designed to detect nuclear explosions. The satellite provided sufficient detail for reports suggesting it was an atmospheric nuclear explosion of two-to-three kilotons.

The Carter Administration established an ad hoc panel of scientific and engineering experts to examine the data from the Vela. In its final report, the panel concluded, "careful examination reveals a significant deviation in the light signature of the 22 September event that throws doubt on the interpretation as a nuclear event." But while they could not rule out the possibility that the Vela signal was of nuclear origin, "based on our experience in related scientific assessments, it is out collective judgment that the September 22 signal was probably not from a nuclear explosion." Subsequent to the report, other experts have questioned this conclusion, with one suggesting that the decisions of the ad hoc panel were politically motivated. The Vela Incident remains one of the small mysteries in the development of nuclear weapons.

The author of this book was with the Canadian Embassy in Washington at the time of the Vela Incident and had conversations with a variety of American experts. The information from the Vela of most interest in the conversations was the "double flash" of light reported by the satellite. The double flash is one of the most distinctive features of a nuclear explosion: an approximately six-second time gap between two flashes. The information from the Vela, according to those who had seen the data, clearly showed the double flash with the six-second interval. In the subsequent discussions of the incident, there are no references to the double flash, the most damning piece of evidence from the Vela that it detected a nuclear explosion.

According to estimates by the Bulletin of Atomic Scientists in 2013, Israel has approximately 80 nuclear weapons and enough fissile material to produce 190 more, but it stopped production of additional weapons in 2004.

Iran

Iran is the only country today creating serious concerns over the development of nuclear weapons. Some ten years ago, this led to the creation of the P5+2 grouping (the five permanent members of the Security Council plus Germany and the European Union) that began negotiations with Iran in order to bring its potentially nuclear weapons proliferation activities to an end. This resulted in the Joint Comprehensive Plan of Action (JCPOA) of 2015, agreed to by all of the seven involved countries and the EU. This was an unprecedented moment since the JCPOA included the United States, Russia, and China in their first ever collective agreement on nuclear weapons. The agreement provided for ongoing IAEA inspection of Iranian nuclear facilities and significant limitations on its uranium enrichment activities. The agreement was for 15 years, up to 2030, but could be extended. In exchange, Iran obtained significant relief from political and economic sanctions. The early years of the agreement provided internationally verified evidence that Iran was honouring the agreement.

There was widespread support in the region and elsewhere for the JCPOA. The most significant opposition came from Israel, the only nuclear weapons state in the Middle East. The Israeli government under Benjamin Netanyahu labelled the agreement a "historic mistake" and found support for this view within the American Republican Party. John Baird, the Canadian foreign minister at the time, was quoted as saying Iran "has not earned the right to have the benefit of the doubt." Donald Trump opposed the agreement in his pre-2016 electioneering, so it was no surprise when he withdrew the United States from the agreement in 2018. Since then, the other five parties to the agreement have sought to keep it active with little success. In recent months, Iran has resumed full-scale uranium enrichment activities and has limited IAEA inspections.

The collapse of the JCPOA was accompanied by assassinations, sabotage of cyber facilities associated with enrichment, and attacks on Iranian military personnel in Syria, Lebanon, and Iraq by Israel and the United States. Iran, in return and, in cooperation with its allies in those countries, Hezbollah and Hamas, carried out attacks both on American bases in the region and Israel. There is now nearly a state of clandestine war between the various parties.

The election of Joe Biden two years ago came with a commitment to re-negotiate and rejoin a recreated JCPOA. There is strong international agreement in doing so, but the renewed American interest came with new conditions and demands. Iran, for its part, is insisting on non-reversable American guarantees, not subject to the results of the next presidential election. These demands have yet to be bridged, and there is significant uncertainty as to the renewal of the JCPOA. In late September, the Iranian foreign minister reported renewed indications from the United States of "will and goodwill" in Washington to reach a new agreement. Whether President Biden's success in the November 8, 2022 midterm congressional elections will lead to a new agreement remains uncertain.

This impasse with Iran is a danger to the control, if not the spread, of nuclear weapons. It could end any possibility of some measure of calm, let alone peace, in the Middle East. Despite some efforts by President Biden along with the Europeans to see the Accord re-energized, the Iranians have demanded guarantees from the United States on its permanency; Iran does not want to again be a victim of the vagaries of American electoral politics. Iran has also demanded the elimination or reduction in sanctions and the removal of Iran's Islamic Revolutionary Guards Corps (IRGC) from the American list of terrorist groups. The September death of a Kurdish woman in governmental custody and the consequential widespread unrest directed at the government has created hesitation in Tehran on the agreement as well. The Kurdish Regional Government in northwestern Iran has been subject to verbal criticism as well as military action by the IRGC, contributing to a fragile political environment for a revised agreement on nuclear non-proliferation to emerge.

Israel has been consistent in its objection to the Accord. This to many is self-injurious, but Jerusalem persists in its strong objections to any renewal of an international agreement with Iran on nuclear matters. The success of Benjamin Netanyahu in the November general election will see a renewal of Israeli objections to the Iranian arrangement. In the United States, the matter is a third rail in American political decision making. In some measure, the objections are driven by the existence of Israel's own nuclear weapons program, which has been enormously successful in avoiding international attention.

But already the disastrous consequences of the collapse of the agreement with Iran have become apparent. Iran has now fully reactivated its uranium enrichment program and has fissile material available for upgrading to the 90% range needed for the construction of nuclear weapons. Experts suggest it is only a matter of weeks before the construction of an actual weapon, although there is skepticism with such projections given the complexities involved in bomb construction.

Comments from Iran on the situation are rare, but on July 17, 2022, a senior adviser to Supreme Leader Ayatollah Ali Khamenei told Al-Jazeera that Iran was capable of making a nuclear weapon, but a decision to do so has not yet been made. The adviser said, "In a few days we were able to enrich uranium up to 60 percent and we can easily produce 90 percent enriched uranium... Iran has the technical means to produce a nuclear bomb but there has been no decision by Iran to build one." The JCPOA provides an upper limit of below 4 percent for enrichment, but 90 percent would provide material for a nuclear bomb.

Already, there are suggestions that should the renegotiations fail (see Eric Brewer's article in the June 17, 2022 *Foreign Affairs*), the United States would use its massive ordnance penetrator 30,000-pound "bunker buster" bomb on Iran's deep underground enrichment and weapons facilities. Available American military facilities throughout the region lend some credence to such a scenario. Unfortunately, there is no one involved with memories of the last time the United States militarily entered Iran. That happened in December 1979, when President Carter authorized a mission to rescue American embassy staff held hostage by the new government. The Iranians did not fire a shot, but the American effort ended ignominiously in flames on the desert of southern Iran. Washington, in the following days, was etched in dark foreboding, and it took the entry of Ronald Regan into the White House a few weeks later to create the conditions in Tehran for the release of the hostages.

Even more troublesome is Israel's historic assertion that "it will not tolerate a nuclear-armed Iran." This claim remains central to its security policy. Its earlier attacks on nuclear facilities in Syria and Iraq and its ongoing sabotage and assassinations against Iran and Iranians gives ample evidence of its willingness to enforce this doctrine. More broadly, efforts to create a military alliance of Arab and other states against Iran last March saw American and Israeli security officials meeting with those from Egypt, Jordan, Qatar, Bahrain, Saudi Arabi, and the United Arab Emirates. In these evolving circumstances, Israel would obtain support from the United States for a bombing mission and most likely one or two of the Gulf States would offer serious objections.

An article in the July 1, 2022 *Foreign Affairs* by Maria Fantappie and Vali Nasr also highlights the fragile political environment attending the flailing negotiations for the renewal of the JCOPA. Fantappie and Nasr write that the Biden Administration still argues that the revival of the JCPOA is the best way to control Iran's nuclear weapons program, "But failing that, it appears prepared to adopt Israel's current approach to containing Iran. That entails further tightening the economic noose around Iran's neck by forcing the country out of the oil market. And it means the United States would support Israel in carrying out attacks inside Iran and in its effort to weave a coalition of Arab states to contain the country."

Other Middle East Countries

The Israeli nuclear weapons program created incentives and ambitions for Egypt, Syria, Iraq, and Libya to establish their own nuclear weapons programs.

Egypt

Egypt was the first, with activities starting in the mid-1950s to obtain facilities associated with the production of nuclear energy. In 1954, it acquired a 2 MW research reactor from the Soviet Union for the Inshas Nuclear Research Centre in Cairo and a second research reactor of 22 MW for Inshas from Argentina. Both reactors are still operational and under IAEA safeguards.

There has been an incipient effort to develop nuclear power program, and a Nuclear Power Plant Authority was established in 1976. In 1964, 1983, and 2006, plans were announced for specific nuclear power plants, but little happened. Again, in 2015 and 2017, plans were announced for a power plant at El Dabaa with Russian Rosatom, and in 2022 it was announced that the Korean Hydro Nuclear Power agency would help with the construction. Local opposition to the use of the land has delayed if not eliminated the possibility of the plant being constructed. Earlier, Canada's AECL and the American company Bechtel expressed interest in nuclear power plant development, but these did not result in any specific plans.

Egypt has ratified the 1970 Non-Proliferation Treaty but has not signed the 2022 Treaty on the Prohibition of Nuclear Weapons (TPNW), and it is one of the eight countries whose signature is needed for its entry into force. A former Foreign Minister of Egypt and Secretary General of the Arab League, in a meeting in Washington a number of years ago, summed up the situation when he stated, "If there is a nuclear program in Israel, then we can blame nobody and no country if they want to acquire the same . . . this is an invitation to an arms race – a very, very serious and dangerous policy."

That belief permeates the issue and there will be occasional developments giving rise to allegations of Egyptian interest in acquiring nuclear weapons. The IAEA has investigated allegations of undeclared nuclear activity at the Inshas Nuclear Research Centre, including the presence of low and highly enriched uranium. It ultimately reported that Egypt was in conformity with its obligations. Egypt fully cooperated with the IAEA in its investigations.

Iraq

Activities by Iraq, as with Syria, created strong indications of efforts to develop nuclear weapons. But their activities involving the use of chemical weapons were of greater concern, especially when used against its own people and in Iraq's eight-year war with Iran, and this in some measure minimized their nuclear weapons activities.

Early Iraqi nuclear activities included the establishment of an Atomic Energy Commission in 1956, and a 1959 agreement with the Soviet Union for the construction of a nuclear power plant. This eventually came to fruition in 1968 when the Soviet Union supplied a nuclear research reactor, IRT-2000, which was constructed at the Tuwaitha Nuclear Research Centre at Osirak, southeast Baghdad. Several western countries in these early years were also involved in providing Iraq with equipment associated with nuclear energy. These nations included France, Italy, Germany, the United States, and the United Kingdom. In 1976, France signed an agreement with Iraq to provide two research reactors for Tuwaitha, along with a pilot plutonium separation laboratory. Most of these arrangements were covered by IAEA safeguards. Italy, however, provided a laboratory, also at Tuwaitha, for a plutonium handling facility, outside the bounds of IAEA safeguards.

Construction of the French reactors was nearing completion in early 1980. The largest was a 40MW highly enriched uranium, light-water-moderated Osiris-class nuclear reactor, while the second was an ISIS open-pool reactor of 700KW intended for teaching and training purposes. The agreement with France also included the provision of 72 kg of 93% enriched uranium and associated training for the operation of the reactors, the first shipment of which arrived in Iraq in July.

Israel and Iran, nervous allies at the time, followed these developments closely, and eight days after the start of the Iraqi war with Iran on September 22, 1980, Iranian F-4 American-made aircraft, provided when the Shah was still on the Peacock Throne, attacked the Tuwaitha site, damaging the reactors and, more critically, the Nuclear Research Centre. The Iranian attack, code named *Scorch*

Sword, was a world's first: a successful air attack on nuclear reactors without releasing nuclear radiation. But Israel considered the attack insufficient, so, nine months later, the Israelis flew into Iraq on June 7, 1981, completely destroying the Research Centre and eliminating any future possibility of an Iraqi nuclear weapons program.

The Israeli attack was audacious. Again, American-made aircraft, F-16As and F-15As, travelled nearly a thousand miles, violating hostile Jordanian, Saudi, and Syrian airspace, without midair refueling, and attacked a defended nuclear site in Iraq. The Israeli military thought it could be done, but many in the government felt otherwise; there was considerable debate as to the value of the attack, especially given the inevitable international fallout. In the end, Prime Minister Menachem Begin approved the attack on the basis of the worst-case scenario that the Iraqis could have nuclear weapons in a one-to-two-year time frame. This reasoning was bolstered by the possibility that the reactors, if operational, could cause the dispersal of radioactive materials. The decision to attack became known as the Begin Doctrine and was used again by Israel as justification for its attack on the Al Kibar nuclear site in Syria on 2007.

The attack became a textbook example for such operations. The aircraft took approximately two hours to reach the Nuclear Research Centre, spent less than two minutes over the site, released sixteen 2,000 lb bombs, eight of which hit the reactor containment dome. The dome and its associated facilities were completely destroyed. Two hours later, all aircraft were safely on the ground in Israel. Twenty-two later years, American troops further reduced the rubble when they entered the site in the aftermath of their 2003 invasion. Today, Saddam's nuclear ambitions are as with Shelley's Ozymandias:

> My name is Ozymandias, king of kings:
> Look on my works, ye Mighty, and despair!
> Nothing beside remains. Round the decay
> Of that colossal wreck, boundless and bare
> The lone and level sands stretch far away.

International reaction to the attack was intense and widespread. Resolutions in both the UN General Assembly and the Security Council were condemnatory. The attack was a "clear violation of the Charter of the United Nations and the norms of international conduct," with the Assembly describing it as a "premeditated and unprecedented act of aggression." The IAEA sought to expel Israel from the Agency but was opposed by the United States on the grounds that it was beyond the rules and could affect future of non-proliferation efforts. Along with the 2007 bombing of the Syrian nuclear reactor, the bombing of Osirak reflected Israel's absolute determination to be the only nuclear weapons state in the Middle East.

Syria

Over the years, Syria has demonstrated an interest in developing nuclear weapons along with development and production facilities for mass destruction chemical weapons, especially ricin. In 1991, China provided a miniature nuclear research reactor, and there was interest in additional research reactors. Early in this century, there were reports of the construction of a nuclear weapons facility at Al Kibar (also known as Dair Alzour) in the Deir ez-Zor province of eastern Syria. In the spring and summer of 2007, Israel, in cooperation with the United States, obtained information confirming suspicions the site was being prepared for the development of nuclear weapons. In addition to support from North Korea, it was believed that Iran was also assisting.

There is conflicting information on the degree of American involvement, with one report saying that the United States did not agree to the attacking of the site, but, in any event, on September 6, 2007, Israel attacked the Al Kibar site in an operation codenamed *Outside the Box*. The attack was carried out by eight aircraft of the Israeli Air Force using Maverick missiles and 500 lb bombs, with four of the aircraft entering Syria. The facility was destroyed. Surprisingly, everyone involved – the Israelis, the Americans, and the Syrians

– downplayed the attack, and, other than increasing the popularity of the Israeli Prime Minister, the event became just another episode in the ongoing conflicts in the Middle East.

A month after the attack, the American non-governmental organization Institute for Science and International Security, founded by a former IAEA nuclear inspector, released a report on the nuclear work at Al Kibar. The report included speculation that the facility was constructed with help from North Korea as it was similar to a facility at Yongbyon, the main nuclear facility for the country. IAEA inspectors were permitted to visit the bombed site in mid-2008 and subsequently reported that they found "a significant number of natural uranium particles." At the time, the IAEA did not speculate as to whether or not the site was intended for the development of nuclear weapons. Later in 2009, the IAEA reported that the analysis of collected material from the site suggested that it had the "features" of a nuclear reactor, but went on to report that Syria had refused to provide the necessary cooperation for a firm conclusion.

Libya

Libya, in 1968, was an early signature country of the NPT and went on to ratify the treaty in 1975. In 1969, the monarchial government established in the aftermath of the Second World War was overthrown while King Idris was outside of the country; thus, the world began its 40-year fascination with Muammar Ghaddafi, Brotherly Leader and Guide of the Revolution of Libya. While he died ignominiously in a drainage ditch in October 2011, he roiled regional and world politics throughout his rule, including efforts to obtain nuclear weapons to bolster his role and influence in the fight against Israel.

In the aftermath of his revolution, there were reports of efforts to buy nuclear weapons, without success, from China, India, and Pakistan. As well, according to later reports from the IAEA, Libya began activities that could lead to the use of uranium and plutonium for nuclear weapons. Uranium was imported outside of its obligations under NPT and efforts were begun to obtain enrichment facilities. In the late 1980s, Libya was able to obtain equipment for small-scale uranium enrichment from Pakistan. It also made arrangements with a "nuclear weapon state" for the processing of uranium compounds that could have been used in the development of nuclear weapons. At Tajoura, a few miles the east of Tripoli, a nuclear research centre was established, along with a 10 MW research reactor obtained from the Soviet Union. Discussions were later initiated with the Soviet Union, France, and Belgium for a larger research reactor and a nuclear power plant, but international objections prevented the purchases. The Soviet reactor was covered by IAEA safeguards. Hundreds of students went abroad for studies in nuclear physics, some to the United States, until entry was denied in 1983.

In the 1990s, Libya intensified its efforts to "reinvigorate its nuclear activities." This included efforts to obtain gas centrifuge uranium enrichment equipment, according to an IAEA 2004 report. Dr. A Q. Khan, the developer of Pakistan's nuclear weapons program, was involved in assisting Libya, as were representatives from North Korea and Russia, with an emphasis on the development of uranium enrichment facilities.

These efforts toward production of nuclear weapons ended in 2003. On December 19, President Ghaddafi announced his decision to dismantle Libya's nuclear weapons activities and to provide the international community with details. In a letter to the UN Security Council, Libya's commitments under the NPT were reaffirmed and, significantly, it agreed to the IAEA Protocol providing for additional and more intrusive inspections of sites where nuclear weapons research was underway. There was also an invitation for IAEA inspectors to enter the country in order to verify the abrupt change in Libya's nuclear policy. IAEA inspectors began visits in late 2003 and inspected 18 sites where nuclear weapons development activities had been underway. In its early reports, the Agency concluded its "initial inspections of these locations did not identify specific facilities currently dedicated to nuclear weapons component manufacturing."

Separate agreements with the United States and the United Kingdom resulted in thousands of documents transferred to the American Oak Ridge National Laboratory in Tennessee, along with containers of uranium hexafluoride used for enrichment, plus associated centrifuges provided by Pakistan.

On February 20, 2004, the Director General of the IAEA issued a report on the findings of his inspectors:

> Starting in the early 1980s and continuing until the end of 2003, Libya imported nuclear material and conducted a wide variety of nuclear activities, which it had failed to report to the Agency as required under its Safeguards Agreement
>
> ...
>
> As part of verifying the correctness and completeness of Libya's declarations, the Agency is also investigating ... the supply routes and sources of sensitive nuclear technology and related equipment and nuclear and non-nuclear materials ... It is evident already that a network has existed whereby actual technological know-how originates from one source, while the delivery of equipment and some of the materials have taken place through intermediaries, who have played a coordinating role, subcontracting the manufacturing to entities in yet other countries.

The 2003 decision by Libya to publicly dismantle its nuclear weapons activities and to provide complete details is unique in non-proliferation terms. It was not, however, self-generated or a benevolent act. Rather, it followed years of efforts by the non-proliferation community and the international agencies involved that increasingly made the cost, both politically and economically, of the Libyan nuclear program too high to maintain. Sanctions, both political and economic, increased the difficulty for Libya to obtain the needed equipment and material to manufacture its own weapons. Its international political isolation became more intense as awareness of its nuclear activities became known. This was particularly evident following the release of information relating to the Pan American flight 103 from London to New York on December 21, 1988, which exploded midair over Lockerbie, Scotland, killing 270 onboard and on the ground. The subsequent identification of those involved, along with details of the involvement of the government of Libya, intensified the pressure.

Two years before the destruction of Pan Am 103, the American air raid on April 15, 1986, against air and military facilities in Tripoli and Benghazi, demonstrated the willingness of the United States to use its military resources in the United Kingdom and especially in the Mediterranean to counter Libyan naval activities along its coast. Three NATO allies of the United States – France, Italy, and Spain – refused overflight permission for aircraft from the United Kingdom. But despite considerable additional distance, the raid was successful. The raid also came 10-days after the bombing of a nightclub in West Berlin blamed on Libya. This was the first indication that the United States was willing to use its military against Libya. In the aftermath of the 9/11 attacks on the World Trade Centre in New York and the Pentagon, the speed of the United States' invasion of Afghanistan, and the planning for the invasion of Iraq provided renewed evidence of the willingness of the US government to counter its adversaries militarily. It was only nine-months after the invasion of Iraq on March 19, 2003, that Ghaddafi announced the ending of his nuclear weapons activities, realizing the tenuousness of his position in the perspectives of Washington.

In the final ten years of rule, with his influence in the Middle East largely at an end, Ghaddafi shifted his attention to Africa and was chair of the African Union in his final year of life. The turmoil in the Middle East associated with the Arab Spring of 2011 spread to Libya, and protests were widespread, first in eastern Libya, and then descending into a civil war. NATO forces ultimately intervened in support of the anti-Ghaddafi National Transitional Council. Ghaddafi's government was overthrown and he retreated to Sirte, only to be captured and executed. With his death, the last example of a Middle East nuclear weapons program disappeared.

The March 19, 2011 NATO Libyan military intervention was an operation involving several states providing support for UN Security Council Resolution of 1973 passed two days earlier, on March 17, acting under the authority provided by Chapter VII of the UN Charter. The Resolution called for "an immediate ceasefire in Libya, including an end to the current violence against civilians, which it said might constitute 'crimes against humanity' ... [imposing] a ban on all flights in the country's airspace – a no-fly-zone – and tightened sanctions on Qahafi regime and its supporters."

Canada joined the forces of the United States, the United Kingdom, Italy, Belgium, Denmark, France, Norway, Spain, and Qatar in support of the anti-Ghaddafi coalition. The operation ended seven months later, on October 31, following the death of the President and a vote by the Security Council. Canadian naval and air force units were directly involved and engaged in the 7,000 bombings into Libya against Ghaddafi's forces.

President Ghaddafi was captured and killed on October 20, 2011 during fighting around the city of Sirte, halfway between Tripoli and Benghazi on the Gulf of Sirte. Ghaddafi was part of a large military convoy escaping the area when it was attacked by British, American, and French aircraft. The President, along with his son, took shelter in a nearby drainage pipe where he was captured. There are conflicting accounts of the events surrounding his capture and his subsequent death. In any event, his treatment did not correspond to any of the acceptable rules in such situations, and there have been calls for an investigation by the UN, the United States, and the United Kingdom on the grounds that it was extrajudicial and a war crime. Nothing of any consequence came from the questions associated with his death, and in the meantime, President Ghaddafi and his son were buried in secret in the Libyan desert, a place of comfort for him throughout his life.

The Libyan civil war of 2011 rages on. There are a variety of contending factions in play, and there are few signs these will come to any sort of acceptable solution. In many ways, Libya today resembles

Somalia, where only time and endless frustration might provide some measure in which an acceptable government might emerge. In this, there are no indications whatsoever of any interest among any of the contending parties for a renewal of Ghaddafi's nuclear weapons program. The IAEA continues to maintain an interest in Libya's legacy nuclear materials, and there have been periodic inspections, but there is no danger that these materials will or can be used in connection with nuclear weapons.

Algeria

Algeria, on the western border of Libya, is still largely preoccupied with internal political issues and an abundance of oil and gas that offers lucrative trade opportunities as Europe looks for new sources amidst sanctions on Russia. There have been few significant developments relating to nuclear power, but Algeria has two nuclear research reactors. The first was a 1MW pool-type unit at Draria built by INVAP of Argentina in the late 1980s. The second is a heavy water reactor at Ain Ouessara built with assistance from China and operational since 1992. A 2014 agreement with Russia provided for assistance in the construction of nuclear power plants and additional research reactors, but there are few signs the agreement has turned into construction contracts. Earlier agreements with the United States and discussions with France have not made any progress.

Algeria was the main test site in the development of French nuclear weapons in 1960. This arrangement continued after independence in 1962 until 1968 and remains a matter of ongoing bitterness in the bilateral relationship. approximately 17 nuclear test explosions were involved. The French government has been unusually difficult (as were the Americans in compensation for the Marshall Islanders) in providing compensation for those affected, apart from the French soldiers. Only a few hundred Algerians have been compensated, and the testing region in the centre of the country remains largely out of bounds.

Saudi Arabia

There is little information available supporting the idea that Saudi Arabia or other states in the Gulf have undertaken activities related to the development of nuclear weapons. There is, however, occasional speculation of Saudi interest in the purchase of nuclear weapons. This is largely a result of the Saudis' relationship with Iran and the failure of the international community, especially the United States and Israel, to provide verifiable assurances and limits on Iranian activities and intentions.

There are also media reports alleging Saudi Arabia financed the nuclear weapons program of Pakistan in exchange for weapons at some future date. Similar stories were earlier written about the Iraqi nuclear program. The Iraqi nuclear program no longer exists, but a nuclear weapon sharing agreement between Pakistan and Saudi Arabia may be a concern. The close political and military relationship between the two countries and the existence of Israeli nuclear weapons, along with the ongoing possibility of Iran developing nuclear weapons, makes such an agreement valuable to Saudi Arabia. The Saudi Crown Prince, Mohammed bin Salman, speaking on CBS' *60 Minutes* in late 2018 warned that if Iran develops nuclear weapons, "without a doubt ... we will follow suit as soon as possible."

In recent years, Saudi Arabia has sought to develop facilities that would increase its understanding and experience with nuclear power issues, including the use of its own uranium resources. In 2019, there was an agreement with the Trump Administration that would allow Saudi Arabia access to information on nuclear matters, but few details on what information was released is available. In the same time period, there was a report that China had provided assistance in the construction of a uranium yellowcake production facility, a preliminary process in the conversion or raw uranium before use for fuel fabrication or uranium enrichment.

In 2018, Saudi Arabia began construction of its first nuclear research reactor at King Abdulaziz City, near Riyadh. The light-water research reactor, which produces 10KW of power using 2.1% enriched uranium, is being assisted by INVAP of Argentina and is now close to completion. There are no reports as to where the needed low-level enriched uranium will be sourced. The reactor is part of Saudi Arabia's emerging developments efforts beyond the use of oil, including renewable and atomic energy, water desalination, genetic medicine, and aircraft manufacturing. The reactor as presently envisioned would have no direct role in the production of nuclear weapons; yet, it would form part of the pool of expertise needed should a decision be made to obtain them.

The fueling of the research reactor with low-level enriched uranium engages IAEA safeguards that have yet to be developed. The Saudis and the Agency have been discussing the matter, but so far nothing specific has emerged. Saudi Arabia is a signatory to the 1970 Non-Proliferation Treaty, but in the absence of nuclear facilities, it has only required an appropriate low-level safeguards agreement. The research reactor changes that, and the IAEA is now encouraging Saudi Arabia to sign a more comprehensive safeguards agreement. It is possible the July 2022 agreement with the South Korean Institute of Nuclear Safety for regulatory support will provide advice leading to an improved agreement with the IAEA.

Nuclear events and activities covering both power and weapons involving Iran, Pakistan, Israel, the United States, and the IAEA require close monitoring as they are related to and conditional for Saudi nuclear intentions. Saudi nuclear intentions are, at this time, appropriate for the circumstances, but the conditioning factors, especially those of Iran, remain uncertain and provide the impulse for serious efforts by Saudi Arabia to obtain and or develop nuclear weapons. At this time, they are well short of that capacity.

Saudi Arabia's close allies in the Persian Gulf – the United Arab Emirates, Iraq, Oman, Kuwait, and Oman – are equally concerned with the collapse of the 2015 Iranian agreement on non-proliferation. They nervously regard recent developments as being directly inimical to their interests, and, along with the Arab League, have promoted the idea of a nuclear-weapons-free zone for the region. This initiative has not attracted support, mainly due to Israel's nuclear weapons and the near nuclear capacity of Iran. However, at some point, it is an idea that might be helped by such a plan; it remains as only an idea until such time as there is support from countries such as Saudi Arabia and Egypt.

South Africa

South Africa successfully developed nuclear weapons, but its program was terminated during the period when minority rule gave way to majority rule between 1989-91. At the time, it had seven nuclear weapons (six operational and one in development). All were destroyed. It is the only country in which an active nuclear weapons program was terminated and its entire arsenal destroyed. In 1994, the IAEA confirmed the dismantling of the one partially completed and six operational weapons. South Africa has retained most of the weapons-grade enriched uranium used in its nuclear weapons, repurposing it for the production of medical isotopes.

South Africa's disarmament was controversial at the time and remains so. Some critics suggest that the termination was motivated by fears in the apartheid government of leaving nuclear weapons for the incoming African National Union (ANU) government, even though the ANU had a long-established policy of rejecting such weapons. Africa remains the only continent that is completely free of nuclear weapons and the only one not part of a nuclear umbrella protection system.

In the development of its nuclear weapons, South Africa collaborated with Israel and Taiwan. Support from Israel was significant, including exchanges of fissile material as well nuclear and ballistic missile technologies. There is speculation that the September 22, 1979 nuclear test in the southern Indian Ocean was a joint Israeli-South African operation. In 2010, the British newspaper *The Guardian* released documents from the South African government dated 1975 that confirm Israel's possession of nuclear weapons and detail an offer to sell some to South Africa. Israel denies such an offer occurred, and critics have said that the documents do not support the conclusion that a sales offer was on the table. Taiwan and South Africa agreed in 1983 to cooperate on uranium enrichment technologies, but since this agreement occurred when both programs were under stress, it is unlikely that the exchanges took place.

South Africa was an early supporter of the Treaty on the Prohibition of Nuclear Weapons and provided ratification on February 25, 2019. It was one of the original 50 states-party when the treaty came into effect of January 23, 2021. At the first meeting of the states-parties in Vienna in June of 2022, the South African delegate noted, "It is [sic] indeed been a long journey and now we are finally here, working on the implementation of this vital treaty." He went on to say, "We much recognize that this treaty is the democratic wish of the overwhelming majority of UN member states and the people of the world. No longer should the world's peoples be held hostage to the unspeakable terror of these weapons." South Africa and Malaysia, at the Vienna conference, were appointed to co-chair a working group promoting universal acceptance of the treaty before its next meeting of states-party.

Russia-Ukraine War

Since the war began on February 22, 2022, there have been statements from President Putin and others alluding to the availability of Russia's nuclear weapons, especially if foreign support for Ukraine were to escalate beyond the provision of "defensive" weapons. To some extent, that barrier has been breached without seeing an increase in the Russian nuclear threat. Nevertheless, there have been some changes in Russia's political demands and military objectives. But it is far too early to eliminate the possibility that Russia would deploy nuclear weapons should support for Ukraine significantly escalate or if Russia faces a complete failure in it "special military operation."

Forecasting in the midst of a war such as that in Ukraine comes with little confidence. As Richard Betts, Professor of War and Peace

Studies at Colombia University wrote on July 4 in *Foreign Affairs*, "But NATO policymakers should not bank on Moscow's restraint. Putin has more at stake in the war than Ukraine's nuclear-armed supporters outside the country do, and he could bet that in a pinch, Washington would be less willing to play Russian roulette than he is. He could play the madman and apply nuclear shock as an acceptable risk for ending the war on Russian terms."

As well, the disappearance of successful American-Russian historic unity on nuclear arms control throughout the period of détente contributes to the threats of the possible use of nuclear weapons. Both countries have allowed relationship issues and the Russian invasion of Ukraine especially to downplay the value of and need for ongoing unity on nuclear weapons.

That unity was central to the maintenance of stability and security attending the disintegration of the Soviet Union and the emergence of today's Russia. It was as well the foundation for the fifteen newly independent states where "self-determination" became a central factor in their independence and continued existence. Some have argued the traditional approach on nuclear arms control has come to an end. But that will not be the final word as the control of nuclear weapons by the United States and Russia, with 90% of such weapons, is essential for any progress in their reduction and elimination.

In the 2022 summer months of the war, the safety and security of nuclear power plants became an issue of significance for the first time. There has always been a justification, however flimsy, that nuclear power plants provide legitimacy for nuclear energy. This idea of positive utility has been used to counter the dangerous utility of nuclear weapons. Experience has shown that the positive utility is the minor partner in the duality, and since interest in nuclear power is on the decline globally, the excuse wears more and more thin. To once again quote the long-term chair of the Israeli Atomic Energy Commission, "There is no distinction between nuclear energy for peaceful purposes or warlike ones."

Ukraine, more than most countries, illustrates the problem of the power plant excuse. Ukraine has relied on nuclear power for over 20% of its power needs, with its first plants dating from the early 1970s. Before the Russian invasion, it had four major nuclear power complexes with 16 operational reactors, along with 3 research reactors; there were another four-dozen decommissioned, unfinished, or planned reactors located in all parts of the country. And there was, of course, Chernobyl, the exemplar of the dangers associated with nuclear power. When Chernobyl's four power reactors accidentally exploded in 1986, two years after they were operational in 1984, the environmental and human cost was catastrophic, with lingering fatal radiation making the area surrounding Chernobyl a danger zone even today. While Chernobyl is the most severe and famous example of nuclear meltdown, Ukraine is not alone, as many countries using nuclear power reactors have experienced disasters or near disaster.

To the Chernobyl disaster itself we can now add the decision by Russia that nuclear power plants are appropriate targets for its invading military force, or to use its description of what is happening, "limited military operation." In that operation, Russian troops took control of the destroyed reactors at Chernobyl on February 24. It was three weeks before they left and control returned to the Ukrainian operators. On March 3, Russian forces took control of the territory around the Zaporizhzhia nuclear plant, marking the first time an operational nuclear power plant was attacked militarily. Zaporizhzhia is the largest nuclear power plant in Europe, with six reactors. A day later, outside power supply to the plant was lost, followed by the rocket strike of an on-site training building. On July 22, Ukrainian forces launched drone strikes against the Russian forces at the plant. It took until September 1 before IAEA inspectors were able to visit the plant, and they decided to keep two staff members in place.

The IAEA Director General stated it was "obvious that the plant and the physical integrity of the plant has been violated several times. [...] This is a reality that we have to recognize and this is something that cannot continue to happen." In his report to the UN Security

Council on September 6, he emphasized, "We are playing with fire, and something very, very catastrophic could take place." In its written report, the IAEA noted "The presence of Russian military personnel, vehicles and equipment at various places [at the plant] including several military trucks on the ground floor of the unit 1 and unit 2 turbine halls and military vehicles stationed under the overpass connecting the reactor units." The IAEA went on to demand the "immediate establishment of a nuclear safety and security protection zone" for the nuclear power site.

The Director General in his speech to the Security Council emphasized the need for the observance of the indispensable pillars for ensuring nuclear safety and security at Zaporizhzhia, chiefly that

- operators be allowed to perform safety and security tasks without undue pressures;
- all safety and security systems and equipment should be fully functional;
- an off-site power supply be maintained and military activity that could interfere would halt;
- uninterrupted logistical supply chains to and from the site be operational;
- fully functional radiation monitoring systems be maintained;
- and uninterrupted and reliable communications between operations and regulators be in effect.

The failure of the Russian invasion and the surprising success of the Ukrainian forces have created a significantly different security policy environment in September than that which existed in March. In September, Russia accepted that its initial effort to decapitate the Ukrainian government in Kiev had failed. Russia had failed to annex the eastern provinces, mainly east of the Dnipro River, of Kharkiv, Luhansk, and Donetsk. Even more troublesome were military activities indicating the war had spread to Russia itself and, significantly, to Crimea, which had been annexed in 2014. Occasional bombing attacks by Ukrainian forces in neighbouring Russian territory and in the Crimea created unexpected security problems. The sinking of the Russian flagship in the Black Sea, the *Moskva,* near Crimea on April 14 provided dramatic evidence of the overall Russian failure. The cause of the sinking and the casualties involved remains disputed between Ukraine and Russia. Regardless, the event demonstrates the tenuousness of the Russian military in the region.

The Russian reaction and its efforts to regain the military initiative for its invasion have been significant and perhaps unique. President Putin, in an address to the Russian people on September 21, tried to place the war, which he continued to refer to as a "special military operation" or a "pre-emptive military operation," into its historical context of the NATO "offensive infrastructure close to our borders. They used indiscriminate Russophobia as a weapon, including by nurturing the hatred of Russia for decades, primarily in Ukraine, which was designed to become an anti-Russia bridgehead."

It was in this context that President Putin announced the partial mobilization of Russia's military reserves in late September 2022. In his announcement, the President broadened the context by reiterating references to the use of nuclear weapons back at the start of the war in late February. In September, he sharpened the reference by stating that "this was not a bluff." Others in the Russian government have also emphasized the nuclear threat, including former President Dmitry Medvedev, who is now deputy head of the Russian Security Council.

The United States was quick to respond to the renewed Russian threat on the use of nuclear weapons, with President Biden's national security adviser, Jake Sullivan, telling the press that there would be "catastrophic consequences" should nuclear weapons be used and the United States would "respond decisively." Biden also responded by messaging Putin through the press, saying, "Don't. Don't. Don't. You will change the face of war unlike anything since World War II." And in his September 21 speech at the UN General Assembly, Biden stated, "Let us speak plainly. A permanent member of the United Nations Security Council invaded its neighbor, attempted to erase a sovereign state from the map. Russia has shamelessly violated the core tenets of the United Nations Charter, no more important than the clear prohibition against countries taking the territory of their neighbor." In a specific reference to the nuclear threat, Biden stated that this was "reckless" and contrary to Russia's non-proliferation responsibilities.

Compounding the folly of continuing to fight what is now, probably, an unwinnable war, Russia is mobilizing its citizens, or, to put it in more familiar terms, drafting a military. The decision may represent the end of Putin's success in steering the country out of the morass created by the disintegration of the Soviet Union, the collapse of its Communist Party, and its loss of world-wide primacy. Putin has commanded special military operations since 2014 to rescue Russians adrift in neighbouring countries. The once-celebrated effort to return citizens and territory to "the great Motherland" has now generated opposition at home and abroad, capable of sundering all that he had succeeded in doing.

There is a historical example of this self-injuring syndrome by a major power. Not so many years ago, the United States, as much by inadvertence as by design, was mired in a conflict even more complex than the one that President Putin created. This was the Vietnam War, a military disaster in which the United States confronted enemies it did not understand, resulting in a lost war exacerbated by the erosion of support by its own people. Tens of thousands refused to obey draft orders or deserted the armed forces. Many of these objectors to the war moved to Canada where there was an understanding of non-extradition. Even though Canada was an ally of the United States, it accepted these mobile Americans who were prepared to emigrate rather than fight in a war they did not believe in.

Tens of thousands of Russians, in the face of the mobilization call, have left the country or want to do so. Some argue that this defiance may be enough to reverse Putin's policies. While there may be merit to such claims, they miss the larger dimensions of what is happening. The left-behind families, friends, and supporters of these mobile Russians are influenced by the people moving, and, in the

Russia created by President Putin, that is as important as the call by the President to support the Motherland. The President's call is more a figment of historical memory than of today's Russia; educated and mobile citizens are unwilling to fight for the ideals of an overreaching President whose concept of Russia was formed when Russians strode throughout the conquered lands of Eastern Europe and Central Asia.

A worrisome aspect of this movement of Russians voting with their feet has been the reaction of the countries of the European Union. There was almost an instinctive "closing of the doors" to these Russians that undermines the larger goals of protecting the independence of Ukraine. Rather than seeing this movement of Russians as an important manifestation in their support for Ukraine, the EU has rebuffed the good intentions of these émigrés, potentially reverting their support to Putin. As in the United States fifty years ago, the erosion of domestic opposition to an unwinnable foreign war is a central factor in promoting peace.

4. Nuclear Weapons and Their Science

"One Great Mistake"

Albert Einstein, *comment on his 1939 letter to President Roosevelt, following the 1945 bombings of Hiroshima and Nagasaki.*

Richard Feynman, the American physicist who received the shared Nobel Prize in Physics in 1965, strongly believed in sharing the wonders of science and physics in understandable terms with the world. In a 1961 lecture, he proposed an answer to the question of the single most important bit of scientific knowledge to share with the future. His answer was, "All things are made of atoms – little particles that move around in perpetual motion, attracting each other when they are a little distance apart, but repelling upon being squeezed into one another."

The history of physics, even when it was called natural philosophy, has been the essence of Feynman's answer. The Greeks, and the Indians, and the Chinese before them, provided preliminary answers centred around the question of what we are made of and what surrounds us. From the Greeks the word "atom" originated, meaning unbreakable or impossible to cut. For the early Greeks there were the fundamentals elements of earth, water, air and fire. Characteristically, other Greeks did not agree and suggested these were not really fundamental to our physical world. These were themselves made up of small units of ordinary matter, and though it took a long time to get there, this led to the modern understanding of atomic chemistry.

The early interpretations from the ancients were largely lost to the western world; for nearly two-thousand years, there was instead a preoccupation with an imaginary place associated with our afterlives and whether or not angels could dance on small surfaces. Far less attention was given to the physical world of here and now. Modern science began when Isaac Newton associated mathematics with natural philosophy, leading to an ongoing conflict between those who contend with the idea of an afterlife and those who offer answers based on what is in our existing physical world. Newton's work reflected the earlier works of Copernicus, Galileo, Kepler, and Descartes, and it was over two-hundred years later before his interpretation of our physical world were supplemented with the concepts of quantum mechanics and relativity, described by Planck and Einstein and refined by Bohr, Heisenberg, and others.

Even during this period of transition, there were many who promoted ideas from metaphysics, romanticism, and mechanicalism as answers to Feynman's question. But when Darwin completed his long cruise and gave us answers based on science for an understanding of human physical development, the battle between evolution and the role of a god was not significantly different from the reception of works by Copernicus to Newton. Today, the acceptance of the universality of our physical environment suffers from the same reluctance these pioneers encountered when the products of the mind overcame the lingering influence of false faith.

It is from the understanding of the now-fundamental theory of quantum mechanics that nuclear weapons emerged. The theory provides the scientific understanding of the physical properties of atoms and subatomic particles – the opposite end of the physical world as described by Copernicus, Galileo, and Kepler – and in doing so provided the science to contain an extraordinary amount of energy within a transportable container: a nuclear weapon. Our understanding of the world of the quanta continues as the concept of the Higgs boson elementary particle demonstrates. It was first theorized by Peter Higgs and a number of other researchers, but its transitory existence was only confirmed nearly fifty years later. Unfortunately, it was popularly misnamed the God Particle, continuing the historical damage done to science by associating it with faith.

Nuclear weapons emerged in the twentieth century as a direct product of nuclear physics. The discovery of radioactivity by the French physicist and engineer Henri Becquerel in 1896 and the associated work of Marie Salomea Sklodowska-Curie and her husband Pierre (the trio was awarded the Nobel Prize in Physics in 1903), along with the work of J. J. Thomson, who discovered the electron in 1897, created the modern understanding of the atom as having an internal structure. By 1911, Ernest Rutherford was able to demonstrate that the nucleus of an atom contained its energy, and in less than a decade, created a nuclear reaction and discovered the proton. Rutherford, from New Zealand, worked in Canada and the United Kingdom and is considered the father of nuclear physics. His 1908 Nobel Prize in Chemistry was based on his work at McGill University for his "investigations into the disintegration of the elements, and the chemistry of radioactive substances."

The distinction between nuclear physics and atomic physics is worth exploring. Atomic physics examine atoms in isolation, each with a single nucleus surrounded by one or more satellite electrons, while the focus of nuclear physics is the examination of the atomic nuclei, and the interactions of their constituents or satellites. The application of these nuclear studies created the foundation for nuclear weapons and explains the evolutionary language from "atomic" to "nuclear" bombs, and more generally nuclear weapons. The rapid developments in these sciences owe much to the urgency of weapons development during the Second World War. Thus, in two-to-three decades, nuclear science had sufficiently evolved to produce nuclear weapons. While other non-lethal uses of the nuclei of the atom were recognized, their refinement and application were largely post-war initiatives.

The early work of Becquerel, the Curries, Thompson, Bohr, and especially Rutherford, laid the preliminary foundations of nuclear physics. Their work led two British physicists, John Cockcroft and Ernest Walton, to create the modern construction for the new science. On April 14, 1932, working at the Cavendish Laboratory, Cambridge University, headed by Ernest Rutherford, Cockcroft and Walton artificially disintegrated an atomic nucleus, now popularly called "splitting the atom," for the first time.

Cockcroft and Walton designed and built one of the earliest particle accelerators and were able to transform one element into another. Their machine could produce protons and accelerate them through 300,000 electron volts, thereby penetrating atomic nuclei. They used the work of Ukrainian born physicist George Gamow, whose mathematical calculations laid the theoretical basis for the accelerator. The 1951 Nobel citation for Cockcroft and Walton read, "Thus, for the first time, a nuclear transmutation was produced by means entirely under human control." Today the Large Hadron Collider (accelerator) near Geneva can accelerate beams of electrons 6.5 teraelectronvolts; that is trillions of electron volts as compared to the 300-thousand available to Cockcroft and Walton.

IN 1938-39, shortly after Cockroft and Walton's invention of the accelerator, a German chemist, Otto Hahn, and his associates discovered that the splitting of nuclei created chain reactions releasing extremely large amounts of energy, mainly kinetic. This was nuclear fission and became the energy source for the very rapid, uncontrolled explosion of nuclear weapons. When it is controlled, it is the energy source in a nuclear reactor. After Hahn, the war in Europe was underway, and Einstein, reflecting the views of European scientific émigrés, wrote to Roosevelt, alerting him to the dangers of the atom and the possibility that Germany had undertaken research for the weapons. The Americanization of nuclear physics was underway.

In 1940 there was one further development relating to nuclear weapons. Enrico Fermi and a team at the University of Rome discovered element 94 in 1934, but it was not until 1940 that the team at Berkley under Glen T. Seaborg was able to produce and give it its modern name: plutonium. By then, the American National Defence Research Committee on Uranium was organized by Roosevelt and within a few months it became the Office of Scientific Research and Development. Immediately after the attack on Hawaii in December 1941, it was renamed again, this time as the Manhattan Project. For the next six years until the Project was dismantled and its responsibilities taken over by the civilian Atomic Energy Committee in 1947, nuclear physics research was dedicated to the production of an atom bomb. A deep and heavy security blanket covered everything underway relating to nuclear physics. It was not until 1948 that public recognition was given to the scientists at the University of California for their 1940 work on plutonium.

The European and Pacific wars were over by August 15, 1945. At this point, the United States had manufactured three nuclear weapons, two of which were dropped on Japan, the third being used for training purposes. The USA had the global monopoly on nuclear weapons for the next four years. Within twenty years, the United States was joined by five other countries with nuclear weapons – Soviet Union, United Kingdom, France, China, and Israel. The miracle of the next nearly sixty years was that only three additional countries have joined them – India, Pakistan, and North Korea. The science associated with nuclear weapons is now universal, but the international effort to see the elimination of the end of these world-threatening weapons is also universal. It must continue until they are eliminated from the arsenals of all countries.

Weapons are but "sticks and stones" without the human mind and hand to guide them toward their dangerous purpose. They have always been near at hand for use when violence is needed to settled disputes, conflicts, and war. Nuclear weapons, by their very nature, are not an extension of the sticks and stones road; they are a road all their own.

The Scary World of Nuclear Weapons

Their road consists of frustration, demonstration, retaliation, escalation, annihilation, and universal bereavement. Their understanding and application provide a dramatic and dangerous illustration of where minds and hands can lead when under extreme pressure and urgency from the fears associated with the sharing of planet Earth. The physicists and chemists of the late nineteenth and twentieth centuries, along with their predecessors in natural philosophy, dedicated research into the understanding of our physical world. Inevitably, the initial search was cosmological, fueled by looking deeper and deeper into our heavens. But, more recently, the search was directed to where we lived, or to pun, the matter of matter.

As with all weapons, research associated with the energy of the nucleus of the atom has dual purposes. There are considerable benefits in the development of nuclear power, such as the development of nuclear medicine, or, more fundamentally, in the understanding of matter and its importance in our continued existence. The problem arises in ensuring that the gargantuan negatives associated with nuclear weapons do not overwhelm these benefits. By establishing collective international agreements against the development and use of nuclear weapons the duality can be eliminated. The variety of existing and proposed treaties on testing, non-proliferation, export controls, and elimination of nuclear weapons must emerge as *jus cogens,* or peremptory norms.

The discovery of nuclear fission in 1938 by four German scientists Otto Hahn, Fritz Strassman, Lise Meitner, and Otto Frisch (Lise Meitner was originally from Austria and then living in exile in Sweden) established the basic scientific foundation and understanding for the production of nuclear weapons. This was atom splitting, or fission as it is now known. Seven years later, the United States dropped two nuclear bombs on Japan as a demonstration of its power; eleven years later, the Soviet Union had its first test explosion in Kazakhstan, demonstrating that the United States was not alone in the ownership of this new weapon. The nuclear arms race was underway; today, containment and elimination should remain a priority.

Nuclear fission has two dominant characteristics. The first is the vast amount of energy produced, and second, the production of more neutrons than are consumed, resulting in chain reactions. The released energy is several million times more than that produced by burning coal or fossil fuels. Uranium, particularly the rare isotope U-235, was unique in its splitting or undergoing fission. It was the understanding of this fundamental science that emerged in the years just before 1939 and established the belief that weapons could be created using U-235, and such weapons would be the most powerful in the history of the world.

Scientists at the time were concerned about the dangers. The letter written in late August 1939 by Leo Szilard, Edward Teller, and Eugene Wigner, all physicists from Hungary and living in the United States, signed by Albert Einstein, and sent to the American President, presaged the possible production of such weapons. Scientists in Germany, the Soviet Union, France, and the United Kingdom were equally alarmed. Their national political and defence authorities were forewarned of the looming dangers represented by such weapons. Even with the beginning of a world war, efforts were initiated to exploit the possibility of these new weapons with national defence programs. The authority of the Einstein letter, along with perceptions of President Roosevelt, were sufficient for the United States to investigate the dangers leading to the creation of the comprehensive Manhattan Project and ensuring the United States would be first to achieve nuclear weapon status.

The Manhattan Project faced four large problems, and these remain endemic in the development of nuclear weapons. The first was to obtain sufficient supply of the needed fissile material, still U-235 and plutonium, whether 239 or 241 isotopes, essential for the creation of nuclear weapons and the associated technologies in production, processing, and containment. The second issue was the construction of the facilities in which these activities could take place, along with the moderating or controlling materials including heavy water and graphite for nuclear reactors. The third issue was the recruitment and seclusion of a work force that would come to exceed one-hundred-thousand workers.

The fourth and still unresolved problem involved the moral and political considerations associated with developing and using these kinds of weapons.

The weapons designs have been more-or-less unchanged since 1945. Essentially, they consist of fissile material in a controlled chain reaction, leading to supercriticality and explosion. Any changes over time have largely been in terms of size, explosive equivalents, and specificity of use. Delivery systems, however, have changed dramatically in the intervening decades, adding significantly to the dangers of use. More importantly, the major policy issues have remained, especially regarding whether to grant legitimacy to five countries' supply under treaty law. Such legitimacy is conditional on efforts to eliminate the weapons. That condition, unmet by any of the five nations, is described in the chapter dealing with the treaties on testing, non-proliferation, and elimination.

5. The Manhattan Project

"I found this data of such import that I have convened a Board ... to thoroughly investigate the possibilities of your suggestion regarding the element of uranium."

President Roosevelt's *response to the Einstein letter on October 14, 1939*

In any discussion of nuclear weapons, the most concentrated and consequential development program was The Manhattan Project. In less than six years after President Roosevelt was made aware of the possible development of such weapons by Germany, the response was national, urgent, coherent, constant, and focused. Ultimately, the efforts resulted in the attacks on Nagasaki and Hiroshima.

The legitimacy of using the two nuclear weapons on largely civilian populations is still debated. There will be no complete nor final answers on that decision, one of the most consequential of the 20th century. The words of President Harry S. Truman announcing the dropping of the bomb on Hiroshima remain the most authoritative:

> Sixteen hours ago, an American airplane dropped one bomb on Hiroshima, an important Japanese Army base. That bomb had more power than 20,000 tons of T.N.T. It had more than two thousand times the blast power of the British "Grand Slam" which is the largest bomb ever yet used in the history of warfare.

The Japanese began the war from the air at Pearl Harbor. They have been repaid many fold. And the end is not yet. With this bomb we have now added a new and revolutionary increase in destruction to supplement the growing power of our armed forces. In their present form these bombs are now in production and even more powerful forms are in development.

It is an atomic bomb. It is a harnessing of the basic power of the universe. The force from which the sun draws its power has been loosed against those who brought war to the Far East.

Before 1939, it was the accepted belief of scientists that it was theoretically possible to release atomic energy. But no one knew any practical method of doing it. By 1942, however, we knew that the Germans were working feverishly to find a way to add atomic energy to the other engines of war with which they hoped to enslave the world. But they failed. We may be grateful to Providence that the Germans got the V-1's and the V-2's late and in limited quantities and even more grateful that they did not get the atomic bomb at all.

The battle of the laboratories held fateful risks for us as well as the battles of the air, land, and sea, and we have now won the battle of the laboratories as we have won the other battles.

The story of the Manhattan Project stands as a monument to the unique ability of a government to command and mobilize vast resources. There was American collaboration and cooperation with only two close allies – Canada and the United Kingdom – otherwise, there was complete secrecy. The endeavour required the exploitation of a science still in its infancy; life-threatening conditions in exploration and application; the construction of complex, air transportable explosive devices to a distant battlefield; and the logistics of dropping a bomb into the middle of two large cities. These attacks remain among the most outstanding yet troublesome achievements of the United States in the twentieth century. The success of the effort in forcing a capable, focused enemy to an early and complete surrender shaped today's warfare and the modern world.

The effort began a few days before the German army marched into Poland on September 1, 1939. Two scientist, political emigrees from Europe, drafted a letter to the President of the United States, Franklin D. Roosevelt, warning of the possible development of "extremely powerful bombs of a new type." The two scientist, Leo Szilard and Eugene Wigner, both from Hungary, drafted the letter and were able to have a colleague, Albert Einstein sign. Szilard and Einstein had worked together in Europe and remained friends after arriving in the United States.

All three scientists, then working in the United States, were educated in Europe and were part of the open exchange of information within the European scientific community. Germany was a recognized leader on most scientific issues and that of nuclear fission in particular. At the time, there was research and discussion in Germany on the discovery of the unique properties of uranium.

Szilard and Wigner had the professional experience to provide the warning on the state of science in Germany leading to the construction of atomic bombs. Wigner was awarded the Nobel prize in Physics in 1963 for "his contributions to the theory of the atomic nucleus and the elementary particles," while Szilard was associated with the development of the concept of nuclear chain reactions in 1933. The letter was not a warning from the uninformed, but involved two of the world's most outstanding nuclear physicists. The Einstein signature provided assurance that the issue would receive the desired attention.

Their unique and historical letter is transcribed here:

The Scary World of Nuclear Weapons

Albert Einstein
Old Grove Road
Peconic, Long Island
August 2nd, 1939

F.D. Roosevelt
President of the United States
White House
Washington, D.C.

Sir:

Some recent work by E. Fermi and L. Szilard, which has been communicated to me in manuscript, leads me to expect that the element uranium may be turned into a new and important source of energy in the immediate future. Certain aspects of the situation which has arisen seem to call for watchfulness and if necessary, quick action on the part of the Administration. I believe therefore that it is my duty to bring to your attention the following facts and recommendations.

In the course of the last four months it has been made probable through the work of Joliot in France as well as Fermi and Szilard in America–that it may be possible to set up a nuclear chain reaction in a large mass of uranium, by which vast amounts of power and large quantities of new radium-like elements would be generated. Now it appears almost certain that this could be achieved in the immediate future.

This new phenomenon would also lead to the construction of bombs, and it is conceivable–though much less certain–that extremely powerful bombs of this type may thus be constructed. A single bomb of this type, carried by boat and exploded in a port, might very well destroy the whole port together with some of the surrounding territory. However, such bombs might very well prove too heavy for transportation by air.

The United States has only very poor ores of uranium in moderate quantities. There is some good ore in Canada and former Czechoslovakia, while the most important source of uranium is in the Belgian Congo.

In view of this situation you may think it desirable to have some permanent contact maintained between the Administration and the group of physicists working on chain reactions in America. One possible way of achieving this might be for you to entrust the task with a person who has your confidence and who could perhaps serve in an unofficial capacity. His task might comprise the following:

a) to approach Government Departments, keep them informed of the further development, and put forward recommendations for Government action, giving particular attention to the problem of securing a supply of uranium ore for the United States.

b) to speed up the experimental work, which is at present being carried on within the limits of the budgets of University laboratories, by providing funds, if such funds be required, through his contacts with private persons who are willing to make contributions for this cause, and perhaps also by obtaining co-operation of industrial laboratories which have necessary equipment.

I understand that Germany has actually stopped the sale of uranium from the Czechoslovakian mines which she has taken over. That she should have taken such early action might perhaps be understood on the ground that the son of the German Under-Secretary of State, von Weizsacker, is attached to the Kaiser-Wilhelm Institute in Berlin, where some of the American work on uranium is now being repeated.

Yours very truly,

A. Einstein

By the time the Einstein letter was delivered to Roosevelt in early October 1939, the German army was marching on the roads of Poland. The President was fully engaged with the war, fearing it was only a matter of time before the United States was directly engaged; he fully understood that the information on extremely dangerous new weapons required urgent attention. In the reply to Einstein dated October 14, 1939, Roosevelt wrote, "I found this data of such import that I have convened a Board consisting of the head of the Bureau of Standards and a chosen representative of the Army and Navy to thoroughly investigate the possibilities of your suggestion regarding the element of uranium."

The Board had its first meeting within a week of the letter to Einstein and included Szilard and Wigner. They were joined by a third émigré scientist from Hungary, Edward Teller, also with a background in the emerging science of nuclear power. Today, he is regarded the "father of the hydrogen bomb." There was some skepticism from the military representative on the warning, but research funds were provided to Szilard and Enrico Fermi, a refugee physicist from Italy, who together began construction of a nuclear reactor using natural uranium at Colombia University.

The established Board was replaced by the National Defence Research Committee and a few months later by the Office of Scientific Research and Development in 1941. Before the invasion of Hawaii in December 1941, President Roosevelt was sufficiently alarmed of the possibility of nuclear weapons to order the Research Committee to begin a program for the production of the weapons. Roosevelt included himself in the new grouping, but day-to-day work was done by Vice President Henry A Wallace, along with the chair, Vannevar Bush from MIT, and various departmental secretaries, including the chief of staff for the army, George C Marshall.

The Research Committee held its first meeting on December 18, 1941, ten days after the attack on Pearl Harbour and seven days after entering the war with Germany. It was then called the S-1 committee and was "pervaded by an atmosphere of enthusiasm and urgency," according to one participant. The Research Committee created the Manhattan Project eight months later, on August 13, 1942, to coordinate all activities relating to the development of nuclear weapons, and it was placed under the control of the Army Corps of Engineers. The Project was initially managed from the Corps' headquarters in New York, hence the name.

At the time of the formal creation of the Manhattan Project, significant research on nuclear energy was already underway in the United States and of direct relevance to the ultimate production of nuclear weapons. Ernest Lawrence was directing research at the University of California that lead to the invention of the cyclotron, which accelerated atoms through a vacuum using electromagnets to create collisions at speeds up to 25,000 miles-per-second. It was this machine that would permit the production of uranium isotopes, especially Uranium-235, essential for a nuclear explosion. At the same university, two other researchers, Emilio Segre and Glenn Seaborg, established that element 94, which they named plutonium, could also be used as a fuel for nuclear weapons. Elsewhere, the 1940, $6,000 grant provided to Fermi and Szilard at Colombia University was used to construct a nuclear reactor, then called "piles" in these early days of nuclear research. This research ultimately provided information on the amount of fuel needed for nuclear explosions.

Throughout this period, the Americans were aware that research in the United Kingdom on nuclear energy was ahead of that in the United States, so it initiated contact to strengthen cooperation. The British had created the MAUD Committee early in 1940 to establish whether it was possible to construct an atomic bomb. The Committee was established in response to a report written by two refugee scientists from Germany, Rudolf Peierls and Otto Frisch, working at the University of Birmingham. The report sought to answer the question of the amount of natural uranium needed to create a bomb more powerful than thousands of tons of TNT. The prevailing view in the United Kingdom at the time was that the smallest amount of natural uranium needed to sustain a chain reaction was a matter of tons.

In the meantime, Niels Bohr, a Danish nuclear scientist working at the University of Copenhagen, held that rather than using natural uranium, the Uranium-235 isotope could be used for an atomic bomb. Frisch experimented with uranium enrichment using thermal diffusion and found that when using the earlier theoretical work done by Peierls, less than a kilogram of U-235 was needed for a chain reaction. In their report, Frisch and Peierls wrote that five kilograms of U-235 would create a bomb equal to several tons of TNT.

Using the research of Frisch and Peierls, the MAUD Committee initiated research to establish the use of uranium and provide appropriate recommendations on the technical issues involved. The work was divided among four universities: Birmingham, Liverpool, Cambridge, and Oxford. Many of the researchers involved were refugees from Europe, especially Germany, and this presented problems in obtaining security clearances. But these were largely overcome given the experience they represented for the research. Before long, the conclusions of Frisch and Peierls were confirmed. In July 1941, the MAUD Committee wrote:

> We should like to emphasize . . . we entered the project with more skepticism than belief . . . As we proceeded, we became more and more convinced that release of atomic energy on a large scale is possible that conditions can be chosen which would make it a very powerful weapons of war. We have now reached the conclusion that it will be possible to make an effective uranium bomb which, containing some 25 lb of active material, would be equivalent as regards destructive effect to 1,800 tons of TNT and would also release large quantities of radioactive substances which would make places near to where the bomb exploded dangerous to human life for a long period.

Additional information in the report provided technical details along with the estimates on cost. It also warned Germany had shown interest in heavy water and might also be working on the construction of an atomic bomb.

The British government accepted the conclusions of the MAUD report and immediately initiated action for a program to develop nuclear weapons. The program was named Tube Alloys to disguise its purpose, and exchanges were organized with the newly established Manhattan Project. Ironically, the exchanges were not significant as there were concerns in the UK as to American security. But before the end of 1941, substantial contact was established between members of the Tube Alloys project and the pre-Manhattan group then working as the Office of Scientific Research and Development and the earlier Uranium Committee.

The British Technical and Scientific Mission, or Tizard Mission, to the United States in September 1940 provided the opportunity for the United Kingdom to display its scientific and technological wares and thereby obtain American cooperation and support. There was considerable overlap between the state of research in both countries in such areas as radar, microwaves, and bombsights, but it was the work of the British in developing the cavity magnetron, which was small enough to allow for the installation of radar units on military aircraft, that attracted attention. Within six weeks of the visit, the Bell Telephone Company of New York was awarded a contract for the manufacture of magnetrons and produced the first by October 30. A million were made before the end of the war.

Members of the mission also met with Enrico Fermi at Columbia University, who was deep in his own research on the possible manufacture of an atomic bomb. At the time, Fermi was doubtful such a weapon could be created, despite being provided with information on the Frisch and Peierls research.

The Tizard Mission also went to Ottawa, where they met with George Laurence of the National Research Council (NRC). Laurence had studied with Ernest Rutherford in the United Kingdom following his completion of degrees from Dalhousie University in Halifax. In 1939, he had been researching nuclear fission at the NRC. He overlapped with Fermi in generating a man-made chain reaction using a graphite-uranium reactor. Laurence was the first to induce fission by neutrons in a large quantity of uranium and carbon, demonstrating the potential use of these materials for the creation of nuclear energy, similar to what Fermi was doing at Columbia. Laurence later joined the research team at the Montreal Laboratory of McGill University. In 1946, Laurence was part of the Canadian delegation to the United Nations Atomic Energy Commission, and four years later he was involved in the design and construction of the Canadian CANDU nuclear power system based on natural uranium and heavy water.

The United Kingdom initially rejected American overtures for a joint program on nuclear weapons, and it was not until mid-1942 that the British accepted they could not afford to continue alone with their Tube Alloys efforts. First, London transferred most of their efforts to McGill University and the National Research Council involving Canadians in the common effort. A few months later, in the realization that the American effort was more coherent and better funded, the Canadian-British project became part of the Manhattan Project. The British minister responsible for Tube Alloys, in a memorandum to Churchill in late July 1942, wrote, "We must face the fact that . . . our pioneering work . . . is a dwindling asset and that, unless we capitalize it quickly, we shall be outstripped. We now have a real contribution to make to a 'merger.' Soon we will have little to none." The Quebec Conference in August 1943, involving Canadian Prime Minister Mackenzie King, Churchill, and Roosevelt, agreed to a united effort for the production of nuclear weapons within the Manhattan Project.

The Army Corps of Engineers had long experience in civil engineering work, having supervised the construction of the Panama Canal as well as involvement in flood control and other projects throughout the United States. It built the headquarters for the American military, the Pentagon, in less than sixteen months in the early days of the war, and its completion overlapped with the Corps' involvement in the Manhattan Project. Lieutenant General Leslie Groves supervised the Pentagon project and his success there led to his appointment as the general in charge of the Manhattan Project. His appointment was fortuitous, but more fortuitous was the appointment of Robert

Oppenheimer as Chief Scientist for the Project, eventually becoming the driving scientific force at the Los Alamos Laboratory in New Mexico. At the time, he was professor of physics as the University of California, Berkeley, and along with Groves is credited with the success of the Manhattan Project. As distinct from Teller, the "father of the hydrogen bomb," Oppenheimer, is generally credited as the "father of the atomic bomb."

By late 1941, there was scientific consensus among nuclear physicists in the United States and elsewhere providing reasonable promise for the construction of nuclear weapons. The dire military situation in Europe combined with the uncertainty of the Asian theatre motivated the feelings of urgency at the potential of Germany possessing new, more powerful weapons. The first task of the Manhattan Project was to create the common physical facilities in which the scientists, engineers and technicians could turn the scientific consensus into weapons. It was an enormous task involving hundreds of thousands of workers and the construction of the facilities never before accomplished.

The principal American sites of the Manhattan Project follows:

Los Alamos Laboratory. Los Alamos housed the centralized research laboratory where a broad range of scientists representing physics, chemistry, metallurgy, ordnance, and engineering could work in complete secrecy. It was located at what was then a private ranch school at Los Alamos, near Santa Fe, New Mexico. It was originally intended as a military installation and the scientists even received military ranks despite some objections among the researchers. The laboratory was operated by the University of California under contract with the Department of War in Washington. In 1943, there were a few hundred personnel working at the site, and by 1945, there were over 6,000.

Clinton Engineering Works, Tennessee. Early in the Manhattan Project, Groves and Oppenheimer began work to establish facilities to produce the fuel for nuclear weapons. Enriched uranium and plutonium were the only known fissionable substances, and their production involved untested and unknown technologies. Oak Ridge, twenty miles west of Knoxville, was sufficiently isolated to suit the necessary research. In September 1942, its local population of roughly three-thousand was ordered to leave the area designated as Project Y.

Within weeks, construction began on the plants necessary for the enrichment of uranium to be used in nuclear weapons. There were three processes available for the level of enrichment needed for a nuclear explosion. All three processes – electromagnetic isotope separation, thermal diffusion, and gaseous diffusion – were new and had never before been used on the necessary scale. It was early in 1945 before enough enriched uranium-235 could be sent to Los Alamos for experimentation. At the time the bombs were dropped on Japan, there were nearly 100,000 people working at Oak Ridge

Hanford Engineer Works Reactor, Pasco, Washington. There were lingering concerns that Oak Ridge was too close to civilians. So, in late 1942, a site near Richmond, Washington State, near the Columbia River, was selected and approved in early 1943 under the name Hanford Engineer Works. Its primary purpose was to produce sufficient plutonium for use in nuclear weapons as an alternative to enriched uranium. The construction of the production reactors started almost immediately; by April 1943, there were 25,000 workers at the site. A year later, there were 51,000 and some 1200 buildings, including three plutonium production reactors. By early February 1945, the first plutonium was sent to Los Alamos, but it wasn't until after the bombing of Hiroshima and Nagasaki that the three reactors were fully operational.

Alamogordo Trinity Test Site. Located some 200 kilometres from Albuquerque, New Mexico, the Alamogordo Air Base was the testing site for the first atomic bomb on July 16, 1945. Oppenheimer chose the name in mid-1944, later stating it was from one of John Donne's Holy Sonnets. Two days before the test, in indirect justification for his work on the first bomb, he quoted the *Bhagavad Gita:*

> In battle, in the forest, at the precipice in the mountains
> On the dark great sea, in the midst of javelins and arrows,
> In sleep, in confusion, in the depths of shame,
> The good deeds a man has done before defend him.

Scandia National Laboratories. Further laboratories were established at the Albuquerque Army Air Base, relatively close to the Los Alamos Laboratories. The Scandia National Laboratories were responsible for the non-nuclear aspects of nuclear weapons. Today they serve a different purpose, to guarantee nuclear safety through research and development in arms control and non-proliferation technologies. The laboratories are operated by the National Technology and Engineering Solutions of Sandia, which is a wholly owned subsidiary of Honeywell International.

Heavy Water Production Plants in the United States and Canada. Heavy water is an important component of nuclear arms and power plants, and production in high enough quantity was critical. In addition to facilities constructed in the United States, there were associated facilities in Canada. The first was largely a commercial endeavour through Cominco, a Canadian mineral producer with an electrolytic hydrogen plant at Trail, B.C., which in 1941 was enlarged to produce heavy water. It produced its first shipment of heavy water in 1944, which was used in the Chicago Reactor No 3 [Pile]. The production of heavy water at Trail continued until 1956.

The Canadian government only became aware of the production of heavy water in 1942, a year after the work started. Cominco (at the time it was called Consolidated) was chosen because it already had an electrolytic hydrogen plant, a natural concentrator of heavy water. The company shipped 100 pounds of heavy water a month to Ohio. In 1945, the plant began supplying heavy water to a uranium facility owned by the Canadian government at Chalk River, Ontario.

Chicago Reactor 3 (actually located outside Chicago in Palos Hills, Illinois) was the world's first using natural uranium and heavy water; it went operational on May 15, 1944. The facility was associated with the work of the Metallurgical Laboratory at the University of Chicago for the Manhattan Project and decommissioned in 1954.

Following the 1943 agreement to combine the nuclear research efforts of Canada and the United Kingdom, Canada established a separate dedicated facility at Deep River, Ontario. It was located on the Ottawa River near Camp Petawawa, a large military base. The Zeep (zero-energy experimental pile) was constructed and was the first reactor to be constructed outside of the United States. It went operational in September 1945 and remained in use until 1970. A larger 10MW NRX (National Research Experimental) reactor was completed at the site and it went operational in July 1947. It was a heavy-water-moderated, light-water-cooled nuclear research reactor. For a time, it was the world's most powerful nuclear research reactor, especially in terms of the free neutrons it generated. It had a major accident in 1952, but it was repaired and continued to operate until 1993.

Germany and Nuclear Weapons

The concerns in the United States and elsewhere with Germany initiating a nuclear weapons program in the early days of the Second World War were accentuated by developments in Norway in 1934. The 108MW hydroelectric power plant at Vemork in the Telemark district, southwest of Oslo, opened in 1911 and was the largest in the world. It was designed to support the processing of nitrogen into artificial fertilizers. Later in 1934, an electrolysis unit was added to produce heavy water, which was emerging as a critical element in nuclear reactors.

Before the German invasion of Norway on April 9, 1940, arrangements had been made for lending the heavy water to France. This was done via the United Kingdom, who would then transfer the heavy water to France for use by Frédéric Joliot-Curie and his wife Irène Joliot-Curie at the Radium Institute in Paris.

It was a fortuitous arrangement, as Germany was already investigating the manufacturing of an atomic bomb, and while the evidence is slight, the possibility of using heavy water in the process was explored. The German scientific community was constricted before 1939, given the elimination of Jewish scientists from most research centres, many of whom took refuge in the United States and elsewhere.

Nevertheless, the remaining scientific community was fully aware of the developments associated with nuclear energy.

Once the war was underway and Norway occupied, there was Allied concern with the continued production of heavy water at Vemork. By early 1940, German and French scientists had concluded that graphite used in the production of Plutonium 239 was not pure enough and that heavy water was the only alternative. The Allies realized the dangers and launched five ground and air attacks on the site between October 1942 and February 1944 to prevent Germany from obtaining heavy water. The ground raid on February 28, 1943, partially destroyed the electrolysis plant, resulting in the loss of 500kg of heavy water, yet production resumed a few months later. The American Air Force began air raids with B-17 Flying Fortress and B-24 Liberator heavy bombers on November 1943. Of the 711 bombs dropped by 143 B-17s, 600 missed the target, suggesting just how inaccurate such air raids can be.

The raids nevertheless convinced the German authorities to abandon the plant along with its heavy water production. Today, the original hydroelectric plant is an industrial museum including exhibits on the production of heavy water. There is a new hydroelectric plant now buried into the mountain.

The raids on Vemork and the significance of its heavy water production were subjects of numerous books, film and even a video game scenario. However, postwar analysis of the German nuclear weapons program suggests that while there was a substantial nuclear weapons program, it was far from producing nuclear weapons. After the closure of the Vemork heavy water plant, Germany built a new plant near the Swiss border in 1944, but with the retreat of German troops from the far reaches of Europe, time was running out on the program. As well, there was a concentration of scientific and technical resources in the production of the rockets that were expected to protect Germany from impending defeat. There was an understanding that the rockets could carry nuclear weapons, especially in their use against the United

Kingdom, but both programs eroded under the speed, intensity, and scope of the Allied attacks.

At the beginning of the war, the German nuclear program was probably more advanced than what was underway in the United States. However, the shortage of heavy water probably became the limiting factor, and, during the remainder of the war, Germany was unable to find alternative supplies to do much more than limited nuclear reactor experiments. As well, by mid-1942, the German offensive into the Soviet Union was meeting effective opposition in Stalingrad; by the end of January 1943, the German army surrendered, and the two-year Soviet westward advance began. The German nuclear program never progressed much beyond the laboratory experimental stage, lacking both the resources and the time to move into the manufacturing phase.

During this period, German science and technology was also preoccupied with the development and production of self-propelled unmanned missiles, largely used in 1944 and '45 to undermine and weaken British determination to continue with the war. These V-1 and V-2 missiles (the "V" represents the German word *Vergeltungswaffe* or Retaliation Weapon or Weapon of Reprisal) dominated German scientific work in these years and the possibility of nuclear weapons faded. On June 13, 1944, Germany began the V-1 phase of the war, launching over eight-thousand at the United Kingdom with less than 60% arriving, a reasonable success effort in wartime. The successor to the V-1, the V-2, was first launched in September 1944. This "Second Blitz" caused considerable death and destruction in southern England.

The two weapons were unique in the world at the time. The initial V-1 was a "pilotless, jet-propelled plane that flew by air-driven gyroscope and magnetic compass, capable of unleashing a ton of . . . explosives." The range was 1,500 miles, easily reaching the United Kingdom from Germany. The V-2 was the world's first long-range guided ballistic missile, powered by a liquid-propellant rocket engine. It was the first artificial object to travel into space, crossing the Karman line, at the edge of space.

These unique weapons demonstrated the depth and scope of German science as it dominated the final phase of the war. The power of these weapons was recognized by the Allies and the Soviet Union. Both had programs in place to capture many of the Germans involved in both the nuclear and rocketry programs in the expectation they could be used in their own programs. For the Soviet Union, it was called Operation Osoaviakhim. As late as October 1946, it "relocated" over eight thousand Germans, 2,200 them scientists and technicians with their dependents. The Soviets even relocated complete scientific facilities to the Soviet Union.

The United States had two programs. The first were based in Italy in 1943. These "Alsos Missions" were named for a Greek rendering of Brigadier General Leslie Groves, who had been in charge of the construction of Pentagon before heading the Manhattan Project. The Alsos were devised as an extension of the Manhattan Project to obtain information on nuclear energy developments in Europe during the war. General George Marshall, Chief of Staff for the Army, explained the Alsos Missions in late 1943:

> While the major portion of the enemy's secret scientific developments is being conducted in Germany, it is very likely that much valuable information can be obtained thereon by interviewing prominent Italian scientists in Italy. [. . .] The scope of inquiry should cover all principal scientific military developments and the investigations should be conducted in a manner to gain knowledge of enemy progress without disclosing our interest in any particular field. The personnel who undertake this work must be scientifically qualified in every respect. It is proposed to send at the proper time to allied occupied Italy a small group of civilian scientists assisted by the necessary military personnel to conduct these investigations. Scientific personnel will be selected by Brig. Gen. Leslie R. Groves with the approval of Dr. [Vannevar] Bush. . . . This group would form the nucleus for similar activity in other enemy and enemy-occupied countries when circumstances permit.

The Alsos II mission landed in France in early August 1944 with the objective of interviewing Frédéric Joliot-Curie and his wife Irène Joliot-Curie, the eldest daughter of Pierre and Marie Curie. They were jointly awarded the Nobel Prize in Chemistry in 1935 with a citation for "recognition of their synthesis of new radioactive elements." They both worked at the Radium Institute at the College of France and were at the centre of the investigation of nuclear energy in France. Over the duration of the war, they got to know the German nuclear research scientists. Joliot-Curie created a large inventory of heavy water for his research, 185.5kg of which came from Vemork, Norway. He also obtained a supply of natural uranium from the Belgian Congo; this allowed him to become one of world's leading researchers on nuclear energy for both civil and military uses.

Joliot-Curie provided the Alsos II interview team with the names of German physicists and established part of the agenda for the Alsos III team that worked in Germany from February 1945. By this time, the team was aware of the Soviet efforts to identify German scientists and arrange for their relocation to the Soviet Union. As a result, there were several actions by the Allies, especially the United States, to reach into the Soviet zone of occupation and either eliminate facilities related to nuclear research or to arrange for designated Germans to move westward and be interviewed for possible relocation to the United States.

This became known as Operation Paperclip and was the American equivalent of Operation Osoaviakhim. From 1945 into the late '50s, 1600 German scientists, engineers, and technicians were removed to the United States. Among these was Wernher von Braun, the co-developer of the V-2 program; in the United States, he developed the rockets for the first American space satellite in 1958, following the 1957 Soviet launch of the Soviet Sputnik. In both the United States and the Soviet Union, the work of the German scientists was recognized with various national awards.

The successful end of the war in Europe and the use of nuclear weapons in Japan created interest and controversy in the United States related to the management of nuclear energy and weapons. Various inquiries and reports in 1945 and 1946 resulted in the Atomic Energy Act of 1946, which became law on January 1, 1947. The Act passed unanimously in the Senate and by a large majority in the House of Representative. It established the principle that the management and development of nuclear weapons and nuclear power would be transferred from the military to civilian control. This was effectively the end of the Manhattan Project.

The surrounding discussion of these changes overlapped with the defection of Igor Gouzenko from the Soviet Embassy in Ottawa on February 16, 1946. The defection and associated stories created significant fears in the United States that the Soviet Union was stealing American nuclear secrets. This resulted in high security standards for information relating to nuclear matters, which are still in effect today. These standards also resulted in the exclusion of the United Kingdom and Canada as partners of the United States in future nuclear energy and weapons development.

It was a dozen years before the United States relented with a 1958 amendment to the 1946 Act that provided permission for the United States to share nuclear information with allies making "substantial and material contributions to the national defense and security." In the meantime, the United Kingdom had developed its own nuclear weapons with the first test taking place in western Australia in 1952. Canada, by contrast, decided to forgo developing its own nuclear weapons and concentrated on the use of nuclear energy for medicine and power.

At the time, Soviet espionage relating to western nuclear developments generated paranoia and over-reaction in the United States, Canada, and the United Kingdom amounting to an exercise in self-deception. To some extent, the paranoia is responsible for the belief that the first Soviet nuclear test explosion in 1949 was possible because of the theft of nuclear secrets. There were prosecutions in the three countries relating to the spying, but a lack of detail suggests that the early Soviet success was not due to successful espionage.

The Soviet Union had world class physicists involved in nuclear fission and related subjects. In the pre-war climate of world-wide cooperation on scientific matters, Russian scientists were contributors as much as users. A sampling of those scientist includes Pyotr Kapitsa, Georgy Flyorov, Yakov Frenkel, and George Gamow:

> Pyotr Kapitsa studied under Ernest Rutherford at the Cavendish Laboratory at Cambridge and spent more then ten years in the United Kingdom. He was the first director of the Mond Laboratory and on his return to the Soviet Union he established the Institute for Physical Problems and studied liquid helium for which he was awarded the Nobel Prize for Physics in 1978.
>
> Georgy Flyorov, another physicist was known for his discovery of spontaneous fission. He warned Stalin in 1942 of the lack of information coming out of the United States, the United Kingdom and Germany on issues associated with nuclear fission. He went on to urge Stalin "to build the uranium bomb without delay."
>
> Another physicist at the time was Yakov Frenkel known for his work in the area of condensed matter physics. In 1930, he was a visiting professor at the University of Minnesota.
>
> George Gamow began his scientific work in the Soviet Union before he defected to the United States while visiting Belgium. He has been described as a polymath, theoretical physicist and cosmologist and was credited by Francis Crick (of DNA double helix structure fame) with providing suggests in solving the problems of genetic coding.

The Soviets' development of nuclear weapons was delayed following the intensity and depth of the German invasion in 1941. Nevertheless, the Soviet scientific community was fully aware of the developments of 1938 when four German scientists – Otto Hahn, Fritz Strassman, Lise Meitner, and Otto Frisch – established the existence of nuclear fission. When the Soviets began their march on Germany in 1943, it can be assumed that their nuclear weapons program was underway. The capture of hundreds of German scientists and technicians and the associated shipment of research facilities back to the Soviet Union contributed to the test of a nuclear weapon four years after the end of the war. It is comforting to believe this was done with the occasional bit of espionage, but given the complexity involved, it seems more likely that the efforts of their scientists are what made the difference. The Americans, however, did provide an impulse for the Soviet program, and that was the demonstration provided by the two bombs dropped on Japan – they dramatically showed that successful nuclear weapons could be made.

6. Nuclear Weapons and Hiroshima and Nagasaki

"The lighting effects beggared description. The whole country was lighted by a searing light with the intensity many times that of the midday sun. It was golden, purple, violet, gray and blue. It lighted every peak, crevasse and ridge of the nearby mountain range with clarity and beauty that cannot be described but must be seen to be seen to be imagined."

Brig. General Thomas Farrell, *VIP Observer of the Trinity Test*

The Trinity Test – The Gadget

At 5:29:21am on July 16, 1945, the Atomic Age and that of Nuclear Weapons began. It was at the Trinity test site in the Jornada Del Muerto Valley, 35 miles (56km) southeast of the town of Socorro and 60 miles north of the White Sands National Monument, New Mexico. The test bomb consisted of a plutonium core surrounded by an array of 20 small explosive charges called the lens. The explosive lens was made with Baratol (TNT and barium nitrate) and Composition B (TNT and RDX – Research Department eXplosive, commonly used in C-4 plastic explosive). The array concentrated diverging detonation waves into a single spherical converging wave that uniformly compressed the plutonium core.

At the centre of the core was an initiator, code named "Urchin," consisting of beryllium and polonium; between the core and the explosive charges was a layer of uranium. The explosive charges, detonated concurrently, compressed the plutonium core to several times its original density, making it supercritical and activating the initiator, producing neutrons, leading to a fission chain reaction and a nuclear explosion.

The device was nicknamed "the Gadget," its official name being Y-1561. From photographs, it resembled something Rube Goldberg might have depicted in his cartoons. It consisted of a sphere with external wiring for the twenty explosive charges (lens) and weighed 48 kg (105 pounds). The steel testing tower was 30m (100ft) high with its four legs buried into the ground. The initial analysis of the explosion concluded that it had produced the energy equivalent of 18.6 kilotons of TNT. In a 2021 re-analysis of the data, the earlier conclusion was rejected, and the new conclusion was that the explosion produced a yield of 24.8 kilotons of TNT with a plus/minus factor of 2 kilotons.

The explosion created a crater almost 5 feet deep and 88 yards wide and melted the surrounding desert sand. The melted sand was named "trinitite" in honour of the device. The light from the explosion was "brighter than daytime" for one-to-two seconds, in the words of one observer, and the heat was "as hot as an oven" at the base camp, ten miles (16km) away. The colours of the illumination changed from purple to green and eventually to white. The sound of the shock wave took 40 seconds to reach the observers (10,000 yards or 9100 metres away) and was felt over 100 miles away; the mushroom cloud reached 7.5 miles high.

The test explosion was witnessed by a ten-person VIP group chosen by General Groves. They were all American except for two scientists from the United Kingdom, Sir Geoffrey Taylor and Sit James Chadwick. Taylor and Chadwick were at the centre of the British effort to develop an atomic bomb and were seconded to the Manhattan Project under the 1943 Quebec Agreement between Roosevelt and Churchill. Chadwick was awarded the 1935 Nobel Prize in Physics for his discovery of the neutron in 1932 and was the principal author of the MAUD report, which concluded that a nuclear weapon was possible. Taylor was a physicist and mathematician concentrating on fluid dynamics and wave theory. He was described as "one of the most notable scientists" of the 20th century.

The Quebec Agreement provided for the United States and the United Kingdom to pool their resources in developing nuclear weapons and share information. It was also agreed such weapons would not be used against a third country without common consent. Canada had hosted the Quebec City conference but was not party to the bilateral agreement. However, at the insistence of the United Kingdom, Canada was asked to nominate a Canadian member for the Combined Policy Committee, which provided oversight for the development of nuclear weapons. Mackenzie King selected C. D. Howe, his minister of Munitions and Supply, for the position. Before the decision to drop the nuclear bomb on Japan, the United States sought the agreement of the United Kingdom, which was provided. As far as can be ascertained, Canada was not invited to the Trinity test.

The date for the test was determined by the planned Potsdam Conference scheduled to start in Germany on July 18. President Truman wanted the test done before the start of the conference when he, Stalin, and Churchill/Attlee were to discuss the post war administration of Germany. In was clear by July 18 that the British Conservative Party had lost the General Election with voting starting on July 5 and ending on July 19. Final results were only available on July 26. Clement Attlee replaced Churchill as Prime Minister while the Potsdam Conference was still under way. Truman informed Stalin of an unnamed "powerful new weapon" but provided no other details. Churchill and Attlee were informed of the successful July 16 Trinity test in accordance with the Quebec Agreement. The United Kingdom, China, and the United States issued a joint declaration at the end of the conference demanding an unconditional surrender by Japan or it would meet "prompt and utter destruction" but gave no indication of new weapons. The Soviet Union did not sign on to the declaration, and it was only after the two nuclear explosions in Japan that it declared war on Japan.

The Trinity explosion was hard to conceal, and in order to limit speculation, Groves had the following statement issued: "Several inquiries have been received concerning a heavy explosion . . . this morning. A remotely located ammunition magazine containing a considerable amount of high explosives and pyrotechnics exploded. There was no loss of life." Truman was notified in Potsdam with two messages: "Operated on this morning. Diagnosis not yet complete but results seem satisfactory and already exceed expectations." The second message read, "Doctor [Groves] has just returned most enthusiastic and confident that the little boy is as husky as his big brother. The light in his eyes discernible from here to High Hold and I could have heard his screams from here to my farm."

There were many personal and official reports on the Trinity test. Robert Oppenheimer, the Senior Scientist in charge, famously quoted the holy book of the Hindus, the Bhagavad Gita. At the time, he said, "If the radiance of a thousand suns were to burst at once into the sky, that would be like the splendor of the mighty one." His most quoted line involved Vishnu trying to persuade the Prince to do his duty and, to impress him, takes on his multi-armed form. He introduces the quote, "We knew the world would not be the same. A few people laughed; a few people cried. Most people were silent": and the famous quote itself, "Now I am become Death, the destroyer of worlds." Oppenheimer personalized the quote: "I suppose we all thought that, one way or another."

In 1962, Oppenheimer wrote about the choice of "Trinity" as the name for the test: "Why I chose the name is not clear, but I know what thoughts were in my mind. There is a poem of John Donne, written just before his death, which I know and love. From it a quotation:

> As West and East
> In all flat Maps – and I am one – are one,
> So death doth touch the Resurrection.

That still does not make a Trinity, but in another, better known devotional poem Donne opens,

> Batter my heart, three-person'd God.

A Navy transport pilot flying at 10,000 feet east of Albuquerque on his way to the west coast observed the explosion: "My first impression was, like, the sun was coming up in the south. What a ball of fire! It was so bright it lit up the cockpit of the plane." He radioed the tower in Albuquerque but did not get an explanation, only the instruction, "Don't fly south."

Brig. General Thomas Farrell, one of the VIP observers, initially exclaimed, "The long-hairs [scientists] have let it get away from them." In his official report, he wrote, "The lighting effects beggared description. The whole country was lighted by a searing light with the intensity many times that of the midday sun. It was golden, purple, violet, gray and blue. It lighted every peak, crevasse and ridge of the nearby mountain range with clarity and beauty that cannot be described but must be seen to be seen to be imagined."

A reporter for the *New York Times*, William Laurence, was temporarily attached to the Manhattan Project and was witness to both the test and the bombing of Japan. He wrote the official press releases but later was quoted as saying, "A loud cry filled the air. The little groups that hitherto had stood rooted to the earth like desert plants broke into dance, the rhythm of primitive man dancing at one of his fire festivals as the coming of spring."

But perhaps the true measure of the reaction to the test explosion was a comment by Kenneth Banbridge, a professor of physics at Harvard who, in speaking to Oppenheimer, said, "Now we are all sons of bitches." Isidor Isaac Rabi, an American physicist who won the 1944 Nobel Prize in Physics for his discovery of nuclear magnetic resonance and a VIP observer at the test, watched Oppenheimer's reaction: "I'll never forget his walk; I'll never forget the way he stepped out of the car . . . his walk was like *High Noon* . . . this kind of strut. He had done it."

The First Atomic Bomb: Little Boy

The first atomic bomb used in war, named *Little Boy*, exploded at 1900 feet over the Japanese city of Hiroshima at 8:16am, on August 6, 1945, twenty-one days after the Trinity test explosion.

Technically, *Little Boy* was significantly different from the test bomb, *the Gadget*, exploded on July 16. Early in the process, scientists with the Manhattan Project created two distinctively different designs for nuclear weapons. The one for the Trinity test was a plutonium implosion device as described above, while *Little Boy* was a uranium gun-type device. In the description of *Little Boy* provided by Atomic Heritage, "the fission reaction occurred when two masses of uranium [U-235] collided together using a gun-type device to form a critical mass that initiated the reaction. In effect, one slug of uranium hit another after firing through a smooth bore gun barrel. The target was in the shape of a solid uranium spike measuring seven inches long and four inches in diameter, [both weighing 64 kg (141 lb)]. The [containment] cylinder [fitted] precisely over the spike as the two collided together creating the highly explosive fission reaction. While the theory of the gun firing concept was not fully tested until the actual bomb dropped on Hiroshima, scientists concluded successful lab test on a smaller scale that gave them confidence the method would be successful."

The delivery system for *Little Boy*, along with two other bombs, was equally unique. The components were assembled at the Los Alamos Laboratory in New Mexico and shipped by train to San Francisco. The components were then loaded on the US Navy heavy cruiser *USS Indianapolis* which went direct to Tinian Island, Marianas Islands. The U-235 enriched uranium and plutonium cores for the bombs were shipped separately from Los Alamos on three C-54 Skymaster aircraft (in civilian use, it was the DC-4) direct to Tinian Island. Both the *Indianapolis* and the C-54 arrived at Tinian on July 26.

Tinian is one of three large islands that today form the Commonwealth of the Northern Marianas Islands at the eastern edges of the Philippine Sea. The island of Guam is at its southern reaches, but it is administered separately as a territory of the United States. Tinian and the Northern Marianas became the United Nations Trust Territory of the Pacific Islands. In 1978, it obtained Commonwealth Status with the United States, ending the trusteeship in 1986. It has its own elected governor and legislature and is represented in the American House of Representative by one non-voting representative. It has, in essence, status similar to that of Puerto Rico within the American system of government.

Tinian was captured by American forces a year before the Trinity test, on August 1, 1944, along with Saipan, a nearby island of the Marianas. The loss of life, 300 Americans and 6,000 Japanese, was typical of the island-taking-war in the Pacific. There were 25,000 American casualties in the capture of Iwo Jima, with only one percent of the 22,000 Japanese soldiers, about 220, captured in February 1945; all the others were killed. Later, in the three months war for Okinawa (Operation Iceberg from April to June) which was only 400 miles from the main islands of Japan, the casualties were astronomical – 50,000 American and Allied soldiers, an estimated 84,166 to 117,000 Japanese soldiers, and an estimated 150,000 civilian Okinawans killed.

The capture of Tinian and the other islands of the Marianas was made possible with the earlier American success in the Pacific War. Initially, this was the capture of Guadalcanal and the other islands of the Solomons in the second half of 1942 and early 1943. The Guadalcanal campaign signaled the transition of the defensive operations in the Pacific to a broad offensive campaign directly aimed at the defeat of all Japanese forces outside of Japan and, ultimately, the invasion of Japan. The forces dedicated from both sides and the casualties provide understanding of the difficulties involved in the planned island-to-island campaign. The United States had 15,000 casualties, while Japan suffered loses of almost 30,000. But it was the loss of naval and air resources that demonstrated the difficulties of the Pacific war; the Americans lost 29 ships, including 2 carriers, 6 heavy cruisers, and 17 destroyers, along with 615 aircraft; the Japanese lost 38 ships, including one carrier, 17 cruisers and destroyers, and 683 aircraft. Japan was able to evacuate only 11,000 troops.

The changing security dynamics in the Pacific is also illustrated by the politics of the Solomon Islands, independent since 1978. The various islands with differing political, economic, and social interests have had a contentious existence with related security problems. The United States has shown little interest over the years in these problems, while Australia has been ineffective, if not heavy-handed, in its relations with the government in Honiara. Today's Solomon Islands has switched its allegiance to Beijing and has recently signed an agreement with China dedicating a portion of its police force to the protection of the significant Chinese community in the capital. There is also a draft proposal for broader cooperation on security matters. Recently, ships of the United States Navy were advised that they were not welcome.

These activities reflect the interest of China in broadening its security footprint in the western Pacific and is seen as an important element in its international security arrangements. Other islands see a closer relationship as an important element in their economic development and a willingness to balance Australian and American interests with those of China.

The massive casualties and the forecast of more to come with an invasion of the main islands of Japan (Operation Downfall) provided incentive for using the atomic bomb. The decision centred around predictions of a million American casualties and that of untold number of Japanese military and civilians should an invasion take place. These estimates have been questioned, but for those involved in the decision making at the time, they were influential in the final decision to use the new atomic weapons.

President Roosevelt died on April 12, 1945, less than four months into his fourth term following his re-election the previous November. There was now a new president, new not only in not being an inner member of the government and the management of the war, but new to the existence of the developing atomic weapons. On April 24, the Secretary of War, Henry L Stimson, and General Leslie Groves met with Truman and provided a detailed briefing on the Manhattan

Project. The written report for the President opened with the words, "Within four months, [August] we shall in all probability have completed the most terrible weapon ever known in human history." The briefing detailed the state of the American project with emphasis on the fact that it was unique in the world and there were no fears Germany had such weapons. Truman was also briefed that the Soviet Union did not have the weapons but would likely have them within four years.

Truman agreed to the continuation of efforts for a workable bomb but realized there was also need for further information, advice, and guidance on the role of post-war nuclear energy. More urgently, he needed information on the use of the new weapons in the continuing war with Japan. In May, Stimson with Truman's concurrence, created the "Interim Committee" under his chair. The Committee included former Senator James Byrnes, soon to be Secretary of State, as the President's personal representative. The other Committee members included seven others, well known political, scientific, and industrial figures. On the use of the bomb in the war with Japan, the Committee reported within a few days of its creation, on June 1, 1945:

> Mr. Byrnes recommended, and the Committee agreed, that the Secretary of War [Stimson] should be advised that, while recognizing that the final selection of the target was essentially a military decision, the present view of the Committee was that the bomb should be used against Japan as soon as possible; that it be used on a war plant surrounded by workers' homes; and that it be used without prior warning.

The four scientists closely associated with the development of the bomb supported the decision. They were Enrico Fermi and Arthur Compton, of the Metallurgical Laboratory at the University of Chicago; Ernest Lawrence, of the Radiation Laboratory at the University of California at Berkeley; and Robert Oppenheimer, the scientific director at Los Alamos. On June 16 they wrote,

> The opinions of our scientific colleagues on the initial use of these weapons are not unanimous: they range from the

proposal of a purely technical demonstration to that of the military application best designed to induce surrender. Those who advocate a purely technical demonstration would wish to outlaw the use of atomic weapons, and have feared that if we use the weapons now our position in future negotiations will be prejudiced. Others emphasize the opportunity of saving American lives by immediate military use, and believe that such use will improve the international prospects, in that they are more concerned with the prevention of war than with the elimination of this specific weapons. We find ourselves closer to these latter views; we can propose no technical demonstration likely to bring an end to the war; and we see no acceptable alternative to direct military use.

The political and scientific consensus was sufficient for Byrnes to meet with the President immediately after the June 1 meeting of the Interim Committee. Truman agreed with the consensus, so the planning for the bombing took on urgency. In a new report, the Committee advised that

> The weapon be used against Japan at the earliest opportunity, that it be used without warning, and that it be used on a dual target, namely, a military installation or war plant surrounded by or adjacent to homes or other building most susceptible to damage.

Several scientists continued to present views in opposition to the use of the new weapons. The most prominent was Leo Szilard and his colleagues Walter Bartkey and Harold Urey at the universities of Chicago and Colombia. Szilard was the main author of the August 1939 letter to President Roosevelt, signed by Albert Einstein, warning of the development of the new weapons and the possibility Germany was involved in such work. Szilard and his colleagues sought a meeting with Truman following the June 1 consensus but were deflected to a meeting with Byrnes. And so, they were not successful in creating any hesitation in the use of the weapons. Their views were not widely shared either within the government nor beyond, and while the debate on the justification for use in 1945 continues today, the consensus remains that Truman was right to use the new weapon.

Nevertheless, the range of views in the June 16 report remain of interest. The arguments sum up the continuing issues associated with nuclear weapons and especially the comment, "they are more concerned with the prevention of war than with the elimination of this specific weapons." The question of deterrence remains at the centre of debates about the proliferation of nuclear weapons and their ownership by nine countries today.

The capture of Tinian, located 1600 miles south of Tokyo, provided a base for roundtrip bombing attacks on Japan using the B-29, which entered service in May 1944. The components for *Little Boy* were assembled on Tinian and the tactical decision to bomb Hiroshima was taken by General Curtis LeMay, the Commander of Pacific Air Combat on August 4. It was given the codename Operation Centerboard.

The Boeing B-29 Superfortress was the largest aircraft of World War II. It had four engines powering a high altitude strategic heavy bomber. It was also used at low altitudes for night incendiary bombing throughout Japan and the dropping of naval mines around the islands. It had state-of-the-art technology, including pressurized cabins, dual wheeled tricycle landing gear, and a fire-control system using an analog computer. It could fly to Tokyo from Tinian and return in twelve hours. The design and production cost for the aircraft was $3 billion, the equivalent of $45 billion today. Its cost exceeded that of the Manhattan Project, which was $1.9 billion ($30 billion today). Nearly 4,000 of the aircraft were built, and the B-29 remained in service in various iterations until the early 1960s; today, only two still fly.

General LeMay used the newly available B-29s to begin the decimation and incineration of Japan from the air with massive, continuing attacks on 67 Japanese cities. The most intensive and destructive was the firebombing of Tokyo on March 9-10, 1945. The attack involved 325 B-29s loaded with incendiary clusters, magnesium, and white phosphorus bombs and napalm. The bombing killed 100,000, destroyed 250,000 buildings, and incinerated 17 square miles (42 square kilometres) of the city. One subsequent report noted that, while precise figures were not available, the bombing campaign may have killed more than 500,000 Japanese civilians in the five months before the nuclear bombing. The official estimate by the United States reported 220,000 persons killed, with 40% of the centres of 66 cities destroyed.

General LeMay, in characteristic fashion, (he went on to head the Strategic Air Command of the USAF during the early days of the Cold War), said, "if the war is shortened by a single day, the attack will have served its purpose." He later said, "If I had lost the war, I would have been tried as a war criminal." In the ambiguities of war, LeMay dropped leaflets on possible targets, saying, "Unfortunately, bombs have no eyes. So, in accordance with America's humanitarian policies, the American Air Force, which does not wish to injure innocent people, now gives you warning to evacuate the cities named and save your lives." In the aftermath of the war, neither the Americans nor its allies prosecuted military personnel for the bombings that failed to distinguish between civilians or war related production facilities. In the aftermath of the dropping of the bombs on Hiroshima and Nagasaki, efforts were made to relate both cities to the production of war materials. Both Presidents Roosevelt and Truman supported the strategy of killing civilians and used as justification the anticipated death of a million Americans if Japan was invaded.

Hiroshima

Enola Gay, the B-29 bomber that carried *Little Boy*, left Tinian at 2:45am on August 6, 1945. The bomb's components were assembled shortly before take-off in the underground weapons storage area, which allowed for the direct loading of the device into the aircraft. The assembled bomb weighed 10,000 lbs and the B-29 needed the full two miles of runway to get airborne. In addition to the Pilot, Col. Paul Tibbets, there was a twelve-man crew inclusive of a co-pilot, mission commander, bombardier, navigator, and tail gunner. *Enola Gay* was accompanied by two other B-29s flying out of Iwo Jima. The *Great Artiste*, piloted by Major Charles W. Sweeney, was equipped to measure the atomic explosion, while the *Necessary Evil*, piloted by Captain George W. Marquardt, was to photograph the explosion and observe the results. In flight, the mission commander and bombardier on the *Enola Gay*, Navy Captain William Parsons, armed the bomb.

Flying north by northwest out of Tinian, the *Enola Gay* flew towards Iwo Jima in the Bonin Islands at 31,000 feet; there it made the rendezvous with the *Great Artiste* and *Necessary Evil*. Flying in loose formation, the trio flew directly to Hiroshima. Some thirty minutes out from Hiroshima, Second Lieutenant Morris Jeppson removed the safety devices from the bomb.

Hiroshima was the principal city on southwestern Honshu Island, the largest and most populous of Japan's five main island. It was on the Ota River Delta, facing eastward onto the Inland Sea of Japan. It had a civilian population of near 500,000 and was the military headquarters for the defence of the island, with 43,000 soldiers, and a number of industries associated with the war. At 8:15am, *Little Boy* was dropped and exploded forty-four seconds later at 1900 feet above the ground. The chain reaction explosion of 64 kg of U-235 created a force estimated at 15 kilotons, or the equivalent of 15,000 tons of TNT. The radius of destruction was 1.6 kilometres, with fires radiating across 11 square km. In subsequent analysis by the *Atomic Heritage Foundation*, the weapon was "considered very inefficient," as only 1.7 percent of its enriched uranium fissioned.

The forty-four seconds for the delay allowed the B-29 to fly eleven miles beyond. Looking back, the crew recorded their impressions of the first atomic bomb used in war. The pilot, Col. Paul Tibbets, said,

> We turned back to look at Hiroshima. The city was hidden by that awful cloud. . . boiling up, mushrooming, terrible and incredibly tall. No one spoke for a moment, then everyone was talking. I remember (co-pilot Robert) Lewis pounding my shoulder, saying "Look at that! Look at that! Look at

that!" (Bombardier) Tom Ferebee wondered about whether radioactivity would make us all sterile. Lewis said he could taste atomic fission. He said it tasked like lead.

The navigator, Theodore Van Kirk, recalled the shockwaves from the explosion: "(It was) very much as if you've ever sat on an ash can and had somebody hit it with a baseball bat . . . The plane bounced, it jumped and there was a noise like a piece of sheet metal snapping . . . I don't believe anyone ever expected to look at a sight quite like that. Where we had seen a clear city two minutes before, we could not no longer see the city. We could see smoke and fires creeping up the sides of the mountains."

The tail gunner, Robert Caron, who had an unobstructed view of the explosion, observed, "The mushroom itself was a spectacular sight, a bubbling mass of purple-gray smoke and you could see it had a red core in it and everything was burning inside. As we got farther away, we could see the base of the mushroom and below we could see what looked like a few-hundred-foot layer of debris and smoke and what have you . . . I saw fires springing up in different places, like flames shooting up on a bed of coals."

On the ground, the city was annihilated, with 70,000 out of 76,000 buildings destroyed or damaged. 46,000 had simply disappeared. But in a city that no longer existed, there were survivors and observers. A college history professor said, "I climbed Hikiyama Hill and looked down. I saw that Hiroshima had disappeared . . . I was shocked by the sight. . . What I felt then and still feel now I just can't explain with words. Of course, I saw many dreadful scenes after that – but that experience, looking down and finding nothing left of Hiroshima – was so shocking that I simply can't express what I felt . . . Hiroshima didn't exist – that was mainly what I saw – Hiroshima just didn't exist."

The observation of a medical doctor is much the same, "Nothing remained except a few buildings of reinforced concrete. . . For acres and acres, the city was like a desert except for scattered piles of brick and roof tile. I had to revise my meaning of the word destruction or choose some other word to describe what I saw. Devastation may be a better word, but really, I know of no word or words to describe the view." A writer wrote, "My heart shook like a great wave... the grief of stepping over the corpses of history pressed upon my heart."

A grocer described the people: "The appearance of people was... well, they all had skin blackened by burns... They had no hair because their hair was burned, and at a glance you couldn't tell whether you were looking at them from in front or in back... Many of them died along the road – I can still picture them in my mind – like walking ghosts... They didn't look like people of this world."

A sociologist thought it was the hell for Buddhists: "My immediate thought was that this was like the hell I had always read about... I had never seen anything which resembled it before, but I thought that should there be a hell, this was it–the Buddhist hell, where we were thought that people who could not attain salvation always went ... And I imagined that all of these people I was seeing were in the hell I had read about."

Then there were the children. A fourteen-year-old boy said, "Night came and I could hear many voices crying and groaning with pain and begging for water... The sky was red with flames. It was burning as if scorching heaven."

A sixth-grade girl said, "Bloated corpses were drifting in those seven formerly beautiful rivers, smashing cruelly into bits... the peculiar odor of burning human flesh rose everywhere in the Delta City, which had changed to a waste of scorched earth."

A boy in fifth-grade said, "I had the feeling that all the human beings on the face of the earth had been killed off, and only the five of us were left behind in an uncanny world of the dead."

A six-year -old boy remembered, "Near the bridge there were a whole lot of dead people... Sometimes there were ones who came to us asking for a drink of water. They were bleeding from their faces and from their mouths and they had glass sticking in their bodies. And the bridge itself was burning furiously... The details and the scenes were just like Hell."

[The words of survivors are from the National Museum of Nuclear Science & History, *Voices from Japan*].

The deaths from the explosion and those later ones, victims of radiation poisonings, have never been enumerated with any great accuracy. The incineration of bodies and the destruction of complete families created hesitation for all who have sought to count the deaths occasioned by *Little Boy*. The National Archives of the United States concluded that "70,000 people are estimated to have perished as a result of the initial blast, heat and radiation effects... By the end of 1945, because of the continuing effects of radioactive fallout and other after effects, including radiation poisoning, the Hiroshima death toll was likely over 100,000. The five-year death total may have even exceeded 200,000, as cancer and other long-term effects are considered."

A day after the bombing, on August 7, several Japanese physicists visited Hiroshima for direct examination of the destruction of the city. The group was headed by Yoshio Nishina, considered the founding father of modern physics research in Japan and who headed efforts by Japan in the development of its own nuclear weapons during the war. In their report to Tokyo the next day, they confirmed that a nuclear explosion had destroyed the city. After the war, Nishina became a close friend of the American physicist, Harry Kelly, one of several recruited by the occupation force to examine Japanese nuclear developments. Nishina died in 1951; when Kelly died later, he was buried next to Nishina in a grave in Tokyo's Tama Cemetery attended by both families – a reflection of the value of the fraternization policy of General MacArthur.

Nishina's report was received by Admiral Soemu Toyoda, Chief of the Imperial Japanese Navy General Staff. He, along with the Army, had their own atomic bomb development projects and understood the difficulties in the construction of atomic weapons. It was the belief of the Japanese military that it was unlikely the United States would have any additional atomic bombs. They continued to promote the total defence of the home islands in the very last days of the war. According to records from the time, the Americans expected this reaction, and that entered into their decisions to drop a second bomb as quickly as possible. After the war, Admiral Toyoda was prosecuted "for violating the laws and customs of war" but was acquitted and released in 1949. He was the only member of the Japanese armed forces so charged and acquitted. It was during this period that General Groves promised that a third atomic bomb would be available for use against Japan on August 19.

On August 8, after the nuclear explosion, Truman announced the event, noting that "Providence" ensured that Germany had failed in developing a nuclear weapon but that the United States and its allies had "spent two billion dollars on the greatest scientific gamble in history – and won." His warning to Japan was explicit and dramatic: "If they do not now accept our terms, they may expect a rain of ruin from the air, the like of which has never been seen on this earth. Behind this air attack will follow sea and land forces in such numbers and power as they have not yet seen and with the fighting skill of which they are already well aware."

Earlier, in April, the Soviet Union informed the Japanese government that it was denouncing their Pact of Neutrality of April 13, 1941. The Pact largely covered Manchuria, now mainly northeast China, but at the time, it was an arm of Imperial Japan, known as Manchukuo. It became a puppet state in 1937 following the Japanese military invasion. Before the invasion, it was already under some measure of Japanese control in the aftermath of the Japan-Russia war of 1904-05. Manchukuo was an important part of the resources and industrialization needed by Japan in its preparation for war. In 1939, prior to the start of the war in Europe, there was a brief border conflict between the Soviet Union and Japan, which led to the Pact of Neutrality. Some have suggested that securing its border with the Soviet Union gave Japan confidence in its invasions throughout southeast Asia and ultimately in its attack on the United States in late 1941. The Soviet Union at the time of the Pact was fully preoccupied with events in Europe and with Germany's capture of most of western Europe; Moscow expected they were next on Hitler's agenda.

The legitimacy of Japan's establishment of Manchukuo as a puppet state became a large issue in the weakening of the League of Nations. A League report established that there was no legitimacy for the action of Japan and requested member states refuse to recognize it and pressure Japan to return the area of Manchuria/Manchukuo to China. Japan refused to do so and withdrew from the League, weakening it even further in the last days of peace in Europe and Asia.

Two days after the Hiroshima explosion, early in the night of August 9, the Soviet army and air force crossed the Manchurian border, triggering its war with Japan. The invasion added to both the confusion and difficulty for Japan in those fateful days. The bombing of Hiroshima and the declaration of war by the Soviet Union deepened the divisions within the inner circle of the Japanese leadership, leading to two distinct factions: one for continuing the war to the end and one for an acceptance of the terms of the Potsdam Declaration for unconditional surrender.

Nagasaki

The dropping of the second atomic bomb, three days after Hiroshima, on the city of Nagasaki prompted the Japanese leadership in Tokyo to its ultimate decision of accepting the Potsdam Declaration; they requested one major alteration, however. This was the provision for Emperor Hirohito to remain as part of the structure of the government of Japan.

The decision to use a nuclear weapon on a second Japanese city within days of the first had been delegated to General Curtis LeMay and other senior officers in the region. In consultations, Col. Paul Tibbets was initially scheduled to fly the *Enola Gay* on August 11 to attack the city of Kokura. Kokura was on the northern tip of the island of Kyushu on the Straights of Shimonoseki and the Inland Sea. It was a strategic location, hosting one of Japanese largest military arsenals. The weather forecast for the eleventh called for overcast cloud cover. Since there was a mandated requirement for the target to be visual before the bomb was dropped, the mission was cancelled. The weather looked better for the 9th, and the flight was rescheduled.

For this flight, a B-29 named *Bockscar*, with Major Charles Sweeney as pilot, left Tinian at 3:47am on the ninth, accompanied by two other B-29s carrying instruments for blast measurement and photography. The bomb was *Fat Man,* and apart from the electrical safety plugs, was fully armed at take-off. *Fat Man* was similar to the bomb exploded at Trinity on July 16 in that it was an implosion-type nuclear weapon with a solid plutonium core. Its nickname dates from that explosion as it had a wide, round shape. The shape had been modified for the air drop by adding airfoils at its rear. Like, *Little Boy*, it was 10,000 pounds and measured 128 inches in length with a 60-inch diameter.

Arriving over Kokura, cloud cover and smoke from the incendiary bombing of nearby areas the previous day blocked a visual sighting of the target despite three bombing runs. There were fuel problems, and Major Sweeney decided to proceed to the alternate target of Nagasaki.

Nagasaki had an interesting historical background. During the Edo period of 1600 to 1860, it was the only area of Japan open to Westerners for trade. From 1570 to 1639, it was a trading post for the Portuguese, who were expelled in 1639 following a brief rebellion by Catholic converts. The Dutch, who were unaffected by the rebellion, were nevertheless moved to the small off-shore island of Dejima, where they remained as the only westerners with exclusive access until the Treaty of Kanagawa in 1854 opened the country to foreign trade and diplomatic relations.

Nagasaki was also partially obscured by clouds on August 9, but a bomb run was made anyway. At the last moment, a break in the undercast provided the needed visibility. The bombardier, Captain Kermit Beahan, released *Fat Man* at 11:02am. It exploded following a 43 second fall at an altitude of 1650 feet (500m) but missing the intended target by nearly two miles. The death and destruction, while lesser than at Hiroshima, was still overwhelming.

Fat Man was more powerful than *Little Boy*, producing the equivalent force of 22,000 tons on TNT, much the same as that of the Trinity test explosion on July 16. Most of the damage was concentrated in the Urakami Valley midway between the Mitsubishi Steel and Arms works in the south and Mitsubishi-Urakami Ordnance Works in the north. Over half of the city was destroyed, largely as a result of the traditional use of wood and other flammable materials in building construction.

As with Hiroshima, the number of deaths associated with the nuclear explosion at Nagasaki are imprecise, but they reflect the immediate incineration of thousands plus the short- and long-term deaths of tens of thousands more. The estimates were for 35-40,000 persons killed immediately and approximately the same number dying in the next few days. The immediate death toll was in excess of 80,000. The number of deaths resulting from radiation illnesses over the succeeding years are not known, but they probably exceed a hundred thousand more.

As with Hiroshima, the words of the aircrew offer the most detailed description of the explosion. The co-pilot of *Bockscar*, Fred J. Olivi, published his recollections of the explosion:

> Suddenly, the light of a thousand suns illuminated the cockpit. Even with my dark welder's goggles, I winced and shut my eyes for a couple of second. I guessed we were about seven miles from "ground zero" and headed directly away from the target, yet the light blinded me for an instant. I had never experienced such an intense bluish light, maybe three or four times brighter than the sun shining above us.
>
> I've never seen anything like it! Biggest explosion I've ever seen . . . This plume of smoke I'm seeing is hard to explain. A great white mass of flame is seething within the white mushroom shaped cloud. It has a pinkish salmon color. The base is black and is breaking a little way down from the mushroom.
>
> The Mushroom cloud was coming right at us. I immediately looked up and could see that [Sweeney the pilot] was right,

the cloud was getting close to Bockscar. We had been told not to fly through the atomic cloud because it was extremely dangerous to the crew and aircraft. Knowing this, Sweeney put Bockscar into a steep dive to the right, away from the cloud, throttles wide open. For a few moments we could not tell if we were out-running the ominous cloud or if it was gaining on us, but gradually we pulled away from the dangerous radioactive cloud before it engulfed us, much to everyone's relief.

On the ground, Tatsuichiro Akizuki, offered these observations:

All the buildings I could see were on fire ... Electricity poles were wrapped in flames like so many pieces of kindling ... It seemed as if the earth itself emitted fire and smoke, flames that writhed up and erupted from underground. The sky was dark, the ground was scarlet, and in between hung clouds of yellowish smoke. Three kinds of color – black, yellow, and scarlet – loomed ominously over the people, who ran about like so many ants seeking to escape ... It seemed like the end of the world. [From National Museum of Nuclear Science & History *Voices from Japan*].

American journalist George Weller was one of the first to enter Nagasaki after the bombing. Weller was with the *New York Times* and *Chicago Daily News* and won a 1943 Pulitzer Prize for his war reporting. After the Nagasaki bombing, he was able to enter the city surreptitiously and wrote extensively on the bombing; he was one of the first to identify the mysterious "atomic illness" that was killing people who had survived the initial blast of the nuclear explosion. After spending days on the ground in Nagasaki, Weller wrote a detailed report on the as-yet unrecognized radiation poisoning, but the military censors in Tokyo refused to release the report. It was not until 2006, after his death, that his son, Anthony Weller published the reports along with others by his father. [*First into Nagasaki: The Censored Eyewitness Dispatches on Post-Atomic Japan and its Prisoners of War*, New York, Crown, 2006.]

But Weller's articles from Nagasaki influenced American authorities. Copies were replicated as internal military and Atomic Energy Commission documents – and in time, they became more-or-less gospel. Even General Douglas MacArthur, whose censorship rules led to the confiscation of the report, understood the value of Weller's reporting. MacArthur honoured him by awarding the Asiatic-Pacific Service Ribbon "in view of your long and meritorious services in the Southwest Pacific Area with the forces of this command. You have added luster to the difficult, dangerous and arduous profession of War Correspondent."

Walter Cronkite wrote in the foreword to the Weller's 2006 book:

> This is an important book – important and gripping. For the first time in print, we can read the details of the nuclear bombardment of Nagasaki, Japan, as written by the first American reporter on the terrible scene . . . [George Weller's] reports, so long delayed but now salvaged by his son, at last have saved our history from the military censorship that would have preferred to have time to sanitize the ghastly details . . . Also delayed by MacArthur's censorship were Weller's dispatches from his visits to American prison camps [w]here he uncovered the Japanese military's savage treatment of their American prisoners . . . There is so much in this volume that we never knew or have long forgotten. This volume of the last generation's history is an important reminder, a warning to inspire civilian vigilance.

The bombings of Hiroshima and Nagasaki provided the world with its first understanding of the effects of acute radiation syndrome (ARS) or radiation poisoning. The syndrome is the collection of health effects caused by exposure to high amounts of ionizing radiation in a short period of time and is significantly different than the more common chronic radiation syndrome, which occurs following prolonged exposures to relatively low doses of radiation. The power plant disaster at Chernobyl, Ukraine in 1986 is the only other example of large-scale acute radiation syndrome since the Japanese wartime bombings.

Symptoms of ARS include nausea, vomiting, loss of appetite, infections, bleeding, dehydration, and confusion. It also often results in a variety of cancers. The symptoms can start within hours of exposure, and while there are a variety of treatments, the damage is irreversible. Since the impacts of radiation poisoning are hard to measure and worsen over time, there is no way to determine the true death toll of nuclear weapons or large-scale nuclear accidents like Chernobyl.

According to a Wikipedia article,

> The atomic bombings of Hiroshima and Nagasaki resulted in high acute doses of radiation to a large number of Japanese people, allowing for greater insight into its symptoms and dangers. Red Cross Hospital Surgeon Terufumi Sasaki led intensive research into the syndrome in the weeks and months following the Hiroshima and Nagasaki bombings. Dr Sasaki and his team were able to monitor the effects of radiation in patients of varying proximities to the blast itself, leading to the establishment of three recorded stages of the syndrome. Within 25–30 days of the explosion, Sasaki noticed a sharp drop in white blood cell count and established this drop, along with symptoms of fever, as prognostic standards for ARS. Actress Midori Naka, who was present during the atomic bombing of Hiroshima, was the first incident of radiation poisoning to be extensively studied. Her death on August 24, 1945, was the first death ever to be officially certified as a result of ARS or "Atomic bomb disease." [Wikipedia, August 22, 2022].

Aftermath of Hiroshima and Nagasaki Bombings

The nuclear nature of the Hiroshima bomb, along with the death toll and damage, was available to the authorities in Tokyo a day after the explosion. This knowledge did not affect Japan's basic policy of fighting to the very end. At the time, the leadership of Japan was in the hands of the six members of the Supreme Council for the Direction of the War. The Council was created in 1944, and in 1945 it included Prime

Minister, Admiral Kantaro Suzuki; Foreign Minister, Shigenori Togo; Army Minister, General Korechika Anami; Navy Minister, Admiral Mitsumasa Yonai; Chief of the Army, General Staff General Yoshijiro Umezu; and Chief of the Navy, General Staff Admiral Soemu Toyoda.

The Council, while divided, were under instructions delivered personally by the Emperor on June 22. Emperor Hirohito "desire[d] that concrete plans to end the war, unhampered by existing policy, be speedily studied and that efforts made to implement them." There was no suggestion of surrender. At the time, there was an expectation that the Soviet Union would assist Japan in ending the war through negotiations as there was no state of war between them.

In Moscow, the Japanese Ambassador, Naotake Sato, was attempting to meet the Soviet Foreign Minister, Vyacheslav Molotov, who avoided him until July 11 but provided no indication of Soviet policy or intentions. At the time, the Soviets were preparing to meet with the Americans and the British at Potsdam to make final decisions on the administration of Germany and relations with its wartime allies. The Conference met on July 17 and went on to August 2, 1945. Japan, while discussed, was not on the agenda for specific action as the Soviet Union was not yet at war with Japan.

Following their participation in the Conference, Truman, Churchill, and Chiang Kai-shek, the head of the Nationalist Government of China, met and agreed on the terms for the surrender of Japan. The agreement was also called the Potsdam Declaration and made public on July 26. The Declaration was comprehensive and called "upon the government of Japan to proclaim now the unconditional surrender of all Japanese armed forces, and to provide proper and adequate assurances of their good faith in such action. The alternative for Japan is prompt and utter destruction."

The Declaration was made public by the government of Japan and supplemented by the leaflets dropped by American aircraft, but newspapers reported that the demands had been rejected by the government. At the same time, Prime Minister Admiral Suzuki told the press, "I consider the Joint Proclamation [Potsdam Declaration] a rehash of the Declaration at the Cairo Conference. As for the government, it does not attach any important value to it at all. The only thing to do is just kill it with silence. We will do nothing but press on to the bitter end to bring about a successful completion of the war."

There was disagreement within the Japanese Supreme Council. The Prime Minister, based on advice from Moscow provided by Ambassador Sato, was that "There is no alternative but immediate unconditional surrender if we are to prevent Russia's participation in the war." In response, on August 2, Foreign Minister Togo wrote "it should not be difficult for you to realize that . . . our time to proceed with arrangements of ending the war before the enemy lands on the Japanese mainland is limited, on the other hand it is difficult to decide on concrete peace conditions here at home all at once."

On the same day as the dropping of the atomic bomb on Hiroshima, President Truman made his "rain of ruin" speech. While noting that the Potsdam Declaration was meant to spare the Japanese people from "utter destruction," he went on to note that the leaders of Japan had rejected the surrender ultimatum, and "if they do not now accept our terms they may expect a rain of ruin from the air, the like of which has never been seen on this earth."

The events of August 8 and 9 eliminated any expectation of help from the Soviet Union, who declared war on Japan on August 8; its invasion of Manchuria/Manchukuo was underway on August 9. The Soviet forces also moved into the southern half of Sakhalin Island, a part of Japan since a 1924 treaty. From these invasions, there was the expectation the Soviets would move onto the northern Japanese island of Hokkaido, the second largest of Japan's "home islands," home of the Ainu people, and its capital, Sapporo.

The delayed but direct and significant Soviet involvement in the Pacific War also created concerns in Washington. It was seen as a direct effort by Moscow to involve itself directly into the peace arrangements that were inevitably to follow from the developments of August 8 and 9. There was a fear the Soviets would insist on separate areas of administration, just as they had successfully done in Germany. Today, all of Sakhalin Island remains a part of Russia, as do the nearby Kuril Islands to the southeast. Japan has maintained a claim to four of the Kuril Islands, but in the intervening years, neither the Soviet Union nor Russia has been willing to negotiate their return to Japan.

The second atomic explosion in Nagasaki further hardened the positions of most of the military leadership, but Emperor Hirohito, following developments closely, decided to act on his own in order to prevent the further destruction of his people and country. Over the next four days, the senior leaders of the military, except for Field Marshall Shunroku Hata, Commander of the Second General Army, which had been based in Hiroshima, argued for a continuation of war, largely in opposition to the view by the Prime Minister, the Foreign Minister, and General Hata.

On August 10, the Japanese Foreign Minister responded to the demand for unconditional surrender through the Swiss and stated it would accept the Potsdam Declaration but would not accept any peace conditions that would "prejudice the prerogatives" of the Emperor. On the same day, Washington, again using the Swiss as mediators, responded with direct reference to the role of the Emperor:

> From the moment of surrender the authority of the Emperor and the Japanese government to rule the state shall be subject to the Supreme Commander of the Allied powers who will take such steps as he deems proper to effectuate the surrender terms . . . The ultimate form of government of Japan shall, in accordance with the Potsdam Declaration, be established by the freely expressed will of the Japanese people.

These exchanges, while shared internally with the Supreme Council and the Cabinet, did not resolve either the issue of surrender nor the future role of the Emperor. In the midst of this continuing debate, a group of military officers asked the Minister of War to join them in preventing the acceptance of the Potsdam Declaration. The Minister was non-committal, but the rebelling officers, led by Major Kenji Hatanaka, sought wider support by invading the Imperial Palace and seeking to broadcast their demands on the radio. They were unsuccessful. By the morning of August 14, the rebellion collapsed with Major Hatanaka shooting himself.

The Emperor responded to the ongoing disagreement early in the morning of August 14 to the cabinet and other senior officials:

> I have listened carefully to each of the arguments presented in opposition to the view that Japan should accept the Allied reply as it stands and without further clarification or modification, but my own thoughts have not undergone any change... In order that the people may know my decision, I request you to prepare at once an **imperial rescript** [emphasis added] so that I may broadcast to the nation. Finally, I call upon each and every one of you to exert himself to the utmost so that we may meet the trying days which lie ahead.

"Rescript' is a legal term meaning "to write back." In the context of its use by the Emperor, it was the elimination of all previous imperial decisions relating to the war. The title of the document produced was *Imperial Rescript on the Termination of War* (or *on Surrender* in some translations) and meant precisely that. The emperor had decided to override the continuing disagreements from his advisors and command the end of the war. He accepted the Potsdam Declaration along with the addition dealing with his future role in the government of Japan following the unconditional surrender.

On August 15, Emperor Hirohito, or to use his Japanese name, Emperor Shōwa, spoke to the people of Japan. In his *Jewel Voice Broadcast* he said,

> To "Our Good and loyal subjects:
>
> After pondering deeply the general trends of the world and the actual conditions obtaining in Our Empire today, We have decided to effect a settlement of the present situation by resorting to an extraordinary measure.
>
> We have ordered Our Government to communicate to the Governments of the United States, Great Britain, China and

the Soviet Union that Our Empire accepts the provisions of their Joint Declaration.

To strive for the common prosperity and happiness of all nations as well as the security and well-being of Our subjects is the solemn obligation which has been handed down by Our Imperial Ancestors, and which We lay close to heart. Indeed, We declared war on America and Britain out of Our sincere desire to secure Japan's self-preservation and the stabilization of East Asia, it being far from Our thought either to infringe upon the sovereignty of other nations or to embark upon territorial aggrandizement. But now the war has lasted for nearly four years. Despite the best that has been done by everyone — the gallant fighting of military and naval forces, the diligence and assiduity of Our servants of the State and the devoted service of Our one hundred million people, the war situation has developed not necessarily to Japan's advantage, while the general trends of the world have all turned against her interest.

Moreover, the enemy has begun to employ a new and most cruel bomb the power of which to do damage is indeed incalculable, taking the toll of many innocent lives. Should we continue to fight, it would not only result in an ultimate collapse and obliteration of the Japanese nation, but also it would lead to the total extinction of human civilization. Such being the case, how are We to save the millions of Our subjects; or to atone Ourselves before the hallowed spirits of Our Imperial Ancestors? This is the reason why We have ordered the acceptance of the provisions of the Joint Declaration of the Powers.

We cannot but express the deepest sense of regret to Our Allied nations of East Asia, who have consistently cooperated with the Empire towards the emancipation of East Asia. The thought of those officers and men as well as others who have fallen in the fields of battle, those who died at their posts of duty, or those who met with untimely death and all their bereaved families, pains Our heart night and day. The welfare of the wounded and the war-sufferers, and of those who have lost their home and livelihood, are the objects of Our profound solicitude. The hardships and sufferings to which Our nation is to be subjected hereafter will be certainly great. We are keenly aware of the inmost feelings of all ye, Our subjects. However, it is according to the dictate of time and fate that We have resolved to pave the way for grand peace for all the generations to come by enduring the unendurable and suffering what is insufferable.

Having been able to safeguard and maintain the structure of the Imperial State, We are always with ye, Our good and loyal subjects, relying upon your sincerity and integrity. Beware most strictly of any outbursts of emotion which may endanger needless complications, or any fraternal contention and strife which may create confusion, lead ye astray and cause ye to lose the confidence of the world. Let the entire nation continue as one family from generation to generation, ever firm in its faith of the imperishableness of its divine land and mindful of its heavy burden of responsibilities, and the long road before it. Unite your total strength to be devoted to the construction for the future. Cultivate the ways of rectitudes; foster nobility of spirit; and work with resolution so as ye may enhance the innate glory of the Imperial State and keep place with the progress of the world.

On August 17, Emperor Hirohito directly addressed the members of the armed forces. In doing so, he eliminated the possibility the military at large or elements thereof would attempt to continue the war and, in his words, "endangering the very foundation of the Empire's existence . . . We trust that you officers and men of the Imperial forces will comply with our intention and will . . . bear the unbearable and leave an everlasting foundation of the nation." The war was effectively over.

The creation of peace conditions through the theatre of war was not prolonged even though there was skirmishing in the air and throughout its far reaches still with occupying Japanese troops. One, Teruo Nakamura, only emerged from his retreat in Indonesia in December 1974, while two others fought on in southern Thailand until 1991. General Douglas MacArthur was named Supreme Commander of the Allied Powers; by August 29, he was in Tokyo coordinating the various surrender ceremonies in the Pacific theatre, including New Guinea, Timor, Taiwan, French Indonesia, Singapore, China, and Malaysia. The surrender involved over seven million Japanese soldiers and sailors (out of a population of nearly 80 million) and some were not repatriated until early 1949.

September 2 was established as the date for the main surrender ceremony to take place in Tokyo Bay. It was chosen so as to be as close to Tokyo as possible in order to emphasize the completeness of the surrender. All the symbols of the American victory were in evidence: the largest, fastest, and newest of the American battleships, the *Missouri*, named after President Truman's home state and commissioned by his daughter, Margaret in 1944, was chosen for the signing of the instruments of surrender. The *Missouri* flew the same flag that flew over the American Capitol at the time of the attack on Pearl Harbour. It also displayed the flag flown by Commodore Matthew Perry when he opened Japan to American trade in 1853.

The battleship was in Tokyo Bay by August 29 and at the time of the Instruments of Surrender ceremony at 0900 on September 2. It was accompanied by 250 other ships representing the states involved in the war. There were no ships from Canada as all four were in the eastern Pacific at the time. There was a British ship, *HMS Newfoundland*, a light cruiser named after the Dominion of Newfoundland, among the 250 ships gathered for the surrender ceremony. The *Newfoundland* was launched in 1941, served in the Mediterranean, and was involved in the bombardment of the Japanese home islands and the capture of the Japanese naval base at Yokosuka prior to the surrender.

The signing ceremony was simple but formal. The nine-member Japanese delegation was led by the Foreign Minister, Shigemitsu Mamoru. On the deck of the *Missouri*, they stood facing the American and Allied commanders headed by General Douglas MacArthur. The General invited the Japanese delegation to sign the Instrument of Surrender. It contained the absolute statement, "We hereby proclaim the unconditional surrender to the Allied Powers of the Japanese Imperial General Headquarters and of all Japanese armed forces and all armed forces under Japanese control wherever situated." The Foreign Minister signed on behalf of the Emperor. In turn, MacArthur signed, as did the representatives of the Allied Powers: the United Kingdom, the Soviet Union, China, Australia, Canada, France, the Netherlands, and New Zealand. At 0930, the Japanese delegation departed.

Canada was represented at the ceremony by Colonel Lawrence Vincent Moore Cosgrave. Col. Cosgrave was a wounded veteran (he lost an eye) of the First World War and subsequently was Canadian Trade Commissioner in London, Shanghai, and Melbourne. During World War II, he was appointed Canadian Military Attaché to Australia for the Southwest Pacific and was designated to sign on behalf of Canada. When he signed the Japanese document, he placed his signature a line below that designated for Canada, causing a brief disruption while the lines were adjusted for the subsequent signatures. Col. Cosgrave later explained his loss of an eye led to the error as he had trouble distinguishing the lines. (An easy mistake with which the author can understand, as he lost an eye at an early age and has encountered similar situations).

There were decisions associated with the surrender of Japan that carried import into the present. The first was the American and Soviet agreement in 1945 for a demarcation line along the 38th parallel. American and Soviet troops entered to supervise the departure of the Japanese army, and while there was an understanding of Korea becoming a unified independent country, post-war developments led to a permanently divided country. The Soviet Union established a communist regime in the North under Kim Il-Sung, the grandfather to the Kim Sung-un, the present leader, while the United States established a government in the South under Syngman Rhee. There were attempts in the early years to hold national elections; instead, in 1950, the North sought to unify the peninsula through conquest. Three years of war under UN auspices resulted in a ceasefire agreement that has cemented the 1945 line of demarcation.

The second decision arising out of the war with Japan only became manifest in 1949. In the 1945 departure of Japanese troops from China, inclusive of the island of Taiwan, the Nationalist government of Chiang Kai Shek was given responsibility for the government of both areas. Taiwan had been part of the Japanese Empire since the 19th century. With Japan's defeat in 1945, Taiwan effectively reverted to Chinese sovereignty. This was relatively uncontroversial until 1949 when the Nationalist forces of Chiang were defeated and they withdrew to the Island of Taiwan, still proclaiming to be the government of all of China. In some measure, but with many nuances, that remains the situation today; whenever there is a crisis of some sort with the government in Beijing, there are threats involving Taiwan. In its early years, Taiwan had some expectations of developing its own nuclear weapons but was dissuaded from doing so by the United States.

7. Control and Management of the Scary World

> *In the first place, the [nuclear] secret is possessed by our friends and allies, Great Britain and Canada, whose scientific genius made a tremendous contribution to our original discoveries and the designs of atomic bombs. The secret is also known by the Soviet Union.*
>
> **President Eisenhower, "Atoms for Peace" Speech at the United Nations, December 8, 1953**

Before the dust had settled on the nuclear explosions over Hiroshima and Nagasaki, American scientists and engineers involved in the Manhattan Project began to question what they had achieved. The questioning began with Robert Oppenheimer.

Two months after the explosions in Japan, in October 1945, Oppenheimer met with President Harry Truman, who had given final authority for the use of nuclear weapons. He warned Truman of the dangers of the bombs and the urgent need for international controls on nuclear weapons. In 2011, Paul Ham, an Australian writer, published an account of the two Japanese bombings and reported that Truman refused to accept Oppenheimer's advice, saying, "the blood is on my hands, let me worry about that." There were indications that Truman did "worry," but in the political turmoil of the times, he left office without offering any specific solutions. Oppenheimer's questioning of nuclear weapons continued, and he was fired a few years later from the American Atomic Energy Commission amid unsubstantiated rumours that he was an agent of the Soviet Union.

President Truman's successor, Dwight Eisenhower, reflected the same fears as Oppenheimer. In his first speech to the General Assembly of the United Nations on December 8, 1953, he gave voice to the threat represented by nuclear weapons and urged the world to use atomic energy for peaceful purposes. In one of the most significant speeches of the postwar period, Eisenhower spoke of a program for American foreign policy centered on the control and elimination of nuclear weapons. That policy has been battered and ignored over the last seventy years. The speech called "Atoms for Peace" is worth remembering as the world continues to cope with the scourge of nuclear weapons. Eisenhower opened with these words:

> The atomic age has moved forward at such a pace that every citizen of the world should have some comprehension, at least in comparative terms, of the extent of this development, of the utmost significance to every one of us. Clearly, if the peoples of the world are to conduct an intelligent search for peace, they must be armed with the significant facts of today's existence.
>
> My recital of atomic danger and power is necessarily stated in United States terms, for these are the only incontrovertible facts that I know. I need hardly point out to this Assembly, however, that this subject is global, not merely national in character.
>
> On July 16, 1945, the United States set off the world's first atomic explosion. Since that date in 1945, the United States of America has conducted forty-two test explosions. Atomic bombs today are more than twenty-five times as powerful as the weapon with which the atomic age dawned, while the hydrogen weapons are in the ranges of millions of tons of TNT equivalent. Today, the United States stockpile of atomic weapons, which, of course, increases daily, exceeds by many

times the total [explosive] equivalent of the total of all bombs and all shells that came from every plane and every gun in every theater of war in all of the years of World War II.

A single air group, whether afloat or land based, can now deliver to any reachable target a destructive cargo exceeding in power all the bombs that fell on Britain in all of World War II. In size and variety, the development of atomic weapons has been no less remarkable. The development has been such that atomic weapons have virtually achieved conventional status within our armed services. In the United States, the Army, the Navy, the Air Force and the Marine Corps are all capable of putting this weapon to military use. But the dread secret and the fearful engines of atomic might are not ours alone.

In the first place, the secret is possessed by our friends and allies, Great Britain and Canada, whose scientific genius made a tremendous contribution to our original discoveries and the designs of atomic bombs. The secret is also known by the Soviet Union. The Soviet Union has informed us that, over the recent years, it has devoted extensive resources to atomic weapons. During this period the Soviet Union has exploded a series of atomic devices, including at least one involving thermo-nuclear reactions. If at one time the United States possessed what might have been called a monopoly of atomic power, that monopoly ceased to exist several years ago.

Therefore, although our earlier start has permitted us to accumulate what is today a great quantitative advantage, the atomic realities of today comprehend two facts of even greater significance. First, the knowledge now possessed by several nations will eventually be shared by others, possibly all others.

Second, even a vast superiority in numbers of weapons, and a consequent capability of devastating retaliation, is no preventive, of itself, against the fearful material damage and toll of human lives that would be inflicted by surprise aggression.

The free world, at least dimly aware of these facts, has naturally embarked on a large program of warning and defense systems. That program will be accelerated and expanded. But let no one think that the expenditure of vast sums for weapons and systems of defense can guarantee absolute safety for the cities and citizens of any nation. The awful arithmetic of the atomic bomb does not permit of any such easy solution. Even against the most powerful defense, an aggressor in possession of the effective minimum number of atomic bombs for a surprise attack could probably place a sufficient number of his bombs on the chosen targets to cause hideous damage.

It is with the book of history, and not with isolated pages, that the United States will ever wish to be identified. My country wants to be constructive, not destructive. It wants agreements, not wars, among nations. It wants itself to live in freedom and in the confidence that the people of every other nation enjoy equally the right of choosing their own way of life.

So my country's purpose is to help us move out of the dark chamber of horrors into the light, to find a way by which the minds of men, the hopes of men, the souls of men everywhere, can move forward toward peace and happiness and well-being.

In this quest, I know that we must not lack patience. I know that in a world divided, such as ours today, salvation cannot be attained by one dramatic act. I know that many steps will have to be taken over many months before the world can look at itself one day and truly realize that a new climate of mutually peaceful confidence is abroad in the world.

> But I know, above all else, that we must start to take these steps—now.
>
> The United States would seek more than a mere reduction or elimination of atomic materials for military purposes. It is not enough to take this weapon out of the hands of the soldiers. It must be put into the hands of those who will know how to strip its military casing and adapt it to the arts of peace.

After he left office, Eisenhower was frequently consulted on the possible use of nuclear weapons, especially in the context on the Korean and Vietnamese wars. Despite the caution reflected in his UN speech, Eisenhower is reported to have supported the use of tactical nuclear weapons in both wars. Nevertheless, the language and passion of the 1953 speech remain relevant today, even as American leadership has fallen short of Eisenhower's ideals.

There are two central elements to the speech. The first is to eliminate weaponized nuclear energy; the second is to concentrate exclusively on the peaceful applications. To follow through, Eisenhower called for the creation of an agency under the aegis of the UN. The proposed International Atomic Energy Agency (IAEA) came into existence in 1957. In its 65 years of existence, it has helped in the creation of global standards in the use of nuclear energy and provides continuing focus in the efforts to control the proliferation of nuclear weapons. The IAEA's involvement in providing an international context for Russian threats to use nuclear weapons in Ukraine demonstrates its continuing value.

Non-Proliferation Efforts

Since Eisenhower's speech, there have been international efforts in the control of proliferation. The signature dates of 1963, 1970, 1998, and 2021 demonstrate how difficult progress has been. Those dates represent the years in which significant treaties concerning the testing and non-proliferation of nuclear weapons came into force. The first was the *Partial Nuclear Test Ban Treaty of 1963* which grew out of negotiations involving the United States, the United Kingdom, and the Soviet Union, and which is covered in the next chapter. It was followed seven years later by the foundational **Nuclear Non-Proliferation Treaty** of 1970, which today engages commitments by 191 countries.

At its Review Conference in 1995, the Treaty was unconditionally extended to indefinite status from its original 25-year lifespan. The objective of the NPT was to create a multilateral consensus limiting the spread of nuclear weapons. In doing so, the Treaty established the legal requirements that (a) states without nuclear weapons would not obtain them; (b) states with nuclear weapons would make efforts to eliminate their weapons; and (c) all states were entitled to obtain safeguarded nuclear technology for peaceful purposes. The Treaty also recognized the international legality of the nuclear weapons status of the five states – China, France, Russia, the United Kingdom and the United States–that had nuclear weapons prior to January 1, 1967.

The NPT opened for signature on July 1, 1968, and entered into force on March 5, 1970. Apart from the Chemical Weapons Convention, the NPT has obtained the largest number of state parties to any arms control treaty. Only four states have not signed – India, Israel, Pakistan, and South Sudan. It is expected South Sudan will sign, but it has been preoccupied with an ongoing civil war since its creation on July 15, 2011. India, Israel, and Pakistan are not considered nuclear weapon states as they did not have nuclear weapons prior to January 1, 1967, which was the established termination date for such status. If they were to join the NPT, the three states would have to eliminate their nuclear weapons and accept IAEA safeguards. North Korea was a signatory to the NPT but withdrew on January 10, 2003, three years before it exploded its first nuclear device on October 9, 2006.

In the aftermath of the NPT coming into force, two groupings of nuclear technology exporting countries came together in order to review exports that might be contrary to the provisions of the Non-Proliferation Treaty. The **Zangger Committee** was formed in 1971 in order to ensure IAEA safeguards were applied to nuclear exports in accordance with Article III.2 of the Treaty. The article reads, "Each State Party to the Treaty undertakes not to provide: (a) source or special fissionable material, or (b) equipment or material especially designed or prepared for the processing, use or production of special fissionable material, to any non-nuclear weapons state for peaceful purposes, unless the source or special fissionable material shall be subject to the safeguards required by this Article." There are 39 states in the Committee, including the five designated nuclear weapon states. Canada has been a member from its inception.

A second grouping of states called the **Nuclear Suppliers Group (NSG)** came into existence as a result of concerns created by the May 1974 nuclear explosion by India. The explosion demonstrated that non-weapons-specific nuclear technology could be used in the development of nuclear weapons. The NSG first met in 1975 with seven members, including Canada, and agreed that further export controls were needed. Since then, the group has grown to 48 members, including all five members of the approved nuclear weapons grouping. Both India and Pakistan have sought membership, but China has consistently opposed India's inclusion if Pakistan was not to be included as well. Most other members agree to the inclusion of India but not Pakistan. Opposition to the inclusion of Pakistan increased after 2004, when an illicit network of nuclear related exports to Iran, Libya, and North Korea by Pakistani scientist A. Q. Khan was revealed.

India, Pakistan, Israel, and North Korea remain the only nuclear weapons states to emerge after the 1970 treaty. Israel is not known to have conducted a nuclear explosion (except for its possible involvement in the September 1979 nuclear explosion in the southern Indian Ocean) but most likely had nuclear weapons prior to the NPT coming into force. This limited expansion of only three proliferators since the signing of the Treaty can, in some measure, be attributed to the work of both the Zangger Committee and the Nuclear Suppliers Group.

It was twenty-six years later that the second nuclear weapons treaty was negotiated. This was **The Comprehensive Nuclear Test Ban Treaty (CNTBT)** adopted by the General Assembly of the United Nations on

September 10, 1996. It has been ratified by 186 states, but due to the need for 44 specific states to ratify, the Treaty has not come into force.

The 44 states are involved in treaty negotiations and all must ratify. 36 have ratified so far. Those yet to agree are China, Egypt, India, Iran, Israel, North Korea, Pakistan, and the United States. Two – China and the United States – are recognized as nuclear weapons states under the NPT. Three are self-declared nuclear weapon states – India, North Korea, and Pakistan. One – Israel – is a non-declared nuclear weapon state. Two – Iran and Egypt – do not have nuclear weapons.

The Treaty bans the use of nuclear explosions in all environments (underground, ground, air, or space) for either military or civilian purposes. There are few signs that the United States will ratify anytime soon, nor are their signs North Korea, Pakistan, or India will ever sign. While Israel has signed, it has not ratified the Treaty since it does not officially have nuclear weapons. India, Pakistan, and North Korea have exploded 17 nuclear devices since the Treaty was approved by the General Assembly.

Prior to the completion of the negotiations for the CNTBT, India and Pakistan signed the India-Pakistan Non-Attack Agreement on December 21, 1988. It came into force on January 1, 1991, and both countries committed to refrain from undertaking, encouraging, or participating in, directly or indirectly, any action aimed at causing destruction or damage to any nuclear installation or facility in either country. Both countries are required to inform the other of the precise locations of installations and facilities every year. Starting in January 1992, both countries have exchanged such lists, but there are questions as to their accuracy and completeness.

Egypt has had an ongoing but intermittent nuclear power program since the mid-1950s. Agreements with the Soviet Union, Argentina, and recently with Russia were expected to provide for power reactors, but so far nothing significant has resulted. Egypt signed the NPT in 1968 but has not ratified, claiming that Israel had undertaken a nuclear weapons program. The United States has sought to provide Egypt with assurances on the Israeli program, and to some extent they have succeeded through the agreement for the Egypt-Israel Peace Treaty of March 1979. The treaty provided mutual recognition and elimination of the previous state of war along with various other measures relating to regional issues. It has stood the test of forty years and has provided the basis of treaties and/or understandings by several other countries of the region. In some measure, Israel's nuclear weapons program is seen by some countries as a needed counter-balance against Iran developing its own nuclear weapons.

North Korea is unique in that its nuclear weapons program remains outside of international control or inspection. Its six nuclear weapons tests since 2006, the last on September 3, 2017, are the last such explosions of any country, and There are few signs of any willingness to temper its nuclear weapons developments.

8. Soviet/Russian and American Agreements on Nuclear Weapons

Well, boys, I reckon this is it; nuclear combat toe to toe with the Rooskies. Now look, boys, I ain't much of a hand at makin' speeches, but I got a pretty fair idea that something doggone important is goin' on back there. And I got a fair idea the kinda personal emotions that some of you fellas may be thinkin'. Heck, I reckon you wouldn't even be human bein's if you didn't have some pretty strong personal feelin's about nuclear combat. . . . Now let's get this thing on the hump; we got some flyin' to do."

Slim Pickens as Major T. J. King Kong, B-52 Pilot in
Dr Strangelove

In the aftermath of the 1962 Cuban Missile Crisis, the United States and the Soviet Union, along with the United Kingdom, signed the world's first nuclear control agreement on October 5, 1963. This was the **Limited Nuclear Test Ban Treaty,** which prohibited the testing of nuclear weapons in outer space, underwater, or in the atmosphere. By that time, the dangers of atmospheric testing were evident to all three countries and there was global concern. The negotiations for the Treaty took several years and were interrupted by a variety of incidents; most of all, the requirement for direct inspection of testing facilities created delays from the very start. More than thirty years later, the testing prohibition was extended to "any nuclear weapon test explosion or any other nuclear explosion."

At the time of the signature of the Limited Nuclear Test Ban Treaty, there were over 32,000 nuclear weapons globally. The United States had an inventory of 28,183 weapons, while the Soviet Union had 4,259, and the United Kingdom had 256. That world-wide inventory peaked at over 64,000 in 1986 when the United States had 23,317 weapons, the Soviet Union had 40,159, the United Kingdom had 350. Added to these were the arsenal of France, with 355; China, with 224; and Israel, with 44. Twelve years later, India and Pakistan had inventories of 3 weapons each, and in 2006, North Korea had an inventory of 6.

The Limited Nuclear Test Ban Treaty was the first in a decades-long set of negotiations between the United States and the Soviet Union to control and reduce their nuclear weapons. First were the **Strategic Nuclear Arms Control Agreements,** or SALT I and II. The discussions for SALT I began in 1969 and concluded in May of 1972 with the Anti-Ballistic Missile Treaty (ABM), which banned nationwide strategic missile defenses and capped both American and Soviet Intercontinental Ballistic Missiles (ICBM) and Submarine Launched Ballistic Missiles (SLBM) weapons. In the ensuing SALT II negotiations, concluded in June 1979, additional limitations on American and Soviet ICBM, SLBM and strategic bomber-based nuclear weapons were agreed upon. No treaty was signed for SALT II, but both countries pledged to adhere to the terms of the agreement.

The SALT agreements were followed by the **Strategic Arms Reduction Treaty (START)**, which had three components. START I discussions began in the early 1980s with a treaty signed in July 1991. It required the United States and the Soviet Union to reduce their deployed strategic arsenals to 1600 delivery vehicles with no more than 6,000 warheads. The reduction in weapons was delayed as a result of the collapse of the Soviet Union, but the reduction was completed in December 2001. The negotiations for START II were begun in 1992 with a treaty signed in January 1993. It required further reductions in deployed strategic arsenals to 3,000-3,500 warheads and banned the deployment of destabilizing multiple-warhead land-based missiles. While both countries approved the treaty, it has not taken effect because of a requirement for the United States Senate to agree to several amendments required by Russia.

A START III treaty was proposed by both countries in 1997 and was intended to establish further reductions in deployed strategic warheads. This includes "the destruction of strategic nuclear warheads ... to promote the irreversibility of deep reductions including prevention of a rapid increase in the number of warheads." Direct negotiations did not start because of the delay in the finalization of START II.

Before the START I agreement came into effect, the United States and Soviet Union, on December 8, 1987, signed the ***Intermediate-Range Nuclear Forces (INF) Treaty.*** It verified the elimination and permanent banning of all ground-launched ballistic and cruise missiles with ranges between 500 and 6,000 kilometers. The treaty entered into force June 1, 1988, and the two states completed their reductions by June 1, 1991, just as the Soviet Union collapsed. 2,692 missiles were destroyed with the implementation of the treaty. As a result of the collapse of the Soviet Union, the treaty included Russia, Belarus, Kazakhstan, Turkmenistan, Uzbekistan, and Ukraine, along with the United States. The additional countries were either test sites for the Soviet weapons or had nuclear weapons on their territory at the time the Soviet Union was disbanded.

Twenty years ago, on May 24, 2002, Presidents George W. Bush and Vladimir Putin signed the **Strategic Offensive Reductions Treaty (SORT)**, which commits the United States and Russia to reduce their deployed strategic nuclear forces to 1,700-2,200 warheads each. There are interpretation problems with the treaty (whether it covers only operationally deployed weapons and not warheads removed from service). Neither the American Senate nor the Russian Duma have approved the treaty.

The various bilateral treaties and arrangements involving the United States and the Soviet Union/Russia have been successful in reducing the number of nuclear weapons and their delivery system.

The numbers speak to the success. Less than 40 years ago, the inventory of nuclear weapons peaked at just over 64,000; today there are less than 13,000: an 80% reduction. If only the military stockpiles of such weapons are counted, then there are less than 10,000, while only 3,700 represent deployed strategic weapons. These reductions have occurred during a time when four additional states built nuclear weapons. To a large extent, the provisions of the Non-Proliferation Treaty and the Comprehensive Nuclear Test Ban Treaty have supported these reductions. There are few signs the international opprobrium surrounding nuclear weapons is lessening, and in an increasingly globalized world, it is unlikely that this will change.

Nevertheless, the existence of nearly 10,000 nuclear weapons creates a large impediment in making the world more secure. The existence of such weapons, as recent crises demonstrate, adds a complexity that ensures solutions are often beyond either an easy or an early resolution. Russia's threat of nuclear force should other countries provide assistance to Ukraine is but the most recent example.

The Soviet and Russian-American agreements on nuclear weapons are complicated by the differing profiles they represent in their national security profiles. The United States has 1,664 nuclear weapons classified as being deployed/strategic, while Russia has 1,558. In the deployed/nonstrategic category, (essentially tactical weapons) Russia has reported zero weapons, while the United States has 100. However, significant imbalances appear when we consider that Russia has 2,889 and 4,477 weapons in their reserve and nondeployed military stockpiles respectively. In each of these categories, the United States inventories show 1,964 and 3,708 weapons respectively. Based on current accounting, it will be difficult to reach consensus in future reduction agreements.

Moreover, the increasing nuclear weapons inventory of China adds significant complexity to a permanent solution for the future status of Taiwan that does not involve integration. North Korea's increasing nuclear capabilities ensure it will remain an extraordinary obstacle to the normalization of political arrangements on the Peninsula. Israel's surreptitious inventory of nuclear weapons ensures it will remain the master of arrangements in the Middle East irrespective of its inability to provide acceptable reparations and reconciliation to the tens of thousands of Palestinians who have been uprooted since 1948.

9. Elimination of Nuclear Weapons

Each of the Parties to the Treaty undertakes to pursue negotiations in good faith on effective measures relating to cessation of the nuclear arms race at an early date and to nuclear disarmament, and on a treaty on general and complete disarmament under strict and effective international control.

Article VI of the 1970 Non-Proliferation Treaty

The ongoing Russian and American efforts relating to the management of their nuclear weapons demonstrate how agreements will fall short of their total and absolute elimination. Matters were complicated during the Trump Administration when, in August 2019, the United States withdrew from the 1987 Intermediate-Range Nuclear Forces Treaty (INF) following allegations of Russian violations. At the time, the Trump Administration sought to make the negotiations trilateral with the inclusion of China. The effort failed as there was no benefit for China given their allotment of weapons already being well below that of Russia and the United States.

There are no concerted bilateral efforts underway that promote the elimination of existing nuclear weapons. And the current fractured and deteriorating relationships involving Russia, China, and the United States confirm it will be some time before the efforts of previous years will be resumed. There are various initiatives underway that limit the number of states with legitimate nuclear weapons at only five, and this aspect of nuclear proliferation has been successful.

Mitigating this success is the current fear that one state, Iran, is well underway to achieving nuclear weapons status in the coming months.

Nuclear Weapons Free Zones

Article VII of the NPT provided for the creation of nuclear weapons-free zones. Five such zones have been negotiated and implemented since 1967, starting with the Treaty of Tlatelolco that includes 22 countries in Latin America and the Caribbean. The four other treaties are

- The 1985 Treaty of Rarotonga for the South Pacific (13 signatories),
- the 1985 Treaty of Bangkok for Southeast Asia (10 signatories),
- the 1996 Treaty of Pelindaba for Africa (51 signatories), and
- the 2006 Treaty of Semipalatinsk for Central Asia (5 signatories).

These treaties contain commitments from 114 signature countries not to manufacture, acquire, test, or possess nuclear weapons. As such, they cover 39% or the global population; yet, the nine nuclear weapons states include 47% of the world's population. The 74 other states cover only 14% of the population of the globe.

There are also nuclear free-zone treaties covering the Antarctic, space, and the seabed. Most of the world's oceans above the seabed are not covered due to the freedoms associated with international waters. So far, these do not allow for the restrictions associated with nuclear-free zones. And, while the space nuclear-free zone prohibits the stationing of nuclear weapons there, it does not prohibit the flight of missiles carrying nuclear weapons.

There have been suggestions for Canada to take the lead in the promotion of a nuclear weapons-free zone for the Arctic. Such an effort would engage Canadian responsibilities in its memberships in NATO and NORAD and would create a fundamental disagreement with the United States. To date, little consideration has been given by any of the governments that would be involved, namely Canada, the United States, Denmark, Iceland, Norway, and Russia. Such an effort would engage Canadian responsibilities in its memberships in NATO and NORAD, creating a fundamental disagreement with the United States.

Nuclear Umbrellas

The post-war period and the development of American and Soviet alliance systems resulted in the development of nuclear umbrella arrangements. There are guarantees by nuclear weapons states to provide some measure of assurance that their nuclear weapons would provide protection to client states. At the times of their inceptions, nuclear umbrellas supported limitations on the proliferation of nuclear weapons when many states were investigating the possibility of developing their own nuclear weapons.

Nuclear umbrella arrangements were part of the Warsaw Pact alliance, although there was no diminution of Soviet control over deployed weapons to other countries. There were, however, nuclear weapons in Kazakhstan, Ukraine, and Belarus with total Soviet controls on use at the time of the disintegration of the Soviet Union in 1991. All nuclear weapons were ultimately returned to Russia.

The United States has a more diverse set of alliances and today has umbrella arrangements with more than 30 countries. Most are members of the North Atlantic Treaty Organization (NATO) that decided to forgo their own nuclear weapons programs in exchange for this protection. Canada arranged for the removal of American nuclear weapons in 1984, while France and the United Kingdom have maintained their nuclear weapons status under the NPT largely as a symbolic legacy. An American agreement with the United Kingdom in 1958 arranged for the sharing of American information on weapon designs. France continued with its own nuclear weapons program even though today it is part of the NATO military command.

Beyond NATO, the American nuclear umbrella provides protection to both Japan and South Korea. Both arrangements are sanctioned by security treaties, the latest being the Treaty of Mutual Cooperation and Security with Japan. Similar arrangements are in place with South Korea arising from the 1953 post-war arrangements to defend the country against another invasion from the north. For a time, the United States deployed tactical nuclear weapons in South Korea, but these were withdrawn in 1991. With the development of nuclear weapons in North Korea, that arrangement may be under revision.

There remains some ambiguity as to whether the American nuclear umbrella provides protection for Australia, New Zealand, and Taiwan. Both Australia and New Zealand have signed the NPT, and both are members of the South Pacific Nuclear Free Zone. In the 1980s, New Zealand refused to allow American naval ships to dock if they were nuclear powered or failed to declare whether they were carrying nuclear weapons. The expansion of China into the waters of the South Pacific has created a new security situation for both countries, and there is some question as to whether or not the American nuclear umbrella is still valid based on the ANZUS security treaty of 1951.

The situation with respect to Taiwan is equally ambiguous. Beijing's recent interest in asserting its historical claims places the island under increased military pressure, which could come to include nuclear weapons. The American position is unclear as to whether Taiwan is part of the American nuclear umbrella system, but it likely is not.

10. Nuclear Weapons, Testing and Delivery

> *ICBM is a real-time strategy game of nuclear destruction. Research new technologies, build up your nuclear stockpile and use a combination of ships, planes and missiles to strike at the heart of your opponents' cities while keeping your population safe from harm.*
>
> **Advertisement for the online game ICBM**

The American strategic B-29 bomber, the Superfortress, was developed and manufactured within the same period as the Manhattan Project. The bomber entered service in May 1944, fourteen months before it was used to drop the first atomic bombs in August 1945. At the time of initial design in 1938, the B-29 was meant to carry weights and fly distances envisaged for a war in the Pacific. It easily made the 12-hour round trip from Tinian Island to mainland Japan carrying the 10,000-pound bombs and was ten or so miles away when the nuclear bombs exploded over Hiroshima and Nagasaki.

The B-29 illustrates the complexity of delivery system for nuclear weapons. The dropping of gravity bombs by aircraft was the only means available in 1945 and remains a significant delivery system for all nuclear weapons states. Manned aircraft still provide the assured delivery of the weapons and reasonable accuracy in targeting. In the twenty years after 1945, aircraft were supplemented in nuclear weapons delivery with the intercontinental ballistic (and cruise) missiles (ICBM) and the submarine launched ballistic missile (SLBM). The three form the triad of nuclear weapons delivery systems, and, with a variety of configurations, are used by nearly all the nuclear weapons states.

In the immediate aftermath of the war, nuclear weapons testing in the atmosphere accelerated without understanding or concern for the serious health and environmental dangers. The large and known dangers were ignored or at best incorporated as a necessary element in the frenetic urge to improve the 1945 designs of nuclear weapons by the United States and to master the science and technology by others. For the United States, there was an obsession merging into paranoia of losing its nuclear weapons advantage, knowing that other countries, especially the Soviet Union, would soon have nuclear weapons as well. It took just four years for those fears to come true; three years after that, the United Kingdom exploded its first nuclear weapon. The nuclear arms race was underway.

Characteristic of the period was the frequency and distribution of the atmospheric testing. From 1945 to 2017, there were 528 atmospheric nuclear explosions by the United States and the Soviet Union. During the same period, there were 1,528 underground nuclear explosions. The United Kingdom (21), France (50), and China (23) also conducted numerous atmospheric nuclear test explosions while India (3), Pakistan (2), and North Korea (6) only tested their weapons underground. South Africa did not test its nuclear weapons at all. If Israel tested or was involved in the nuclear explosion in the southern reaches of Indian Ocean in September 1979, then that represents one additional test.

Testing affected all continents. Africa had 17 nuclear test explosions by France in Algeria. The United States tested 1,030 devices, 215 in the atmosphere. Most – 904 – were at the Nevada Test Site in the continental United States, while 106 were at the Pacific Proving Grounds in the Marshall Islands. 36 other tests occurred near Christmas Island (Australia) and the Johnston Atoll, which remains unincorporated territory of the United States. The United States also conducted three tests in the South Atlantic Ocean and 17 other tests in Amchitka, Alaska, Colorado, Mississippi, New Mexico, and Nevada (outside of the main Nevada Test Site).

The Soviet Union conducted 715 tests using 969 devices, with 219 in the atmosphere and 496 underground from 1949 to 2017. Most of the tests were at Semipalatinsk Test Site in northeast Kazakhstan and at Novaya Zemlya, an archipelago in the Arctic Ocean in the northern Soviet Union. There were other tests at locations in Kazakhstan, Turkmenistan, Uzbekistan, and Ukraine. The United Kingdom tested 45 nuclear weapons from 1952 to 2017, with 12 in the Montebello Islands in West Australia and at the Maralinga and Emu sites in South Australia. Nine tests were carried out at Christmas Island, and 24 tests at the American Nevada Test Site.

France conducted 210 nuclear tests, 50 in the atmosphere and 160 underground. 17 of these tests were near Ekker and Reggane in Algeria, while the others were at and around Fangataufa and Moruroa Atolls in French Polynesia in the southern Pacific Ocean. China was the only other country that conducted atmospheric tests, with 23 at its Lop Nur Nuclear Weapons Test Base in western Xinjiang. It also tested 22 devices underground at the same site. India and Pakistan only tested underground, as does North Korea. [All numbers in this section are from the Arms Control Association].

Atmospheric and seabed nuclear testing was terminated by the United States, the Soviet Union, and the United Kingdom with the 1963 partial test ban treaty. China had its first nuclear test in 1964, and it conducted the world's last atmospheric nuclear test in October 1980. France ended its atmospheric testing in 1974 and all its nuclear weapon's testing in 1996. North Korea is the only country with an active nuclear weapon's testing program, having tested six devices since October 9, 2006. Its last test was on September 3, 2017, but there are unconfirmed reports that it will test again in the coming months.

The 1963 Limited Test Ban Treaty was instrumental in ending atmospheric and seabed testing, but it did not ban underground testing. This was achieved with the 1996 Comprehensive Test Ban Treaty, which was endorsed by more than two-thirds of the UN membership. It has yet to enter into force, however, as it lacks endorsement by eight members of the drafting group. These two treaties comprehensively eliminated many of the dangers associated with the development of nuclear weapons. Tens of thousands of people have died or encountered serious medical problems as a result of the more than fifty years of testing, especially from devices exploded atmospherically.

Since the complete ending of the atmospheric tests, the countries involved have sought to provide compensation to victims. The United States has been the most thorough, especially with respect to the ongoing health and medical problems created by its testing in the Marshall Islands. Nearly a billion dollars have been paid, and there are efforts underway, politically and legally, to compensate for the continuing effects of the testing on people and their descendants. Even the crew of a Japanese fishing boat in the testing area in 1954 has been compensated. There is much less known about compensation by the United Kingdom except for legal efforts by veterans who served on Christmas Island during testing. There are continuing efforts to compensate the victims of French testing in Algeria and French Polynesia, with work still ongoing. Russia has offered compensation to some veterans of a 1954 atmospheric test, but there is no information available about compensation to civilians in either Kazakhstan or in Russia. It is unknown if there are efforts for compensation for the victims of Chinese atmospheric testing.

The main purpose behind the prolonged testing of nuclear weapons was to increase their efficiency, reduce their size, and adapt for new delivery systems in use and deployment. This work continues, but it is now confined to computer simulations with occasional suggestions and pleas for further testing. Although North Korea's program remains active, the past five years of no tests suggests a possibility that the world may soon see the end of all nuclear weapons testing.

The Scary World of Nuclear Weapons

Since early August 1945, when a piston-driven aircraft flew six hours to drop one 10,000-pound nuclear weapon, the technology for weapons delivery systems have changed dramatically. Jet engines, rocketry, and nuclear-powered submarines have driven these changes.

Before the Second World War ended, the promises and dangers of the jet engine and rocketry were evident. Both Germany and the United Kingdom had jet-powered aircraft in limited service before the war ended, while Germany's V-2 rockets threatened to drag out the war. The war ended before either could be fully used, but it was not long before the science and technologies involved saw the rapid exploitation of the jet engine, rockets, and nuclear-powered vessels in the military forces of several countries.

The United States led the changes. Within a few years of the war, the six-engine turbojet Boeing B-47 Stratojet replaced the B-29 as America's strategic bomber of choice, outshining the interim B-36, ironically dubbed Peacemaker. The limitations of the B-47 were legendary, as it was slow to take-off and even slower to land. Still, it survived for nearly a decade as the main American delivery system for nuclear weapons. By the mid-1950s, it was replaced by Boeing's six-engine jet-powered strategic bomber, the B-52. In 2015, it completed 60 years of continuous service and is now expected to remain in service into the 2050s. While its official name is Stratofortress, it is commonly referred to as BUFF, or Big Ugly Fat Fucker, or Fella in polite company.

The ending of war came before Germany could fully exploit its unique advantage available with the V-2 rocket. It was the world's first long-range guided ballistic missile, and while more than 3,000 were launched against the United Kingdom, the Netherlands, and Belgium, killing an estimated 9,000 military personnel and civilians, it was too little, too late to affect the march of Allied forces into Germany and force its unconditional surrender. But with the Allied forces came the effort to capture the thousands of German scientists and engineers involved in the development of the V-2 and relocate them to the Soviet Union, the United States and the United Kingdom.

Though Germany never had the chance to implement its V-2 rockets, many of the scientists involved in their development were recruited through Operations Paperclip and Osoaviakhim.

These "relocated" scientists and engineers became the foundations for the rocketry programs of the United States and the Soviet Union, resulting in their space programs in less than a decade and the creation of intercontinental ballistic missiles for the delivery of nuclear weapons to the far reaches of the planet. For the United States, there were also programs for the development of cruise missiles, nuclear-powered submarines with missile launch capacity, and anti-ballistic missile weapons. The Soviet Union did not differ dramatically from the United States in its post-war development of nuclear weapons and associated delivery systems. By the time of the 1963 Partial Test Ban Treaty, both had sufficient weapons and delivery systems to give validity to the idea of mutually assured destruction (MAD) and sufficient confidence to begin the negotiations for reductions in both their inventories of weapons and delivery systems. In many ways, the idea of MAD still permeates the world of nuclear weapons.

Throughout this same post war period, a second type of nuclear bomb was developed. The bombs dropped on Hiroshima and Nagasaki were essentially fission type bombs. These are commonly referred to as atomic or atom bombs and in one description they are

> a mass of fissile material (enriched uranium or plutonium) ... forced into supercriticality – allowing an exponential growth of nuclear chain reactions – either by shooting one piece of sub-critical material into another (the "gun" methods) or by compression of a sub-critical sphere or cylinder of fissile material using, chemically-fueled explosive lenses. The latter approach, the "implosion" methods is more sophisticated and more efficient (small, less massive, and requiring less of the expensive fissile fuel) than the former. [Hansen, Chuck. *U.S. Nuclear Weapons: The Secret History*. San Antonio, TX: Aerofax, 1988}.

The second type of nuclear weapon, often referred to as thermonuclear, produces a large proportion of its energy with nuclear fusion reactions. They rely on fusion reactions between isotopes of hydrogen, deuterium, and tritium, but derive a significant portion of their energy from fission reactions used to "trigger" the fusion reactions, and fusion reactions can themselves trigger additional fission reactions. In detail,

> Thermonuclear bombs work by using the energy of a fission bomb to compress and heat fusion fuel. In the Teller-Ulam design, which accounts for all multi-megaton yield hydrogen bombs, this is accomplished by placing a fission bomb and fusion fuel (tritium, deuterium, or lithium deuteride) in proximity within a special, radiation-reflecting container. When the fission bomb is detonated, gamma rays and X-rays emitted first compress the fusion fuel, then heat it to thermonuclear temperatures. The ensuing fusion reaction creates enormous numbers of high-speed neutrons, which can then induce fission in materials not normally prone to it, such as depleted uranium. Each of these components is known as a "stage", with the fission bomb as the "primary" and the fusion capsule as the "secondary." In large, megaton-range hydrogen bombs, about half of the yield comes from the final fissioning of depleted uranium. [Hansen, Chuck. *U.S. Nuclear Weapons: The Secret History.* San Antonio, TX: Aerofax, 1988].

Only six countries – the United States, Russia, the United Kingdom, France, China, and India – have tested thermonuclear weapons. North Korea claimed to have tested such a weapon, but this is disputed, and it is unknown if Israel and Pakistan have done so. According to the Arms Control Association, almost all of the nuclear weapons deployed today use the thermonuclear design because of its efficiency.

Elsewhere in the book, details are provided on the development of nuclear weapons by each country and the estimated number of weapons they may have. Such numbers are fragile, especially for Israel, Pakistan, India, China and North Korea, while those for the

United States, Russia, the United Kingdom, and France are more reliable as they are based on treaty related reporting requirements. This reporting relates largely to the number of weapons but little on their delivery systems; yet, it largely these systems that give effective understanding to the quality of their weapons.

There has been a number of published reports on the American nuclear bombs and these are provided below for further reference as needed. They provide specific information of the B61 nuclear bomb is the primary thermonuclear gravity bomb used by the United States. There is considerable variation in both its yield (low to intermediate) and its use as both a strategic and tactical nuclear weapon. Hans Kristensen describes it as follows:

> The B61 is of the variable yield design with a yield of 0.3 to 340 kilotons in various modes. It is a Full Fuzing Option (FUFO) weapon, meaning it is equipped with the full range of fuzing and delivery options, including air and ground burst fuzing, and free-fall, retarded free-fall and laydown delivery. It has a streamlined casing capable of withstanding supersonic flight and is 11 ft 8 in long with a diameter of about 13 inches. Its basic weight is about 700 lbs. According to the Federation of American Scientists in 2012, there are 400 B61 bombs in service costing $28 million each.

Further details on specific nuclear weapons can be found in the following references.

> Sublette, Carey (June 12, 2020). *"Complete List of All U.S. Nuclear Weapons"*. Nuclear weapon archive. Retrieved March 18, 2021.

> *"Frequently Asked Questions #1". Radiation Effects Research Foundation.* Archived from the original on September 19, 2007. Retrieved September 18, 2007. total number of deaths is not known precisely ... acute (within two to four months) deaths ... Hiroshima ... 90,000–166,000 ... Nagasaki ... 60,000–80,000

"Federation of American Scientists: Status of World Nuclear Forces". Fas.org. Archived from the original on January 2, 2013. Retrieved December 29, 2012.

The B61 is a specific American nuclear weapon for delivery by a variety of military aircraft, including the B-52 and, in the NATO context, the Panavia Tornado aircraft jointly developed by the German, Italian, and British governments. It can also be dropped from an American F-35 Lightning, which is emerging as the aircraft of choice for many American allies. The Americans have also configured the B-52 as a launch pad for nuclear cruise missiles. One report suggests there is a capacity for 16 such missiles in several aircraft.

There have been a variety of ICBMs in the American inventory going back to the late 1940s, and these are generally based on the V-2 rocket program of Germany. Wernher von Braun was the relocated German scientist for the program, and by 1946, he was in the United States developing ICBM and IRBM for the American Army. An ICBM is by general definition one that has a minimum range of 3,100 miles or 5,000 kilometres. Today, most ICBMs are designed to support several independently targetable re-entry vehicles (MIRVs) capable of being programed to strike different targets. There are other ballistic missiles, all based on distance including intermediate range, medium range, short-range, and tactical.

As with the ICBM, the first iteration of a submarine platform for the launch of a ballistic missile was attempted by the Germans in the last days of the war. In that iteration, a V-2 ballistic missile was to be towed behind a submarine and then launched. The idea never reached fruition, but the idea of marrying a ballistic missile to a submarine went with the relocated Germans to the United States and the Soviet Union where the submarine launched ballistic missile (SLBM) concept was fully developed. The creation of today's nuclear-powered submarines, along with the capacity for nearly 20 MIRVed SLBMs, became the most important advance in the triad of nuclear weapons delivery systems. Today, even with a variety of reductions as a result of agreements with the Soviet Union/Russia, the SLBM remains the dominant strategic element in the nuclear weapons delivery system for both countries.

Today, seven of the nuclear weapons states have created nuclear-powered SLBM systems. The United States and the United Kingdom use the Trident II, with a maximum range of 12,000 kms. Russia has two operational systems, the Layner and the Bulava, with ranges of 12,000 and 9,000 kms respectively. France has two operational SLB missile systems with ranges of 6,000 and 10,000 kms. China has two SLBM systems, one with a range of 8,000 and another still being tested with a range of 12,000 kms. India has one operational system, the Sagarika, with a range of 1,900 kms, and three others under development which will extend the range of its SLBMs out to 8,000 kms. North Korea has tested missile systems that appear to be intended to reach more than 2,000 kms into the Pacific. There have been numerous tests, but so far there is no firm conclusion as to its ultimate range, although North Korea has declared its objective is to reach the continental United States with its ballistic missiles. One report by a Japanese defence official suggested in late November that the ballistic missiles of North Korea had a range of 15,000 kms.

The information concerning the Israeli and Pakistani nuclear weapons program does not include any definitive details on whether they have developed SLBM systems or whether there is an inclination to do so. Both have limited objectives for their nuclear weapons, especially in terms of range, so SLBMs may not be necessary.

Excepting Pakistan and Israel, the weapons of the other seven countries are interrelated. The Soviet/Russian weapons were developed in response to the weapons manufacture in the United States, while those of the United Kingdom and France were developed with a mixture of motivations. These included maintenance of their declining international status in the post war years as well as contributing to the defence of the western world in response to the weapons of the Soviet Union.

For China, its nuclear weapons program developed in response to its political and ideological differences with the Soviet Union and its political differences with the United States. Its 1962 war with India was also a motivating factor. In turn, that war and other differences created the motivation for the Indian nuclear weapons program. The nuclear weapons program of North Korea was motivated by its increasing isolation within the international system and was designed as a threat against the United States. In the change of international relationships, the suicidal nature of the North Korean nuclear weapons program also finds utility in the positioning of Russia and China both regionally and globally. The Pakistani nuclear program is directly related to the Indian program, while that of Israel finds rationality in its "never again" mentality as a recently created unique country in the Middle East.

In the days ahead, the motivations, more so than the capabilities, of nuclear weapons development must be considered if there is expectation that the global inventory be reduced or eliminated. There can be some measure of comfort that only nine countries have developed nuclear weapons and that testing has been nearly halted. There is as well today greater understanding of what can be done to ensure the number of nuclear weapon states does not expand further. With these factors in mind, there is need to further energize the large international consensus supporting the elimination of these potentially world-destroying weapons.

11. Peaceful Uses of Nuclear Energy

"There is no distinction between nuclear energy for peaceful purposes or warlike ones."

Ernst David Bergmann, former Chair of the Israeli Atomic Energy Commission

Despite its first use in nuclear weapons, fusion has been recognized for its applications as nuclear energy and even peaceful nuclear explosions, or PNE. The NPT was largely concerned with the non-proliferation of nuclear energy for weapons, but article V of the treaty specifically highlights the potential benefits of the peaceful applications of nuclear energy as long as "appropriate international observation and through appropriate international procedures." For this reason, the NPT has promoted the sharing of nuclear technology for peaceful purposes.

Soon after the war, experts were forecasting the use of nuclear explosions to build canals, power space exploration, to create wide-area fracking for oil and gas, or to protect the Earth from asteroid impacts. This early enthusiasm for the peaceful applications has been tempered, however, by a more realistic understanding of the limits associated with nuclear energy. The 1976 Treaty on Underground Nuclear Explosions for Peaceful Purposes (PNE Treaty) and the 1996 Comprehensive Nuclear Test-Ban Treaty imposed rational constraints on such thinking; thus, PNE is no longer considered a reasonable approach to civil engineering problems.

Still, nuclear energy continues to make significant contribution to science, engineering, and industry. Research into nuclear science, for example, has allowed for positive applications in agriculture in terms of food storage and preparation, pest controls, precision measurements, air pollution measurement, and desalination.

Using nuclear energy for propulsion has not expanded beyond use for military vessels, mainly submarines and aircraft carriers by the United States and Soviet Union/Russia. In 2022, the United States has eleven nuclear powered aircraft carriers and 70 nuclear powered submarines in active service. The technology has been particularly useful for submarines as it provides both for prolonged underwater endurance as well as enhanced "running silent and deep" features. The 2021 agreement involving the United Kingdom and the United States providing Australia with the technology for the construction of nuclear-powered submarines is a first. But the timelines are estimated to be upwards of twenty years before the first Australian submarine is launched. The Soviet Union/Russia has used nuclear energy for several ice-breaking ships, and as of 2021, it had the only nuclear-powered merchant ship in service.

There are two areas in which the peaceful use of nuclear energy has flourished. The first is in healthcare and medicine. Radiation for treatment and associated services has become a standard procedure. Associated with its use are the global safety standards promoted by the IAEA and the WHO ensuring that patients and medical personnel are appropriately protected.

The second area of widespread use of nuclear energy is the generation of power. From the earliest days of the Nuclear Age, nuclear-generated electrical power was promoted as one great advantage. Enthusiasm has cooled, but nuclear power plants are now in use in 32 countries, with 447 operational nuclear reactors and 53 undergoing maintenance or out of service. Combined, these reactors produce approximately 10% of the world's electricity.

Among the top users of nuclear power are 14 non-nuclear weapons states that generate 20% or more power via nuclear reactors:

- Armenia: 25%
- Belgian: 51%
- Bulgaria: 35%
- Croatia: 37%
- Czech Republic: 37%
- Finland: 33%
- Hungary: 47%
- Slovakia: 52%
- Slovenia: 37%
- South Korea: 28%
- Spain: 21%
- Sweden: 31%
- Switzerland: 29%
- Ukraine: 55%

Of the nuclear weapons states, seven use nuclear power:
- China: 5%
- France: 69%
- India: 3%
- Pakistan: 11%
- Russia: 20%
- USA: 20%
- UK: 15%.

Israel and North Korea do not use nuclear generated power.

China's National Nuclear Corporation (CNNC) is the main supplier for Pakistan's nuclear power efforts. Since 1986, the CNNC has provided Pakistan with five power reactors as well as other civil-use nuclear technologies. Two additional reactors are under construction. The Indian nuclear power program has grown since its 2008 agreement with the United States resulting in a waiver by the Nuclear Suppliers Group (NSG) for India on the transfer of nuclear technology specific for civilian use. It now has 22 nuclear reactors with ten more under construction. As with most countries, there is ongoing opposition at specific sites, particularly after the Fukushima nuclear disaster in Japan.

Safety, cost, complex construction issues, safeguards, spent-fuel storage and disposal, along with local permissions, are significant barriers to nuclear power. These have been balanced to some extent with the technology's benefits in comparison to the use of fossil fuels. The future remains uncertain as several countries have already made plans to eliminate nuclear power from its inventory; these include Germany, Spain, Switzerland, and Taiwan. Conversely, Poland is planning to introduce nuclear generated power. Reflecting this uncertainty, the European Union Parliament gave final approval on July 8, 2022 to a policy that will allow nuclear power projects to be included on its list of environmentally sustainable economic activities.

Over the past two decades, there has been a decline in the use of nuclear power generation. In 1996, over 17% of global power was generated by nuclear power, but by 2020 this had declined to approximately 10%. During this same period, there has been an emphasis on the use of small modular reactors (SMR) and advanced nuclear reactors as a means of countering the declining use of nuclear power. The specific problems associated with nuclear power include its cost in relationship to other means of production, the lengthy period needed for construction, the risk of accidents, the potential link to nuclear weapons proliferation, and the long-term storage of the associated nuclear waste.

At this time, it is uncertain that the potential offered from SMRs is real since they are largely conceptual and there are few signs available that there are serious efforts, including financing, to see them moved beyond that state. As for advanced designs for new reactors, there is even less understanding as to what is on offer other than the dreams associated with Tokamak fusion reactors. The test is whether the designs will reach the point where the heat released through fusion reactions will be greater than the energy supplied by external sources. There are tantalizing suggestions that this can be done, but it remains a scientific expectation with little value as an element in the world of electrical power generation.

Occasional large accidents involving nuclear-power-generating plants have provided graphic illustrations of the dangers. These have occurred throughout the world in 32 countries using such plants. Most accidents are due to the complexities of both the science and the engineering. Among the most known are the following accidents that involved engineering, operations, and most recently, a volcano, an earthquake, and tsunami waves in Japan.

- **Chalk River Laboratories, Chalk River, Ontario:** On December 12, 1952, the world suffered its first nuclear reactor accident when a hydrogen explosion occurred in the reactor core as a result of malfunctions and subsequent operator errors. There were no deaths, but the cleanup was lengthy, involving volunteers and military personnel. A second accident occurred at the same plant on May 24, 1958, when a fuel rod caught fire and broke when being removed from the reactor, spreading radioactive material throughout the building. Chalk River is about two hundred kilometers west of Ottawa.

  After the 1952 accident, military personnel from the United States helped in the cleanup in the reactor building. Then a U.S. navy lieutenant, President Jimmy Carter was part of the American crew working near the nuclear core. In his book *Full Life: Reflections at Ninety,* Carter wrote of the accident.

  > When a Canadian "heavy water" nuclear power plant at Chalk River was destroyed by accident in 1952 by a reactor meltdown and subsequent hydrogen explosions, my crew were volunteered by Rickover [Admiral and father of the American nuclear submarine program] to assist with the disassembly so it could be replaced. The reactor core was below ground level and surrounded by intense radioactivity. Even with protective clothing, each of us would absorb the maximum permissible dose with just ninety seconds of exposure, so we had to make optimum use of this

limited time. The limit on radiation absorption in the early 1950s was approximately one thousand times higher than it is sixty years later.

Much later, one newspaper headlined the story "Did Jimmy Carter Stop a Nuclear Reactor from Destroying Ottawa?" It answered its own question strongly in the affirmative.

- **Windscale Pile, United Kingdom:** Windscale (now Sellafield) was the first nuclear reactor in the United Kingdom. In the spring of 1957, its uranium-filled graphite core caught fire. The fire raged for two days before operators noticed. In the meantime, radioactive material contaminated about 800 farms in the area and subsequently large areas of Europe. The contamination included strontium 90 that spread through the domestic milk supply without any warming to the public.

- **Three Mile Island, Pennsylvania:** The accident began early in the morning on March 28, 1979. It was the most significant malfunction in an American commercial nuclear power plant. The accident was initially mechanical; valves between the non-nuclear secondary and nuclear primary systems failed. This was compounded by operators not noticing a loss-of-coolant failure. The cleanup took 14 years with a cost equivalent of two billion in 2022 dollars. The event was rated Level 5 on the seven-point International Nuclear Event Scale (INES).

- **Chernobyl, Ukraine:** At the time of the accident near Pripyat, on April 26, 1986, Ukraine was a republic within the Soviet Union. The accident was rated level 7 on the INES but was considered beyond the scale. The accident occurred at the Chernobyl Nuclear Power Plant with steam explosions following an unsafe systems test. The explosions lifted the 1,000-ton cover of reactor 4 at the plant. A radioactive plume quickly spread northward over neighbouring Belarus and beyond into Europe. Sheep in portions of the United Kingdom were declared unfit for human consumption as a result of exposure from Chernobyl. In the immediate aftermath of the accident, 32 people died from radiation poisoning. Since 1986, thousands have died from the radioactive debris. It is estimated over 70,000 suffered radiation poisoning.

Invading its 30km "zone of alienation" around the accident site has become a sought-after adventure for many born after the accident. Markiyan Kamysh, author of *Stalking the Atomic City*, has become a cultural icon for adventurists. In the early days of the February 2022 war, Russian soldiers were sent into the disaster area without protection, adding to the disaster legend. Some experts predict the area around Chernobyl will never lose its radioactivity.

- **The Fukushima Daiichi Nuclear Power Plant:** The Okuma, Japan accident occurred on March 11, 2021. It was triggered by the Great East Japan Earthquake with a magnitude of 9.0 centered 130 km offshore from the city of Sendai on Honshu Island. The complex earthquake with a duration of three minutes was followed by tsunami waves nearly 14 metres high that inundated over five-hundred square metres of shoreline. Nearly 20,000 people died, and there was considerable damage to ports and towns.

At the time, there were eleven nuclear reactors operating in the region, and all shut down automatically with no damage when the earthquake struck. However, three reactors lost power for the reactor heat removal system when flooded by successive tsunami waves. There were three nuclear-core meltdowns and three hydrogen explosions with the release of radioactive material into the atmosphere and the Pacific Ocean. A fourth reactor was affected five days after the initial accident. A 20-km wide zone was established around the plant, with over 100,000 residents evacuated. There were no casualties directly attributed to the nuclear accident, but there were associated medical issues for some of the evacuees. The cleanup is expected to last up to 40 years.

12. Agenda and Measures for The Elimination of Nuclear Weapons

The atomic bomb made the prospect of future war unendurable. It has led us up those last few steps to the mountain pass; and beyond there is a different country.

—J Robert Oppenheimer

The 1970 Treaty on the Non-Proliferation of Nuclear Weapons legitimized the nuclear weapons programs of China, France, Soviet Union/Russia, United Kingdom, and United States in exchange for nuclear disarmament. Article VI of the NPT reflects this bargain. In exchange for recognizing the nuclear weapon states, the NPT encouraged negotiations in good faith on effective measures relating to cessation of the nuclear arms race with the eventual goal of eliminating all nuclear weapons. While various efforts have been pursued on non-proliferation, testing of nuclear weapons and nuclear disarmament have not been subject to comprehensive examination or negotiations since the Treaty came into force in 1970. It is time for that to happen and for the world to begin the process leading to the elimination of all nuclear weapons. In twenty-three years, 2045, the world will celebrate the centenary of the ending of the Second World War. It will also be the centenary of the life span of nuclear weapons and of the Nuclear Age.

On December 15, 1994, the UN General Assembly passed a resolution requesting the International Court of Justice to provide an advisory opinion on the question, "Is the threat or use of nuclear weapons in any circumstances permitted under international law?" Reflecting the interest in the question, forty-two states submitted views or "pleadings" on the issue, the largest number of states ever to have done so. Four of the original nuclear weapons states did, with only China not doing so. Of the four other nuclear weapons states, only India participated. Five of the 15 judges hearing the case were from nuclear weapon states.

The judges presented an inconclusive decision: "There is in neither customary nor conventional international law any comprehensive and universal prohibition of the threat or use of nuclear weapons as such." More specifically the court wrote, "A threat or use of nuclear weapons should also be compatible with the requirements of international law applicable in armed conflict, particularly those of the principles and rules of humanitarian law, as well as with specific obligations under treaties and other undertakings which expressly deal with nuclear weapons." But the lack of enthusiasm for the issue was ameliorated to some extent when the court wrote, "there exists an obligation to pursue in good faith and bring to a conclusion negotiation leading to nuclear disarmament in all its aspects under strict and effective international control."

In another case before the ICJ, the Marshall Islands argued in 2014 that the nuclear weapons states were not doing enough in support of the NPT. Initially, all nine nuclear weapons states were named, but the preliminary stages of the case resulted in the removal of six states and the case proceeded against the remaining three: Britain, India, and Pakistan. The Marshall Islands case was predicated on the use of its islands, mainly Bikini, in nuclear test explosions by the United States up until 1958. In an October 4, 2016 decision, the court dismissed the case. It concluded that the Marshall Island had no legal dispute with the three nuclear weapons states.

These decisions by the ICJ demonstrate that the courts are not an effective venue for pursing nuclear disarmament. Rather, the elimination of nuclear weapons remains an intimate element in the warp and woof of international affairs. There are, however, successful models for this work. The Biological Weapons Convention of 1975, the Chemical Weapons Convention of 1997, the 1997 Anti-Personnel Mines Convention (the Ottawa Treaty), and the Convention on Cluster Munitions of 2008 have demonstrated the world can collectively reach agreements on issues of large dangers and provide protective measures and mechanisms. Similarly, the common global-wide efforts to deal with effects of climate change also demonstrates, reluctant as it may seem at times, to create a commonality of purpose and action for this complex planet-saving initiative. The elimination of nuclear weapons can be seen as an appropriate companion for efforts on climate change.

The continuing presence of an extensive inventory of nuclear weapons represents a danger not unlike that of climate change. In some ways, it is a more difficult subject as it has become, for many countries, an essential feature of their national existence and ongoing security. But as many have observed, the sense of security provided by nuclear weapons is a false one, and their continued existence within the global body politic adds to the danger for all. As such, there is an urgent need of action by the global community, comparable to the work associated with the Biological, Chemical, Landmine, and Cluster Munitions conventions and the ongoing global work to eliminate the effects of climate change.

At the same time, these weapons have become essential aspects of national security and international presence by the nine nuclear weapons states. There are a variety of factors in play for a state to maintain and retain their nuclear weapons. The differences are demonstrated by roles these weapons play in the affairs of the United States and North Korea or France and the United Kingdom and Israel. The common denominators are not the weapons themselves, but the reasons for their existence. It is these reasons for the existence of the weapons that the international community must target if there is to be some measure of success in the elimination of nuclear weapons.

Some comfort can be obtained by the efforts over the last decades in limiting the number of states with nuclear weapons. Earlier estimates in the aftermath of the Second World War expected that the number of such countries could increase to more than twenty. Today, there are only nine such states and the possibility of one more. That is ten more than there should be, but it provides the base against which the majority of states can work. That work must be examined, developed, and expanded to both ensure that there are no additions of the number of nuclear weapons states and that existing arsenals are eliminated.

Today, there is no common cause, no country or group of countries to promote and maintain international cohesion and action for the elimination of nuclear weapons. These weapons remain as the largest threat to global security, as demonstrated by the threats emanating from Moscow with respect to its invasion of Ukraine. Nuclear disarmament is as urgent an issue as war and climate change, but there is no indication it will receive comparable international action. Now is the time to rebuild the united international cohesion that emerged to see the Non-Proliferation Treaty come into being, as well as that surrounding the still-pending Comprehensive Test-Ban Treaty. The ongoing and emerging threats represented by the existing and increasing thousands of nuclear weapons needs action today; action is critical, and not just the hope that this will happen without sustained action by the international community. A more peaceful future depends on that action being initiated today.

The delivery of nuclear weapons to distant destinations using intercontinental missiles has dominated public perceptions and intellectual discussions concerning nuclear weapons. During the Cold War, the discussions centered on the validity of the concept of mutually assured destruction (MAD) providing restraint on the use of nuclear weapons for both the Soviet Union and the United States. The fears of nuclear destruction dominate popular culture in the Cold War era, notably Nevil Shute's 1957 novel, *On the Beach* and the 1959 film adaptation

The Scary World of Nuclear Weapons

by Stanley Kramer. Even more enduring is Stanley Kubrick's 1964 film *Dr Strangelove or: How I Learned to Stop Worrying and Love the Bomb*, which fueled widespread public fears of nuclear weapons and prompted efforts for their elimination.

These public concerns and efforts for controls lessened during the latter days of the Cold War. Détente, the numerous Soviet-American-negotiated bilateral control agreements, and the disintegration of the Soviet Union in 1991 lessened the fears associated with nuclear weapons. But the proliferation of nuclear weapons into the inventories of other countries remains of significance. The war in Ukraine, the worsening relationships with Russia and China, along with erratic policies of the United States and the central role of nuclear weapons in the work of the NATO alliance has renewed the earlier fears of conflict involving nuclear weapons. This has increased as Russian intentions in eastern Europe and the war in Ukraine intensifies. It is in this worsening international environment that there is again a need for collective action to support further measures in eliminating nuclear weapons.

This is most evident with the lack of support for the new disarmament treaty, the ***Treaty on the Prohibition of Nuclear Weapons (TPNW).*** Unlike earlier treaties that engaged widespread support for nuclear disarmament issues, there is less than half as much support for the new Treaty. It was negotiated in the first half of 2017 and was supported by a vote of 122 states in the General Assembly, with 69 abstaining. The neutral votes included the five original nuclear weapons states and all NATO members except Netherlands, which voted against the treaty. The TPNW became effective on January 22, 2021 following the reception of fifty instruments of ratification. Today, there are 66 instruments of ratification and 86 signatories.

Support for the treaty is most prevalent in Latin America and the Caribbean, Africa, and Southeast Asia and the Pacific. This support includes Iran, Saudi Arabia, Kazakhstan, Ireland, Austria, Brazil, Indonesia, Mexico, Nigeria, South Africa, and Thailand. Resistance to the Treaty came from all of the NATO members, as well Australia and Japan.

Following the coming into force of the Treaty, the United States and Russia voiced opposition, while the non-nuclear weapon states of NATO issued a statement claiming that the Treaty will be "ineffective in eliminating nuclear weapons" but asked for the advanced implementation of Article VI of the 1970 Non-Proliferation Treaty. Canada joined its NATO partners in this statement but has given indications it would not support the new Treaty.

The United States has given no indication whatsoever of lessening its commitment to the role and use of nuclear weapons. There are few signs it has changed its views on either first use or no use of nuclear weapons in its global security policies. Regarding NATO, the USA's Strategic Concept policy regards nuclear weapons as essential for global security and stability. Canada has taken no steps to counter this approach and emphasized the importance of its NATO and NORAD commitments: "Canada has long held a policy objective of non-proliferation, reduction and elimination of nuclear weapons and other weapons of mass destruction. We pursue this aim steadily, persistently and energetically, consistent with our membership in NATO and NORAD and in a manner sensitive to broader international security context." [http://www.dfait-maeci.gc.ca/arms/nuclear2-en.asp]

Contemplating the elimination of a class of weapons, as demonstrated by the limited success with chemical, biological, landmines, and clustered munitions, is not for the faint of heart. And while there has been some success in limiting the proliferation of nuclear weapons, there are no assurances the various control mechanism negotiated so far, including the TPNW, will provide the level of universal assurance to prevent the world's descent into the lower levels of hell represented by nuclear war.

The world has faced similar challenges, and, in some measure, eliminating nuclear weapons is made possible with the intense globalization of the modern world. The end of colonialism and imperialism led to the emergence of self-determination as the guiding principle of global organization. Combined with efforts for equality and collectivity by and through the United Nations, there is considerable support for action. Instant communication and rapid transportation to all parts of our terrestrial home enlarges and creates the need for the elimination of global dangers through collective efforts. But there is a need for both unilateral as well as collective action.

Reluctance and reticence are characteristics of all nine nuclear weapon states in discussing developments relating to their arsenals. This was even characteristic of South Africa when it was in the same category, just as Iran is reluctant to discuss its objectives with respect to its nuclear program. What can be said with some assurance is in all eleven of these states national actions were central in the successful development of nuclear weapons. There was, as with all complex events, the use of appropriate ideas, materials and processes from elsewhere, some openly, some clandestinely, but it can be concluded this aspect of their successes were never as significant as some would suggest.

Existing and potential nuclear weapon states are motivated by national identity and goals. In reducing the number of such states or ensuring that more states do not join the eleven so far, these factors of national motivation must be addressed head on. Widespread international restrictions and controls help, but in the days ahead, if there is any expectation of eliminating nuclear weapons, then efforts must concentrate on changing those national motivations.

Measures for the Elimination of Nuclear Weapons

The starting point for future action on the elimination of nuclear weapons is already underway in the form of the Stockholm Initiative for Nuclear Disarmament (SIND), which was launched by Sweden in June 2019. Sixteen foreign ministers from non-nuclear weapons states met "to discuss how nuclear disarmament diplomacy can be advanced" by using a constructive, innovative, and creative approaches that respond to the challenges presented by nuclear weapons. The attending foreign ministers were from Argentina, Canada,

Ethiopia, Finland, Germany, Indonesia, Japan, Jordan, Kazakhstan, the Netherlands, New Zealand, Norway, the Republic of Korea, Spain, Sweden, and Switzerland. Six NATO members (plus two who are about to be members) were also in attendance, despite their subsequent opposition of the TPNW, which came into effect two years after the first meeting of SIND.

Despite the changing environment occasioned by TPNW, the SIND met for its Fifth Ministerial Meeting last December and reportedly did not directly address support for the TPNW. Instead, the participants concentrated on the forthcoming NPT Review Conference scheduled to take place at the end of August 2022 in New York. The foreign minister of Sweden, Ann Linde, stated it "is a moment to demonstrate political leadership, honour commitments and achievements made under the Treaty [NPT], and set ourselves on a decisive path towards a world free of nuclear weapons, in the interest of preserving humanity. We remain united in our resolve to achieve the elimination of nuclear weapons in an irreversible, verifiable, and transparent manner, and to reduce the risks they pose in the interim."

The Swedish minister went on to say, "Our message at the Review Conference will be clear: Nuclear weapons states must advance nuclear disarmament, in accordance with Article VI of the Treaty." And, in reflecting the views of all attending minister, Minister Linde stated, "Ministers urged all nuclear weapons states to take clear and decisive steps to lay the groundwork for the next-generation arms control arrangements, to reduce or further reduce nuclear arsenals, to show leadership in putting a definite end to nuclear weapon test explosions, commencing negotiations on a treaty prohibiting fissile material production, as well as to support efforts to develop multilateral nuclear disarmament verification capacities."

Canada and the other members of NATO at the SIND meeting on December 14, 2021 did not object to the statements of the Swedish minister, even with its implicit support of TPNW. It would appear their opposition to TPNW will play out within the context of NATO ministerial meetings, and it would be unrealistic to expect there will be a change in NATO's Strategic Concept in the coming months. Today, creating and maintaining alliance-wide unity to counter the Russian invasion of Ukraine and the possibility of troubles by the NATO members with borders with Russia is the essential objective.

But time will not diminish the importance of the questions associated with nuclear weapons. In some ways, the initial steps start with such questions as "is there any geopolitical reason, rationale or security need for France and the United Kingdom to retain their nuclear weapons?" The United Kingdom was a partner, along with Canada, in the development of nuclear weapons in the Manhattan Project. The involvement of both countries in that Project ended in the months after the conclusion of war as the Americans struggled with the false hope of ensuring their nuclear weapons technology was not duplicated by other countries. The Soviet Union blew that hope to smithereens in 1949, and shortly after the United States decided that it could no longer continue to have foreign countries directly involved in its ongoing nuclear weapons program.

Along with the Soviet nuclear test, China went "red," and the American political system descended into the abyss of self-doubt, recriminations, and false accusations, with everyone questioning everyone else as to their loyalty to the Stars and Stripes. The Soviets' nuclear explosions in the wilds of Kazakhstan in 1949 resulted in American paranoia on the issue of security for its nuclear secrets that has not abated significantly since. Canada and the United Kingdom, partners with Americans in the Manhattan Project, were excluded from such involvement in 1951. For Canada, its exclusion led to the decision to use its nuclear expertise for the peaceful uses of nuclear energy – medicine and power. The first Canadian Deuterium Uranium (CANDU) power reactor was operational by 1958.

For the United Kingdom, in 1952 the lingering images of past glories in running an empire where the sun never sets were still very much in evidence, even with a Labour Government in power and the disappearance of the jewel in its crown. In the middle of the war, the United Kingdom had its own nuclear weapons program but, for security and economic reasons, merged with the Canadian program, and later with the Manhattan Project in 1943. This collaboration assisted the United States with the science that gave birth to the world's first bombs in 1945. Following its exclusion from the American program, along with Canada, the United Kingdom returned to its own program; by 1952, London had nuclear devices and exploded its first over the Monte Bello Islands of Western Australia.

France took slightly longer to arrive at a similar decision. The traumatic defeat in its wars in Indo-China in the early '50s, the nasty war in Algeria trying to protect a million French settlers, along with restive colonies largely to the south of Algeria, destroyed its post-war political system, the Fourth Republic. The cry went out for its only leader of any repute, Charles de Gaulle, and he came out of retirement in May 1958 to herald the creation of a new Fifth republic. Two years earlier, France was an ally of Israel in their short-lived adventure, along with the United Kingdom, to retain western control for the Suez Canal. International pressure put an end to that bit of madness. In the process, France expanded its cooperation with Israel on nuclear weapons and agreed to help build the nuclear research reactor at Dimona in the Negev desert near the Dead Sea.

The international pressure during the Suez crisis is generally considered the seminal event in France taking the decision to develop its own nuclear weapons. In some measure, it was a decision, similar to one taken earlier by the United Kingdom, largely based on the idea that it would cement the country's global standing as a world power. Historically, several French scientists were prominent on nuclear issues, and one invented the now-standard method for extracting plutonium while working with the Manhattan Project. As such, it was only a matter of a few years before France was testing nuclear devices. The first was on February 13, 1960, thirty miles south of the Saharan city of Reganne in central Algeria. The test was named "Gerboise Bleue" or Blue Desert Rat. Before it signed the Comprehensive Nuclear-Test-Ban Treaty in 1998, France exploded more than 200 nuclear devices, fifty in the atmosphere. The tests were in Algeria until 1966 when testing moved to the South Pacific, specifically the Mururoa and Fangataufa Atolls in French Polynesia.

The appeals to France and the United Kingdom for the elimination of their nuclear weapons could be based on the erosion of the national motivation for a return to glory for them in the immediate postwar period. Today, the retention of these weapons by both countries adds nothing to their security or to their position in the world. As the world has changed, their need for such weapons has disappeared. Both countries are comparatively minor players in the affairs of the world, but the elimination of French and British nuclear weapons would effectively enhance their world-wide reputations. Such gestures would also provide support for the essential bargain central to the Non-Proliferation Treaty: the elimination of nuclear weapons.

When Israel decided in the mid-1950s to develop nuclear weapons, Iran was more of an ally than an enemy. Nearly all other countries in the Middle East were enemies. More recently, Iran in its own policies, and Israel in its, are declared enemies. This change reflects efforts involving Israel and other countries in the Middle East, supported and promoted by the United States, to establish reasonable if not friendly relations. The Abraham Accords of 2020 resulted in the establishment of Israeli relations with the United Arab Emirates, Bahrain, Sudan, and Morocco. These agreements, along with the peace treaties between Israel, Egypt, and Jordon, have changed the dynamics of Middle Eastern politics where the nuclear weapons of Israel are seen by some as central to the overall security of the region.

But the historical volatility of the region should provide caution in assigning this value to Israel's nuclear weapons. These recent developments largely resulted in the wake of President Trump's 2018 withdrawal of the United States from the JCPOA, which had imposed effective controls on the ability of Iran to construct its own nuclear weapons. The inability of President Biden so far to negotiate the re-entry of the United States into the agreement has created a situation in which Iran may only be a few months away from having nuclear weapons.

The default position of both Washington and Jerusalem has hardened to the point where they will not permit Iran to have nuclear weapons. In this, there is an emerging willingness to use military means by the United States, Israel, or both to ensure this does not happen. If this were to happen it would require the cooperation of Arab states. Efforts by the United States to negotiate its re-entry into the JCPOA continue, but no one is willing to forecast that this will be successful; the Joint Comprehensive Plan may likely disappear altogether.

This would represent a major disaster in the elimination of nuclear weapons in the Atomic Age. The last time a similar near-disaster occurred was in 1962 with the Soviet-American confrontation over nuclear armed missiles in Cuba. It took a decade or so for that confrontation to result in global discussions on nuclear weapons and resulted in the Non-Proliferation Treaty. It also resulted in a number of Détente-era bilateral agreements between the United States and the Soviet Union resulting in significant reductions in the number of nuclear weapons. Those not-so-long-ago events must be kept in mind in the days ahead as the changes in the Middle East play out. One thing is already evident – the uniqueness of the JCPOA, where the five NPT-sanctioned nuclear weapons states, along with Germany and the EU, created a unique arrangement to limit the proliferation of nuclear weapons by Iran. This concept and associated action must be maintained if there is to be progress on the elimination of nuclear weapons.

In the days ahead, it is important that the world keep sight of the possession of nuclear weapons by Israel. This has to be part of the new agenda on nuclear weapons. Despite vehement Israeli objection to the JCPOA process, it was a reasonable approach in ensuring that the proliferation of nuclear weapons in the Middle East did not worsen. Irrespective of developments in the coming days, the world will have to return to the issue of Iran and nuclear weapons; the attempted destruction of facilities in that country will not provide any lasting security for Israel or its neighbours. The elimination of nuclear weapons by Israel is the only approach that might lead to a more secure existence.

The recent efforts by the United States to engage North Korea in discussions on its nuclear weapons were a disaster. The efforts based on the hopes of an ill-prepared and ignorant President Trump, if anything, has made efforts to see the elimination of nuclear weapons in North Korea even more difficult. Again, the JCPOA-type process, which in some way was modelled on the earlier Six Party Talks on North Korea, offers a reasonable approach on the issues involved. The Six Party Talks have been suspended since 2009, but they could probably be revised if the collective will of the five NPT-sanctioned nuclear weapons states were engaged as they are with the process involving Iran. The continued involvement of Japan and South Korea is essential as they, more than others, would be directly influenced by the process and results.

The overlapping of states mutually rationalizing their nuclear weapons is evident with China, India, and Pakistan. This triangular relationship influenced the development of their nuclear weapons. The degree to which China's relationship with India influenced its first nuclear explosion in 1964 following its 1962 war is still unknown. What is known is India's decision to develop nuclear weapons was very much influenced by its loss in the 1962 war with China; subsequent testing, first in 1974 and later in 1998, demonstrated its success. Pakistan created its nuclear program following the 1974 Indian test and by 1998 was able to match the Indian results a few days after the Indian explosions.

India and Pakistan remain outside of the NPT as well as the Comprehensive Test Ban Treaty, although both have sought to join –unsuccessfully – the Nuclear Suppliers Group. India and Pakistan have approximately 160 and 165 operational nuclear weapons, while China has an inventory of 350 according to one estimate. According to the American Department of Defence, China may have plans for a thousand weapons by 2030. India and Pakistan have entered into a bilateral agreement exchanging information on their nuclear weapons, but for there to be any success in seeing their elimination, China must be involved. As far as it is known, there have not been any discussions involving the three countries on either limitation or elimination of nuclear weapons. There is work to be done in this, and such discussions could be one of the early objectives of countries hoping to promote progress in limiting and/or eliminating nuclear weapons.

The degree to which China would be willing to engage in such discussions is untested even though it has been actively involved in the Pakistani nuclear power sector. Also, China has been active in the Zangger and Nuclear Suppliers Groups, both in protecting the interests of Pakistan and ensuring that the role of India in those groups is not enlarged without equal treatment being applied to Pakistan. The grouping of China, Pakistan, and India should be closely examined as work needs to be done to determine the parameters of where progress could be achieved.

The discussions that saw some early success in reducing Soviet/Russian and American inventories of nuclear weapons have been largely dormant for some time. Yet, there were recent signs of life. In January 2021, the two countries agreed to the extension of the New Strategic Arms Reduction Treaty (New Start). As well, in June of 2021, there was a presidential statement announcing an American-Russian Strategic Stability Dialogue, which included a reaffirmation that "a nuclear war cannot be won and must never be fought."

Whether these developments have survived the Russian invasion of Ukraine has not been established. Nevertheless, the bilateral achievements of the past should be protected from further erosion. The inventories of nuclear weapons controlled by these two states (5,428 for the US and 5,977 for Russia) continue to outdistance the inventories of the other seven nuclear weapon states (1300) by almost a factor of ten.

The bilateral relationship is now wholly dominated by the Russian invasion of Ukraine. There is little expectation the issue of nuclear disarmament will receive attention from the Biden administration.

Even before Biden, President Trump seemed uninterested in the issues involved, insisting that any discussions become trilateral and involve China. China showed no interest in joining such discussions having only a few weapons in comparisons with Russia and the United States. But the war in Ukraine and the associated European defence of Europe, will, it is hoped, soon give way to negotiations that could get the elimination of nuclear weapons elimination back on the table.

13. Canadian Involvement in the Scary World

"Canada has long held a policy objective of non-proliferation, reduction and elimination of nuclear weapons and other weapons of mass destruction. We pursue this aim steadily, persistently and energetically, consistent with our membership in NATO and NORAD and in a manner sensitive to broader international security context."

Press Release, Global Affairs Canada

Canada's involvement in the development and use of nuclear energy and weapons has been long and extensive. Beyond assisting in the development of the first nuclear weapons, there have been few developments in which Canada has not played a role.

- For over twenty-five years, nuclear weapons were stored at locations in Canada, and nuclear weapons were deployed in Europe.
- In the 1950s, Canada was involved in developing the nuclear role for NATO.
- One of the world's first nuclear reactors was operational in Canada in 1958.
- Canadian scientists trained approximately 300 Indian scientists, engineers, and technicians in nuclear technology.

- In 1955, Canada signed an agreement to provide a nuclear research reactor to the Bhabha Atomic Research Centre, India, under grant financing of $10 million and additional fuel rods to be sent in 1960. Plutonium from this reactor was used in India's first nuclear test in 1974.
- Two years later, Canada provided India with Cobalt Beam Cancer Therapy Units.
- Canada provided technical and scientific information and equipment for the construction of Rajasthan Atomic Power Reactor in 1963.
- Construction of a Nuclear Power Reactor at RAPP in 1963 was financed with Canadian export credits of $45 million, with repayments made in Indian currency.
- In 1967, construction of a second nuclear power reactor at RAPP was financed with Canadian export credits of $38 million with repayments made in Indian currency.
- In the mid-1960s, Canada provided Taiwan with a nuclear research reactor similar to the one provided India in 1955. It was decommissioned in the late 1980s, and its fissile material was sent to the United States.
- Canada provided Pakistan with a power reactor in 1965, which remained in service until 2021 and was part of that country's development of expertise on nuclear matters.
- For many years, Canada played a constructive role at the UN on measures promoting nuclear disarmament and was a lead co-sponsor of the annual resolution calling for a comprehensive nuclear test ban treaty.
- Canada was directly involved in the negotiations for the Limited Test Ban Treaty, the Non-Proliferation Treaty, and the Comprehensive Limited Test Ban Treaty, and signed in 1963, 1968, and 1996 respectively. Its signature on the 1996 Treaty carried reservations.
- Canada has not signed the 2001 Treaty on the Prohibition of Nuclear Weapons.

- Following the Indian explosion of a nuclear device in 1974, Canada severed all ties involving nuclear energy and was an organizational member of both the Zangger Committee and Nuclear Suppliers Group. In the aftermath of the Indian test explosion, Canada revised its nuclear cooperation policy and now requires IAEA safeguards on the full scope of a country's nuclear activities.
- Canada has been a member of NATO's nuclear planning group since its inception in 1966. It recently adapted its non-proliferation policy so that it is consistent with NATO and NORAD obligations.
- Over the years, Canada has sold CANDU power reactors to India, Pakistan, Argentina, South Korea, Romania, and China.
- Canada has been the world's largest exporter of uranium ore since the end of the Second World War. Kazakhstan replaced Canada in the top spot in 2009, but Canadian ore is still approximately 20 percent of the world's consumption

Canadian concerns with nuclear weapons peaked in the 1960s when Canada faced a decision on the retention of American nuclear weapons in Canada. Eventually, these weapons were removed, more due to their obsolescence than to a deliberate decision by the Canadian government.

In the current fractured international environment, it may not be a propitious time for Canada to generate public interest on nuclear weapons matters. In another sense, the timing may be especially appropriate in the expectation that the international environment will improve.

Earlier this year, The Senate Standing Committee on Foreign Affairs and International Trade earlier began "to examine such issues as may arise from time to time relating to foreign relations and international trade" with a report to be submitted by June 30, 2025. On May 30, the Minister of Foreign Affairs, Melanie Joly, announced that she was initiating a review to "modernize Canadian diplomacy." Joly noted that "Crises used to be something that happened every once in a decade – but now they're happening every year," and Canada need "to keep up with these challenging times." The Mandate letter for the foreign minister omits any reference to arms control or the elimination of nuclear weapons; this reflects the Mandate letters to her two predecessors, Marc Garneau and F-P. Champagne.

In 1945, before leaving the Manhattan Project, Canada and the United Kingdom publicly raised the need for international action in controlling the development of nuclear weapons. The call suggested an international conference. [See Nelson W Polsby, "Political Innovation in America: The Politics of Policy Initiation," Yale University Press, New Haven, 1984, page 56].

On January 24, 1946, the first resolution of the UN General Assembly created the United Nations Atomic Energy Commission "to deal with the problems raised by the discovery of atomic energy." The Commission was asked

> to make specific proposals: (a) for extending between all nations the exchange of basic scientific information for peaceful ends; (b) for control of atomic energy to the extent necessary to ensure its use only for peaceful purposes; (c) for the elimination from national armaments of atomic weapons and of all other major weapons adaptable to mass destruction; (d) for effective safeguards by way of inspection and other means to protect complying States against the hazards of violations and evasions.

One aspect of Canadian involvement in the development of nuclear weapons has been the mining of uranium in Canada, which affects First Nations communities. Pitchblende, the original name of uraninite, was first discovered on the eastern side of Great Bear Lake in the Northwest Territories in 1930. There are also major deposits in the Athabasca Basin in northern Saskatchewan. Great Bear Lake is significant in the history of the Déline First Nations, and many of its members were involved in the development of the first uranium mine near Port Radium, especially in the carrying of bags of ore to the port. In the process, there have been considerable controversy over the effects of the ore on the wellbeing of the people.

The mine was first developed by Eldorado Mining, which began mining radium in 1932 by the prospectors who first discovered the deposit. It was closed during the war but reopened shortly thereafter as the importance of uranium to nuclear weapons became known. It was nationalized by the federal government and operated as a global source of uranium until 1970. In 2012, the McArthur River uranium mine in northern Saskatchewan was the world's largest producing uranium mine, accounting for 13% of the global production. The mine closed in 2018, but early in 2022, the owners, Cameco, announced that it would reopen.

A 2005 investigation of the health issues associated with uranium mining included some personal histories here recounted:

> My husband went across to the head of Bear River to work transporting ore bags ... After they finished working each day they were always covered with brown dust ... He must have been sick for a while before they found out that he had cancer. The cancer was around his neck ... he passed away (Déline Uranium Team [DUT] 2005:71).

> My dad was a riverboat pilot. He worked the full length of the Bear River for 20 years [transporting uranium ore] ... My dad died of bone cancer ... My older brother died of cancer. He worked a long time for NTCL [transporting ore]. He worked as a deck hand. He also worked on the portage helping to transport ore sacks (DUT 2005:76)

Professor Anna Stanley, University of Guelph, Guelph, Ontario, has written extensively on the impact of the Great Bear Lake uranium mining and the nuclear energy cycle on the Dene First Nation. In a 2015 paper she wrote,

> Internal memos and a report issued in the context of Port Radium suggest that in 1932 the federal government was well aware of the dangers of radioactivity and of the need

for special caution and regular medical examination when handling even low-level radioactive materials. Their decision to operate the transport route without ever communicating this knowledge to the Dene raises the question of whether or not their ability to appropriate Dene life – to transform and exploit it as a source of value – can be understood without reference to deeply entrenched colonial attitudes and arrangements. [Antipode Vol. 47 No. 3 2015]

With the examinations of Canadian foreign policy underway, this book was written to provide Canadians with an understanding of the issues associated with the continued presence of nuclear weapons in the politics of the world. In doing so, it is expected that the announced reviews will accept that the elimination of nuclear weapons is a matter of urgency and should be included in the planned reviews of foreign policy. It is hoped that concerned and interested Canadians come forward promote a more active role for Canada in this needed work.

Annexures

A. Terms Associated with Nuclear Energy and Weapons

B. Agreements on Non-Proliferation, Testing, Delivery and Elimination of Nuclear Weapons

1. Treaty Banning Nuclear Weapons Testing in the Atmosphere, in Outer space and Underwater. 1963.
2. Treaty on the Non-Proliferation of Nuclear Weapons (NPT) 1970.
3. United States – Soviet Union Treaty on the Limitations of Underground Nuclear Weapons Test. 1990.
4. USSR-USA Treaty on Underground Nuclear Explosions for Peaceful Purposes. 1990.
5. Comprehensive Nuclear Test Ban Treaty (CNTBN). 1996.
6. Treaty on the Prohibition of Nuclear Weapons (TPNW). 2021.
7. Summary of United States – Soviet Union/Russia Nuclear Arms Control Agreements.
8. Nuclear Weapons Free Zones. Treaty for the Prohibition of Nuclear Weapons in Latin America and the Caribbean. 1969.
9. India-Pakistan Agreement on the Prohibition of Attacks Against Nuclear Installations and Facilities and the Exchange of Information on Nuclear Facilities. 1991.

A. Terms Associated with Nuclear Weapons

Atom, Nucleus, Sub Atomic Particles: Protons and neutrons together make up the nucleus of an atom and hence are called nucleons. Their properties are: Protons are positively charged subatomic particles; the number of protons in an atom is equal to its number of electrons; and protons can be produced via the removal of an electron from a hydrogen atom. The discovery of protons is credited to Ernest Rutherford.

Electrons are negatively charged subatomic particles that revolve around the nucleus of an atom and the mass of an electron is negligible when compared to the mass of a proton. It is found to have a mass equal to (1/1837) times the mass of a proton. J. J. Thomson is credited with the discovery of electrons since he was the first person to accurately calculate the mass and the charge of an electron.

Neutrons, along with protons, make up the nucleons. They are neutrally charged subatomic particles and provide the basis for isotopic difference of an element. The masses of two different isotopes of an element vary due to the difference in the number of neutrons in their respective nuclei. The neutron was discovered by James Chadwick in 1932.

Chain and Nuclear Chain Reactions: A chain reaction, in chemistry, is a sequence of reactions where a reactive product or by-product causes additional reactions. It is a self-perpetuating chain of events which can continue as long as there is a supply of reactive product.

In nuclear physics, chain reactions occur when a single neutron from fissile heavy isotopes (U-235 or Pu-239) causes one or more subsequent reactions, leading to self-propagating nuclear reactions. These reactions with the splitting of heavy isotopes release several million times more energy per reaction than any chemical reaction. In nuclear physics, a single neutron can cause chain reactions resulting in critical events large enough for use in a nuclear weapon.

Depleted Uranium: Depleted uranium (DU; also referred to in the past as **Q-metal, depletable or D-38**) is uranium with a lower content of the fissile isotope U-235 than natural uranium. Natural uranium contains about 0.72%

U-235, while the DU used by the American military contains 0.3%

U-235 or less. The less radioactive and non-fissile U-238 constitutes the main component of depleted uranium. Uses of DU take advantage of its very high density of 19.1 grams per cubic centimeter (0.69 lb/cu in) (68.4% denser than lead).

Civilian uses include counterweights in aircraft, radiation shielding in medical radiation therapy and industrial radiography equipment, and containers for transporting radioactive materials. Military uses include armor plating and armor-piercing projectiles.

Heavy Water: Heavy water, so named for its higher density, consists of water molecules with deuterium isotopes in the place of hydrogen. Deuterium isotopes are composed of one proton and one neutron, while standard hydrogen contains just one proton. Deuterium is therefore twice as heavy as hydrogen, and pure heavy water has a density about 10.6% higher than that of normal water. Heavy water also has other properties that distinguish it from normal, or "light" water. One of these differences, the lower neutron absorption of heavy water, thrust the material into the center of scientific research during World War II.

Isotopes: The isotope of an element is a variant of a specific chemical element holding the same number of protons and electrons as the atomic number of the element but holds a different number of neutrons when compared to the other variants (isotopes) of the element. Alternately, isotopes are variants of elements that differ in their nucleon numbers due to a difference in the total number of neutrons in their respective nuclei. Isotopes of uranium and plutonium are the main source of fuel for nuclear weapons. Uranium, after it has been enriched, or the U-235 isotope has been removed, is called depleted uranium.

Natural Uranium: This is chemically U-238 and there are two isotopes – U-235 the highly fissile one used in nuclear weapons and U-234, much less fissile and in only limited laboratory use.

Nuclear Fission: Nuclear fission is a kind of nuclear reaction. It occurs when an atom splits into smaller atoms. Some fission reactions provides enormous energy, and are used in nuclear weapon and reactors.

An atom is the smallest particle which makes up a chemical element (e.g., hydrogen, oxygen, magnesium). All atoms are small and are made of three components or particles: Protons, neutrons and electrons. The protons and neutrons are clumped together in a ball called a nucleus, at the center of every atom. The electrons orbit around the nucleus in an electron cloud. ' Elements which have large nuclei, such as uranium and plutonium, can be made to fission.

If a very large nucleus is hit by a slow-moving neutron, it will sometimes become unstable and break into two nuclei. When the nucleus breaks apart (or fissions) it releases energy, mostly as gamma rays and heat. It also causes some neutrons to be released from the nucleus.

For a few isotopes (an atom with the same number of protons but a different number of neutrons) such fission can release many neutrons. If those neutrons then hit other atoms, they will cause other atoms to split repeatedly and is a nuclear chain reaction releasing excessive amounts of energy.

Nuclear fission was discovered in December 1938 by the German nuclear chemist Otto Hahn and his assistant Fritz Strassman in Berlin.

Nuclear Fusion: Nuclear Fusion is a reaction in which two or more atomic nuclei are combined to form one or more different atomic nuclei and subatomic particles – neutrons or protons. The difference in mass between the reactants and products results in either the release or absorption of energy. It is the process that powers the stars, including our sun, where large amounts of energy is released. The first laboratory fusion was done in 1932 and its application for possible nuclear weapons was done during the Manhattan Project. The first self-sustaining nuclear fusion happened in late 1952 in the test of a thermonuclear bomb.

Nuclear Critical Event: The controlled moment at which a nuclear chain reaction results in a nuclear explosion.

Nuclear Reactors: A nuclear reactor, formerly known as an atomic pile (so-called because the graphite moderator of the first reactor was placed into a tall pile), is a device used to initiate and control a fission nuclear chain reaction or nuclear fusion reactions. Nuclear reactors are used at nuclear power plants for electricity generation and in nuclear marine propulsion. Heat from nuclear fission is passed transferred to a fluid or gas, which in turn powers. These drive a ship's propellers or turn the shafts of electrical generators. Reactors are used to produce isotopes for medical and industrial use or for the production of weapons-grade plutonium. In 2019, the IAEA reported 454 nuclear power reactors and 226 nuclear research reactors in operation around the world.

Plutonium: Pu is a radioactive chemical element with the atomic number 94. It is the element with the highest atomic number to occur in nature with trace quantities in natural uranium-238. Two isotopies of Pu 239 and 241 are fissile and can sustain nuclear chain reaction making it applicable for use in nuclear weapons. It was made artificially in 1940 at the University of California.

Plutonium-239: Pu-239 is an isotope of plutonium. It has become the primary fissile isotope used in the production of nuclear weapons, largely replacing enriched uranium or U-235. It is also one of three isotopes used as fuel in thermal spectrum nuclear reactors.

Thermonuclear weapon, fusion weapon or hydrogen bomb (H bomb): This is a second-generation nuclear weapon design. Its greater sophistication affords it vastly greater destructive power than first-generation nuclear weapons and is more compact size with a lower mass, or a combination of these benefits. Characteristics of nuclear fusion reactions make possible the use of non-fissile depleted uranium as the weapon's main fuel, thus allowing more efficient use of scarce fissile material such as uranium-235 or plutonium-239.

Tube Alloy: The code name for the nuclear weapons program of the United Kingdom. It became part of the Manhattan Project in 1943.

Uranium and Enriched Uranium U-235: Natural uranium has three isotopes U-238, U-234, and U-235 and are all fissile. The percentage of enriched uranium is increased by isotopic separation making it a primary source for use in nuclear weapons when it is at the 90% range, in early nuclear weapons. There is about two thousand tons of highly enriched uranium (HEU) in the world and is used for the production of nuclear power, nuclear weapons, research reactors and propulsion in naval vessels.

B. International Agreements on the Non-Proliferation, Testing and Elimination of Nuclear Weapons

****

Treaty Banning Nuclear Weapons Test in the Atmosphere, in Outer Space and Under Water

Signed Moscow August 5, 1963, Effective October 10, 1963

The *Partial Test Ban Treaty (PTBT)* prohibited all test detonations of nuclear weapons except for those underground. It was jointly negotiated by the Soviet Union, the United Kingdom, and the United States. Since the treaty became effective on October 10, 1963, 125 other states became party to the treaty, and another ten have signed but not ratified.

Canada signed the treaty on August 8, 1963 and was part of the initial negotiations in 1955, along with the United States, United Kingdom, France, and the Soviet Union. The negotiations ran into verification issues with respect to underground testing, and it was only in the post-1962 American-Soviet confrontation over Cuba serious negotiations resumed, resulting in the treaty. Of the other nuclear weapon states, France, China, North Korea and Israel have not signed, while India, Israel, and Pakistan have signed.

****

The Treaty

The Governments of the United States of America, the United Kingdom of Great Britain and Northern Ireland, and the Union of Soviet Socialist Republics, hereinafter referred to as the "Original Parties",

Proclaiming as their principal aim the speediest possible achievement of an agreement on general and complete disarmament under strict international control in accordance with the objectives of the United Nations which would put an end to the armaments race and eliminate the incentive to the production and testing of all kinds of weapons, including nuclear weapons,

Seeking to achieve the discontinuance of all test explosions of nuclear weapons for all time, determined to continue negotiations to this end, and desiring to put an end to the contamination of man's environment by radioactive substances,

Have agreed as follows:

Article I

1. Each of the Parties to this Treaty undertakes to prohibit, to prevent, and not to carry out any nuclear weapon test explosion, or any other nuclear explosion, at any place under its jurisdiction or control:

(a) in the atmosphere; beyond its limits, including outer space; or under water, including territorial waters or high seas; or

(b) in any other environment if such explosion causes radioactive debris to be present outside the territorial limits of the State under whose jurisdiction or control such explosion is conducted. It is understood in this connection that the provisions of this subparagraph are without prejudice to the conclusion of a Treaty resulting in the permanent banning of all nuclear test explosions, including all such explosions underground, the conclusion of which, as the Parties have stated in the Preamble to this Treaty, they seek to achieve.

2. Each of the Parties to this Treaty undertakes furthermore to refrain from causing, encouraging, or in any way participating in, the carrying out of any nuclear weapon test explosion, or any other

nuclear explosion, anywhere which would take place in any of the environments described, or have the effect referred to, in paragraph 1 of this Article.

Article II

1. Any Party may propose amendments to this Treaty. The text of any proposed amendment shall be submitted to the Depositary Governments which shall circulate it to all Parties to this Treaty. Thereafter, if requested to do so by one-third or more of the Parties, the Depositary Governments shall convene a conference, to which they shall invite all the Parties, to consider such amendment.

2. Any amendment to this Treaty must be approved by a majority of the votes of all the Parties to this Treaty, including the votes of all of the Original Parties. The amendment shall enter into force for all Parties upon the deposit of instruments of ratification by a majority of all the Parties, including the instruments of ratification of all of the Original Parties.

Article III

1. This Treaty shall be open to all States for signature. Any State which does not sign this Treaty before its entry into force in accordance with paragraph 3 of this Article may accede to it at any time.

2. This Treaty shall be subject to ratification by signatory States. Instruments of ratification and instruments of accession shall be deposited with the Governments of the Original Parties — the United States of America, the United Kingdom of Great Britain and Northern Ireland, and the Union of Soviet Socialist Republics — which are hereby designated the Depositary Governments.

3. This Treaty shall enter into force after its ratification by all the Original Parties and the deposit of their instruments of ratification.

4. For States whose instruments of ratification or accession are deposited subsequent to the entry into force of this Treaty, it shall enter into force on the date of the deposit of their instruments of ratification or accession.

5. The Depositary Governments shall promptly inform all signatory and acceding States of the date of each signature, the date of deposit of each instrument of ratification of and accession to this Treaty, the

date of its entry into force, and the date of receipt of any requests for conferences or other notices.

6. This Treaty shall be registered by the Depositary Governments pursuant to Article 102 of the Charter of the United Nations.

Article IV

This Treaty shall be of unlimited duration.

Each Party shall in exercising its national sovereignty have the right to withdraw from the Treaty if it decides that extraordinary events, related to the subject matter of this Treaty, have jeopardized the supreme interests of its country. It shall give notice of such withdrawal to all other Parties to the Treaty three months in advance.

Article V

This Treaty, of which the English and Russian texts are equally authentic, shall be deposited in the archives of the Depositary Governments. Duly certified copies of this Treaty shall be transmitted by the Depositary Governments to the Governments of the signatory and acceding States.

IN WITNESS WHEREOF the undersigned, duly authorized, have signed this Treaty.

DONE in triplicate at the city of Moscow the fifth day of August, one thousand nine hundred and sixty-three.

For the Government of the United States of America
DEAN RUSK
For the Government of the United Kingdom of Great Britain and Northern Ireland
SIR DOUGLAS HOME
For the Government of the Union of
Soviet Socialist Republics
A. GROMYKO

Gar Pardy

Treaty on the Non-Proliferation of Nuclear Weapons (NPT)

Signed July 1, 1968, In Force Mar 5, 1970

The Treaty is regarded as the cornerstone of the global nuclear non-proliferation regime and an essential foundation for the pursuit of nuclear disarmament. It was designed to further the goals of general and complete disarmament while promoting cooperation in the peaceful uses of nuclear energy

To further non-proliferation the Treaty establishes a safeguards system under the responsibility of the International Atomic Energy Agency (IAEA). Safeguards are used to verify compliance with the Treaty through inspections conducted by the IAEA. The Treaty promotes cooperation in peaceful nuclear technology initiatives and equal access to this technology for all States, while safeguards prevent the diversion of fissile material for weapons use.

The provisions of the Treaty, particularly article VIII, paragraph 3, envisage a review of the operation of the Treaty every five years, a provision which was reaffirmed by the States parties at the 1995 NPT Review and Extension Conference. The 2015 Review Conference of the Parties to the Treaty on the Non-Proliferation of Nuclear Weapons, ended without the adoption of a consensus substantive outcome. There was a successful 2010 Review Conference States where parties agreed to a final document that included conclusions and recommendations for follow-on actions, including the implementation of the 1995 Resolution on the Middle East; the 2015 outcome constitutes a setback for the strengthened review process instituted to ensure accountability with respect to activities under the three pillars of the Treaty as part of the package in support of the indefinite extension of the Treaty in 1995.

On 11 May 1995, in accordance with article X, paragraph 2, the Review and Extension Conference of the Parties to the Treaty on the Non-Proliferation of Nuclear Weapons decided that the Treaty should continue in force indefinitely (see Decision 3). [UN Office on Disarmament Affairs].

****

The Treaty

The States concluding this Treaty, hereinafter referred to as the Parties to the Treaty,

Considering the devastation that would be visited upon all mankind by a nuclear war and the consequent need to make every effort to avert the danger of such a war and to take measures to safeguard the security of peoples,

Believing that the proliferation of nuclear weapons would seriously enhance the danger of nuclear war,

In conformity with resolutions of the United Nations General Assembly calling for the conclusion of an agreement on the prevention of wider dissemination of nuclear weapons,

Undertaking to co-operate in facilitating the application of International Atomic Energy Agency safeguards on peaceful nuclear activities,

Expressing their support for research, development and other efforts to further the application, within the framework of the International Atomic Energy Agency safeguards system, of the principle of safeguarding effectively the flow of source and special fissionable materials by use of instruments and other techniques at certain strategic points,

Affirming the principle that the benefits of peaceful applications of nuclear technology, including any technological by-products which may be derived by nuclear-weapons states from the development of nuclear explosive devices, should be available for peaceful purposes to all Parties to the Treaty, whether nuclear-weapon or non-nuclear-weapons states,

Convinced that, in furtherance of this principle, all Parties to the Treaty are entitled to participate in the fullest possible exchange of scientific information for, and to contribute alone or in co-operation with other States to, the further development of the applications of atomic energy for peaceful purposes,

Declaring their intention to achieve at the earliest possible date the cessation of the nuclear arms race and to undertake effective measures in the direction of nuclear disarmament,

Urging the co-operation of all States in the attainment of this objective,

Recalling the determination expressed by the Parties to the 1963 Treaty banning nuclear weapons tests in the atmosphere, in outer space and under water in its Preamble to seek to achieve the discontinuance of all test explosions of nuclear weapons for all time and to continue negotiations to this end,

Desiring to further the easing of international tension and the strengthening of trust between States in order to facilitate the cessation of the manufacture of nuclear weapons, the liquidation of all their existing stockpiles, and the elimination from national arsenals of nuclear weapons and the means of their delivery pursuant to a Treaty on general and complete disarmament under strict and effective international control,

Recalling that, in accordance with the Charter of the United Nations, States must refrain in their international relations from the threat or use of force against the territorial integrity or political independence of any State, or in any other manner inconsistent with the Purposes of the United Nations, and that the establishment and maintenance of international peace and security are to be promoted with the least diversion for armaments of the world's human and economic resources,

Have agreed as follows:

Article I

Each nuclear-weapons state Party to the Treaty undertakes not to transfer to any recipient whatsoever nuclear weapons or other nuclear explosive devices or control over such weapons or explosive devices directly, or indirectly; and not in any way to assist, encourage, or induce any non-nuclear-weapons state to manufacture or otherwise acquire nuclear weapons or other nuclear explosive devices, or control over such weapons or explosive devices.

Article II

Each non-nuclear-weapons state Party to the Treaty undertakes not to receive the transfer from any transferor whatsoever of nuclear weapons or other nuclear explosive devices or of control over such weapons or explosive devices directly, or indirectly; not to manufacture or otherwise acquire nuclear weapons or other nuclear explosive devices; and not to seek or receive any assistance in the manufacture of nuclear weapons or other nuclear explosive devices.

Article III

1. Each non-nuclear-weapons state Party to the Treaty undertakes to accept safeguards, as set forth in an agreement to be negotiated and concluded with the International Atomic Energy Agency in accordance with the Statute of the International Atomic Energy Agency and the Agency's safeguards system, for the exclusive purpose of verification of the fulfilment of its obligations assumed under this Treaty with a view to preventing diversion of nuclear energy from peaceful uses to nuclear weapons or other nuclear explosive devices. Procedures for the safeguards required by this Article shall be followed with respect to source or special fissionable material whether it is being produced, processed or used in any principal nuclear facility or is outside any such facility. The safeguards required by this Article shall be applied on all source or special fissionable material in all peaceful nuclear activities within the territory of such State, under its jurisdiction, or carried out under its control anywhere.

2. Each State Party to the Treaty undertakes not to provide: (a) source or special fissionable material, or (b) equipment or material especially designed or prepared for the processing, use or production of special fissionable material, to any non-nuclear-weapons state for peaceful purposes, unless the source or special fissionable material shall be subject to the safeguards required by this Article.

3. The safeguards required by this Article shall be implemented in a manner designed to comply with Article IV of this Treaty, and to avoid hampering the economic or technological development of the Parties or international co-operation in the field of peaceful nuclear activities, including the international exchange of nuclear material and equipment for the processing, use or production of nuclear material for peaceful purposes in accordance with the provisions of this Article and the principle of safeguarding set forth in the Preamble of the Treaty.

4. Non-nuclear-weapons states Party to the Treaty shall conclude agreements with the International Atomic Energy Agency to meet the requirements of this Article either individually or together with other States in accordance with the Statute of the International Atomic Energy Agency. Negotiation of such agreements shall commence within 180 days from the original entry into force of this Treaty. For States depositing their instruments of ratification or accession after the 180-day period, negotiation of such agreements shall commence not later than the date of such deposit. Such agreements shall enter into force not later than eighteen months after the date of initiation of negotiations.

Article IV

1. Nothing in this Treaty shall be interpreted as affecting the inalienable right of all the Parties to the Treaty to develop research, production and use of nuclear energy for peaceful purposes without discrimination and in conformity with Articles I and II of this Treaty.

2. All the Parties to the Treaty undertake to facilitate, and have the right to participate in, the fullest possible exchange of equipment,

materials and scientific and technological information for the peaceful uses of nuclear energy. Parties to the Treaty in a position to do so shall also co-operate in contributing alone or together with other States or international organizations to the further development of the applications of nuclear energy for peaceful purposes, especially in the territories of non-nuclear-weapons states Party to the Treaty, with due consideration for the needs of the developing areas of the world.

Article V

Each Party to the Treaty undertakes to take appropriate measures to ensure that, in accordance with this Treaty, under appropriate international observation and through appropriate international procedures, potential benefits from any peaceful applications of nuclear explosions will be made available to non-nuclear-weapons states Party to the Treaty on a non-discriminatory basis and that the charge to such Parties for the explosive devices used will be as low as possible and exclude any charge for research and development. Non-nuclear-weapons states Party to the Treaty shall be able to obtain such benefits, pursuant to a special international agreement or agreements, through an appropriate international body with adequate representation of non-nuclear-weapons states. Negotiations on this subject shall commence as soon as possible after the Treaty enters into force. Non-nuclear-weapons states Party to the Treaty so desiring may also obtain such benefits pursuant to bilateral agreements.

Article VI

Each of the Parties to the Treaty undertakes to pursue negotiations in good faith on effective measures relating to cessation of the nuclear arms race at an early date and to nuclear disarmament, and on a treaty on general and complete disarmament under strict and effective international control.

Article VII

Nothing in this Treaty affects the right of any group of States to conclude regional treaties in order to assure the total absence of nuclear weapons in their respective territories.

Article VIII

1. Any Party to the Treaty may propose amendments to this Treaty. The text of any proposed amendment shall be submitted to the Depositary Governments which shall circulate it to all Parties to the Treaty. Thereupon, if requested to do so by one-third or more of the Parties to the Treaty, the Depositary Governments shall convene a conference, to which they shall invite all the Parties to the Treaty, to consider such an amendment.

2. Any amendment to this Treaty must be approved by a majority of the votes of all the Parties to the Treaty, including the votes of all nuclear-weapons states Party to the Treaty and all other Parties which, on the date the amendment is circulated, are members of the Board of Governors of the International Atomic Energy Agency. The amendment shall enter into force for each Party that deposits its instrument of ratification of the amendment upon the deposit of such instruments of ratification by a majority of all the Parties, including the instruments of ratification of all nuclear-weapons states Party to the Treaty and all other Parties which, on the date the amendment is circulated, are members of the Board of Governors of the International Atomic Energy Agency. Thereafter, it shall enter into force for any other Party upon the deposit of its instrument of ratification of the amendment.

3. Five years after the entry into force of this Treaty, a conference of Parties to the Treaty shall be held in Geneva, Switzerland, in order to review the operation of this Treaty with a view to assuring that the purposes of the Preamble and the provisions of the Treaty are being realised. At intervals of five years thereafter, a majority of the Parties to the Treaty may obtain, by submitting a proposal to this effect to the

Depositary Governments, the convening of further conferences with the same objective of reviewing the operation of the Treaty.

Article IX

1. This Treaty shall be open to all States for signature. Any State which does not sign the Treaty before its entry into force in accordance with paragraph 3 of this Article may accede to it at any time.

2. This Treaty shall be subject to ratification by signatory States. Instruments of ratification and instruments of accession shall be deposited with the Governments of the United Kingdom of Great Britain and Northern Ireland, the Union of Soviet Socialist Republics and the United States of America, which are hereby designated the Depositary Governments.

3. This Treaty shall enter into force after its ratification by the States, the Governments of which are designated Depositaries of the Treaty, and forty other States signatory to this Treaty and the deposit of their instruments of ratification. For the purposes of this Treaty, a nuclear-weapons state is one which has manufactured and exploded a nuclear weapon or other nuclear explosive device prior to 1 January 1967.

4. For States whose instruments of ratification or accession are deposited subsequent to the entry into force of this Treaty, it shall enter into force on the date of the deposit of their instruments of ratification or accession.

5. The Depositary Governments shall promptly inform all signatory and acceding States of the date of each signature, the date of deposit of each instrument of ratification or of accession, the date of the entry into force of this Treaty, and the date of receipt of any requests for convening a conference or other notices.

6. This Treaty shall be registered by the Depositary Governments pursuant to Article 102 of the Charter of the United Nations.

Article X

1. Each Party shall in exercising its national sovereignty have the right to withdraw from the Treaty if it decides that extraordinary

events, related to the subject matter of this Treaty, have jeopardized the supreme interests of its country. It shall give notice of such withdrawal to all other parties to the Treaty and to the United Nations Security Council three months in advance. Such notice shall include a statement of the extraordinary events it regards as having jeopardized its supreme interests.

2. Twenty-five years after the entry into force of the Treaty, a conference shall be convened to decide whether the Treaty shall continue in force indefinitely, or shall be extended for an additional fixed period or periods. This decision shall be taken by a majority of the Parties to the Treaty.

Article XI

This Treaty, the English, Russian, French, Spanish and Chinese texts of which are equally authentic, shall be deposited in the archives of the Depositary Governments. Duly certified copies of this Treaty shall be transmitted by the Depositary Governments to the Governments of the signatory and acceding States.

IN WITNESS WHEREOF the undersigned, duly authorized, have signed this Treaty.

DONE in triplicate, at the cities of London, Moscow and Washington, the first day of July, one thousand nine hundred and sixty-eight.

Note:

On 11 May 1995, in accordance with article X, paragraph 2, the Review and Extension Conference of the Parties to the Treaty on the Non-Proliferation of Nuclear Weapons decided that the Treaty should continue in force indefinitely (see decision 3).

The United States and the Soviet Union Treaty on the Limitation of Underground Nuclear Weapons Test

Signed July 3, 1974, Effective December 11, 1990

The Threshold Test Ban Treaty (TTBT) established a nuclear "threshold" by prohibiting nuclear tests of devices having a yield exceeding 150 kilotons. The threshold was effective for all tests after March 31, 1976. Earlier there were many tests by both the United States and the Soviet Union above 150 kilotons and the treaty imposed mutual restraint on both countries. Under the treaty both countries, for the first time, agreed to make available to each other data relating to nuclear weapons test programs.

Treaty between the United States and the Soviet Union on Underground Nuclear Explosions for Peaceful Purposes

Signed May 28, 1976 and Entered into Force December 11, 1990

The PNE treaty grew out of the Soviet and American discussions for the Threshold Test Ban Treaty (TTBT) in the mid-1970s and the understanding of the need to agree on measures relating to peaceful nuclear explosions. The negotiations were concluded in April 1976 and the agreement applied to all nuclear explosions for peaceful purposes conducted by the parties after March 31, 1976. The Treaty provides both parties with the right to carry out underground PNEs at any location under their jurisdiction or control with the understanding that such explosions will not be used in the developmental testing of nuclear explosive and will not involved test facilities, instrumentation or procedures related only to the testing of nuclear weapons.

Gar Pardy

Comprehensive Nuclear-Test-Ban Treaty (CNTBT)

Signed September 24, 1996

The Comprehensive Nuclear-Test-Ban Treaty (CTBT) bans all nuclear explosions, whether for military or peaceful purposes. It comprises a preamble, 17 articles, two annexes, and a Protocol with two annexes.

Accompanying the Treaty was the Resolution adopted by the Signatory States on November 19, 1996 establishing the Preparatory Commission for the Comprehensive Nuclear-Test-Ban Treaty Organization (CTBTO).

There are 186 states that have signed the Treaty, with 176 having submitting ratification; but for it to come into force, it requires the signatures of eight remaining countries that were party to the negotiations: China, Egypt, India, Iran, Israel, North Korea, Pakistan, United States. Six of these have nuclear weapons.

Summary of the Treaty

Annex 1 to the Treaty lists States by geographical regions for the purposes of elections to the Executive Council.

Annex 2 to the Treaty lists the 44 States that must ratify the Treaty for it to enter into force.

Protocol Part I describes the functions of the International Monitoring System (IMS) and the International Data Centre (IDC).

Protocol Part II sets up the procedures for on-site inspections.

Protocol Part III deals with confidence-building measures.

Annex 1 to the Protocol lists the facilities comprising the IMS network.

Annex 2 to the Protocol lists the characterization parameters for IDC standard event screening.

Articles of the Treaty

Article IV elaborates on the global verification regime to monitor compliance with Treaty provisions. The regime is to comprise a global network of monitoring stations (the International Monitoring System), an International Data Centre in Vienna, a consultation and clarification process, On-site Inspections and confidence-building measures .

Article V outlines measures to redress a situation which contravenes the CTBT provisions and to ensure compliance with the Treaty.

Article VI deals with the settlement of disputes that may arise concerning the application or the interpretation of the Treaty.

Article VII is concerned with amendments to the Treaty.

Article VIII stipulates when a review of the Treaty will take place after its entry into force .

Article IX states that the Treaty is of unlimited duration.

Article X deals with the status of the Protocol and the annexes.

Article XI is concerned with signature of the Treaty.

Article XII deals with ratification of the Treaty.

Article XIII is about accession to the Treaty.

Article XIV is about the Treaty's entry into force . This will take place 180 days after the 44 States listed in Annex 2 to the Treaty have all ratified.

Article XV specifies that the Treaty shall not be subject to reservations.

Article XVI refers to the Depositary of the Treaty.

Article XVII deals with the authenticity of Arabic, Chinese, English, French, Russian and Spanish Treaty texts.

Gar Pardy

Treaty on the Prohibition of Nuclear Weapons (TPNW)

Signed September 20, 2017

Effective January 22, 2021

The TPNW is the first legally binding international agreement to prohibit the existence of nuclear weapons and to call for their total elimination. Parties to the treaty agree to the prohibition on the development, testing, production, stockpiling, stationing, transfer, use, and threat of use of nuclear weapons. As well, the Treaty prohibits assistance and encouragement for any of these activities. For states with nuclear weapons who sign the treaty, there is a time period for negotiations leading to the verified and irreversible elimination of its nuclear weapons. So far, there are 91 signatories to the treaty, with 68 acceding to or ratifying the treaty.

There is widespread support for the treaty from Africa, Latin America, and the Caribbean, as well as ASEAN members except for Singapore and Pacific Island states. However, states with nuclear weapons do not support the treaty, and the three members of NATO with nuclear weapons (the United States, the United Kingdom and France) issued a statement that they did not intend "to sign, ratify or even become party to it." The other non-nuclear weapon states of NATO, including Canada, have indicated that they will not sign the treaty. Russia has indicated that it opposes the treaty, while North Korea supported the negotiations.

****

The Treaty

The States Parties to this Treaty,

Determined to contribute to the realization of the purposes and principles of the Charter of the United Nations,

The Scary World of Nuclear Weapons

Deeply concerned about the catastrophic humanitarian consequences that would result from any use of nuclear weapons, and recognizing the consequent need to completely eliminate such weapons, which remains the only way to guarantee that nuclear weapons are never used again under any circumstances,

Mindful of the risks posed by the continued existence of nuclear weapons, including from any nuclear-weapon detonation by accident, miscalculation or design, and emphasizing that these risks concern the security of all humanity, and that all States share the responsibility to prevent any use of nuclear weapons,

Cognizant that the catastrophic consequences of nuclear weapons cannot be adequately addressed, transcend national borders, pose grave implications for human survival, the environment, socio-economic development, the global economy, food security and the health of current and future generations, and have a disproportionate impact on women and girls, including as a result of ionizing radiation,

Acknowledging the ethical imperatives for nuclear disarmament and the urgency of achieving and maintaining a nuclear-weapon-free world, which is a global public good of the highest order, serving both national and collective security interests,

Mindful of the unacceptable suffering of and harm caused to the victims of the use of nuclear weapons (hibakusha), as well as of those affected by the testing of nuclear weapons,

Recognizing the disproportionate impact of nuclear-weapon activities on indigenous peoples,

Reaffirming the need for all States at all times to comply with applicable international law, including international humanitarian law and international human rights law,

Basing themselves on the principles and rules of international humanitarian law, in particular the principle that the right of parties to an armed conflict to choose methods or means of warfare is not unlimited, the rule of distinction, the prohibition against indiscriminate attacks, the rules on proportionality and precautions in attack, the prohibition on the use of weapons of a nature to cause superfluous injury or unnecessary suffering, and the rules for the protection of the natural environment,

Considering that any use of nuclear weapons would be contrary to the rules of international law applicable in armed conflict, in particular the principles and rules of international humanitarian law,

Reaffirming that any use of nuclear weapons would also be abhorrent to the principles of humanity and the dictates of public conscience,

Recalling that, in accordance with the Charter of the United Nations, States must refrain in their international relations from the threat or use of force against the territorial integrity or political independence of any State, or in any other manner inconsistent with the Purposes of the United Nations, and that the establishment and maintenance of international peace and security are to be promoted with the least diversion for armaments of the world's human and economic resources,

Recalling also the first resolution of the General Assembly of the United Nations, adopted on 24 January 1946, and subsequent resolutions which call for the elimination of nuclear weapons,

Concerned by the slow pace of nuclear disarmament, the continued reliance on nuclear weapons in military and security concepts, doctrines and policies, and the waste of economic and human resources on programmes for the production, maintenance and modernization of nuclear weapons,

Recognizing that a legally binding prohibition of nuclear weapons constitutes an important contribution towards the achievement and maintenance of a world free of nuclear weapons, including the irreversible, verifiable and transparent elimination of nuclear weapons, and determined to act towards that end,

Determined to act with a view to achieving effective progress towards general and complete disarmament under strict and effective international control,

Reaffirming that there exists an obligation to pursue in good faith and bring to a conclusion negotiation leading to nuclear disarmament in all its aspects under strict and effective international control,

Reaffirming also that the full and effective implementation of the Treaty on the Non-Proliferation of Nuclear Weapons, which serves as the cornerstone of the nuclear disarmament and non-proliferation regime, has a vital role to play in promoting international peace and security,

Recognizing the vital importance of the Comprehensive Nuclear-Test-Ban Treaty and its verification regime as a core element of the nuclear disarmament and non-proliferation regime,

Reaffirming the conviction that the establishment of the internationally recognized nuclear-weapon-free zones on the basis of arrangements freely arrived at among the States of the region concerned enhances global and regional peace and security, strengthens the nuclear non-proliferation regime and contributes towards realizing the objective of nuclear disarmament,

Emphasizing that nothing in this Treaty shall be interpreted as affecting the inalienable right of its States Parties to develop research, production and use of nuclear energy for peaceful purposes without discrimination,

Recognizing that the equal, full and effective participation of both women and men is an essential factor for the promotion and attainment of sustainable peace and security, and committed to supporting and strengthening the effective participation of women in nuclear disarmament,

Recognizing also the importance of peace and disarmament education in all its aspects and of raising awareness of the risks and consequences of nuclear weapons for current and future generations, and committed to the dissemination of the principles and norms of this Treaty,

Stressing the role of public conscience in the furthering of the principles of humanity as evidenced by the call for the total elimination of nuclear weapons, and recognizing the efforts to that end undertaken by the United Nations, the International Red Cross and Red Crescent Movement, other international and regional organizations, non-governmental organizations, religious leaders, parliamentarians, academics and the hibakusha,

Have agreed as follows:

Article 1: Prohibitions

Each State Party undertakes never under any circumstances to:

(a) Develop, test, produce, manufacture, otherwise acquire, possess or stockpile nuclear weapons or other nuclear explosive devices;

(b) Transfer to any recipient whatsoever nuclear weapons or other nuclear explosive devices or control over such weapons or explosive devices directly or indirectly;

(c) Receive the transfer of or control over nuclear weapons or other nuclear explosive devices directly or indirectly;

(d) Use or threaten to use nuclear weapons or other nuclear explosive devices;

(e) Assist, encourage or induce, in any way, anyone to engage in any activity prohibited to a State Party under this Treaty;

(f) Seek or receive any assistance, in any way, from anyone to engage in any activity prohibited to a State Party under this Treaty;

(g) Allow any stationing, installation or deployment of any nuclear weapons or other nuclear explosive devices in its territory or at any place under its jurisdiction or control.

Article 2: Declarations

1. Each State Party shall submit to the Secretary-General of the United Nations, not later than 30 days after this Treaty enters into force for that State Party, a declaration in which it shall:

(a) Declare whether it owned, possessed or controlled nuclear weapons or nuclear explosive devices and eliminated its nuclear-weapon programme, including the elimination or irreversible conversion of all nuclear-weapons-related facilities, prior to the entry into force of this Treaty for that State Party;

(b) Notwithstanding Article 1 (a), declare whether it owns, possesses or controls any nuclear weapons or other nuclear explosive devices;

(c) Notwithstanding Article 1 (g), declare whether there are any nuclear weapons or other nuclear explosive devices in its territory or in any place under its jurisdiction or control that are owned, possessed or controlled by another State.

2. The Secretary-General of the United Nations shall transmit all such declarations received to the States Parties.

Article 3: Safeguards

1. Each State Party to which Article 4, paragraph 1 or 2, does not apply shall, at a minimum, maintain its International Atomic Energy Agency safeguards obligations in force at the time of entry into force of this Treaty, without prejudice to any additional relevant instruments that it may adopt in the future.

2. Each State Party to which Article 4, paragraph 1 or 2, does not apply that has not yet done so shall conclude with the International Atomic Energy Agency and bring into force a comprehensive safeguard agreement (INFCIRC/153 (Corrected)). Negotiation of such agreement shall commence within 180 days from the entry into force of this Treaty for that State Party. The agreement shall enter into force no later than 18 months from the entry into force of this Treaty for that State Party. Each State Party shall thereafter maintain such obligations, without prejudice to any additional relevant instruments that it may adopt in the future.

Article 4: Towards the total elimination of nuclear weapons

1. Each State Party that after 7 July 2017 owned, possessed or controlled nuclear weapons or other nuclear explosive devices and eliminated its nuclear-weapon programme, including the elimination or irreversible conversion of all nuclear-weapons-related facilities, prior to the entry into force of this Treaty for it, shall cooperate with the competent international authority designated pursuant to paragraph 6 of this Article for the purpose of verifying the irreversible elimination of its nuclear-weapon programme. The competent

international authority shall report to the States Parties. Such a State Party shall conclude a safeguards agreement with the International Atomic Energy Agency sufficient to provide credible assurance of the non-diversion of declared nuclear material from peaceful nuclear activities and of the absence of undeclared nuclear material or activities in that State Party as a whole. Negotiation of such agreement shall commence within 180 days from the entry into force of this Treaty for that State Party. The agreement shall enter into force no later than 18 months from the entry into force of this Treaty for that State Party. That State Party shall thereafter, at a minimum, maintain these safeguards obligations, without prejudice to any additional relevant instruments that it may adopt in the future.

1. Notwithstanding Article 1 (a), each State Party that owns, possesses or controls nuclear weapons or other nuclear explosive devices shall immediately remove them from operational status, and destroy them as soon as possible but not later than a deadline to be determined by the first meeting of States Parties, in accordance with a legally binding, time-bound plan for the verified and irreversible elimination of that State Party's nuclear-weapon programme, including the elimination or irreversible conversion of all nuclear-weapons-related facilities. The State Party, no later than 60 days after the entry into force of this Treaty for that State Party, shall submit this plan to the States Parties or to a competent international authority designated by the States Parties. The plan shall then be negotiated with the competent international authority, which shall submit it to the subsequent meeting of States Parties or review conference, whichever comes first, for approval in accordance with its rules of procedure.

2. A State Party to which paragraph 2 above applies shall conclude a safeguards agreement with the International Atomic Energy Agency sufficient to provide credible assurance of the non-diversion of declared nuclear material from peaceful nuclear activities and of the absence of undeclared nuclear material or activities in the State as a whole. Negotiation of such agreement shall commence no later than the date upon which implementation of the plan referred to in

paragraph 2 is completed. The agreement shall enter into force no later than 18 months after the date of initiation of negotiations. That State Party shall thereafter, at a minimum, maintain these safeguards obligations, without prejudice to any additional relevant instruments that it may adopt in the future. Following the entry into force of the agreement referred to in this paragraph, the State Party shall submit to the Secretary-General of the United Nations a final declaration that it has fulfilled its obligations under this Article.

3. Notwithstanding Article 1 (b) and (g), each State Party that has any nuclear weapons or other nuclear explosive devices in its territory or in any place under its jurisdiction or control that are owned, possessed or controlled by another State shall ensure the prompt removal of such weapons, as soon as possible but not later than a deadline to be determined by the first meeting of States Parties. Upon the removal of such weapons or other explosive devices, that State Party shall submit to the Secretary-General of the United Nations a declaration that it has fulfilled its obligations under this Article.

4. Each State Party to which this Article applies shall submit a report to each meeting of States Parties and each review conference on the progress made towards the implementation of its obligations under this Article, until such time as they are fulfilled.

5. The States Parties shall designate a competent international authority or authorities to negotiate and verify the irreversible elimination of nuclear-weapons programmes, including the elimination or irreversible conversion of all nuclear-weapons-related facilities in accordance with paragraphs 1, 2 and 3 of this Article. In the event that such a designation has not been made prior to the entry into force of this Treaty for a State Party to which paragraph 1 or 2 of this Article applies, the Secretary-General of the United Nations shall convene an extraordinary meeting of States Parties to take any decisions that may be required.

Article 5: National implementation

1. Each State Party shall adopt the necessary measures to implement its obligations under this Treaty.

2. Each State Party shall take all appropriate legal, administrative and other measures, including the imposition of penal sanctions, to prevent and suppress any activity prohibited to a State Party under this Treaty undertaken by persons or on territory under its jurisdiction or control.

Article 6: Victim assistance and environmental remediation

1. Each State Party shall, with respect to individuals under its jurisdiction who are affected by the use or testing of nuclear weapons, in accordance with applicable international humanitarian and human rights law, adequately provide age- and gender-sensitive assistance, without discrimination, including medical care, rehabilitation and psychological support, as well as provide for their social and economic inclusion.

2. Each State Party, with respect to areas under its jurisdiction or control contaminated as a result of activities related to the testing or use of nuclear weapons or other nuclear explosive devices, shall take necessary and appropriate measures towards the environmental remediation of areas so contaminated.

3. The obligations under paragraphs 1 and 2 above shall be without prejudice to the duties and obligations of any other States under international law or bilateral agreements.

Article 7: International cooperation and assistance

1. Each State Party shall cooperate with other States Parties to facilitate the implementation of this Treaty.

2. In fulfilling its obligations under this Treaty, each State Party shall have the right to seek and receive assistance, where feasible, from other States Parties.

3. Each State Party in a position to do so shall provide technical, material and financial assistance to States Parties affected by

nuclear-weapons use or testing, to further the implementation of this Treaty.

4. Each State Party in a position to do so shall provide assistance for the victims of the use or testing of nuclear weapons or other nuclear explosive devices.

5. Assistance under this Article may be provided, inter alia, through the United Nations system, international, regional or national organizations or institutions, non-governmental organizations or institutions, the International Committee of the Red Cross, the International Federation of Red Cross and Red Crescent Societies, or national Red Cross and Red Crescent Societies, or on a bilateral basis.

6. Without prejudice to any other duty or obligation that it may have under international law, a State Party that has used or tested nuclear weapons or any other nuclear explosive devices shall have a responsibility to provide adequate assistance to affected States Parties, for the purpose of victim assistance and environmental remediation.

Article 8: Meeting of States Parties

1. The States Parties shall meet regularly in order to consider and, where necessary, take decisions in respect of any matter with regard to the application or implementation of this Treaty, in accordance with its relevant provisions, and on further measures for nuclear disarmament, including:

(a) The implementation and status of this Treaty;

(b) Measures for the verified, time-bound and irreversible elimination of nuclear-weapon programmes, including additional protocols to this Treaty;

(c) Any other matters pursuant to and consistent with the provisions of this Treaty.

2. The first meeting of States Parties shall be convened by the Secretary-General of the United Nations within one year of the entry into force of this Treaty. Further meetings of States Parties shall be convened by the Secretary-General of the United Nations on a biennial basis, unless otherwise agreed by the States Parties. The meeting of

States Parties shall adopt its rules of procedure at its first session. Pending their adoption, the rules of procedure of the United Nations conference to negotiate a legally binding instrument to prohibit nuclear weapons, leading towards their total elimination, shall apply.

3. Extraordinary meetings of States Parties shall be convened, as may be deemed necessary, by the Secretary-General of the United Nations, at the written request of any State Party provided that this request is supported by at least one third of the States Parties. After a period of five years following the entry into force of this Treaty, the Secretary-General of the United Nations shall convene a conference to review the operation of the Treaty and the progress in achieving the purposes of the Treaty. The Secretary-General of the United Nations shall convene further review conferences at intervals of six years with the same objective, unless otherwise agreed by the States Parties.

4. States not party to this Treaty, as well as the relevant entities of the United Nations system, other relevant international organizations or institutions, regional organizations, the International Committee of the Red Cross, the International Federation of Red Cross and Red Crescent Societies and relevant non-governmental organizations, shall be invited to attend the meetings of States Parties and the review conferences as observers.

Article 9: Costs

1. The costs of the meetings of States Parties, the review conferences and the extraordinary meetings of States Parties shall be borne by the States Parties and States not party to this Treaty participating therein as observers, in accordance with the United Nations scale of assessment adjusted appropriately.

2. The costs incurred by the Secretary-General of the United Nations in the circulation of declarations under Article 2, reports under Article 4 and proposed amendments under Article 10 of this Treaty shall be borne by the States Parties in accordance with the United Nations scale of assessment adjusted appropriately.

3. The cost related to the implementation of verification measures required under Article 4 as well as the costs related to the destruction of nuclear weapons or other nuclear explosive devices, and the elimination of nuclear-weapon programmes, including the elimination or conversion of all nuclear-weapons-related facilities, should be borne by the States Parties to which they apply.

Article 10: Amendments

1. At any time after the entry into force of this Treaty, any State Party may propose amendments to the Treaty. The text of a proposed amendment shall be communicated to the Secretary-General of the United Nations, who shall circulate it to all States Parties and shall seek their views on whether to consider the proposal. If a majority of the States Parties notify the Secretary-General of the United Nations no later than 90 days after its circulation that they support further consideration of the proposal, the proposal shall be considered at the next meeting of States Parties or review conference, whichever comes first.

2. A meeting of States Parties or a review conference may agree upon amendments which shall be adopted by a positive vote of a majority of two thirds of the States Parties. The Depositary shall communicate any adopted amendment to all States Parties.

3. The amendment shall enter into force for each State Party that deposits its instrument of ratification or acceptance of the amendment 90 days following the deposit of such instruments of ratification or acceptance by a majority of the States Parties at the time of adoption. Thereafter, it shall enter into force for any other State Party 90 days following the deposit of its instrument of ratification or acceptance of the amendment.

Article 11: Settlement of disputes

1. When a dispute arises between two or more States Parties relating to the interpretation or application of this Treaty, the parties concerned shall consult together with a view to the settlement of the dispute by negotiation or by other peaceful means of the parties'

choice in accordance with Article 33 of the Charter of the United Nations.

2. The meeting of States Parties may contribute to the settlement of the dispute, including by offering its good offices, calling upon the States Parties concerned to start the settlement procedure of their choice and recommending a time limit for any agreed procedure, in accordance with the relevant provisions of this Treaty and the Charter of the United Nations.

Article 12: Universality

Each State Party shall encourage States not party to this Treaty to sign, ratify, accept, approve or accede to the Treaty, with the goal of universal adherence of all States to the Treaty.

Article 13: Signature

This Treaty shall be open for signature to all States at United Nations Headquarters in New York as from 20 September 2017.

Article 14: Ratification, acceptance, approval or accession

This Treaty shall be subject to ratification, acceptance or approval by signatory States. The Treaty shall be open for accession.

Article 15: Entry into force

1. This Treaty shall enter into force 90 days after the fiftieth instrument of ratification, acceptance, approval or accession has been deposited.

2. For any State that deposits its instrument of ratification, acceptance, approval or accession after the date of the deposit of the fiftieth instrument of ratification, acceptance, approval or accession, this Treaty shall enter into force 90 days after the date on which that State has deposited its instrument of ratification, acceptance, approval or accession.

Article 16: Reservations

The Articles of this Treaty shall not be subject to reservations.

Article 17: Duration and withdrawal

1. This Treaty shall be of unlimited duration.

2. Each State Party shall, in exercising its national sovereignty, have the right to withdraw from this Treaty if it decides that extraordinary events related to the subject matter of the Treaty have jeopardized the supreme interests of its country. It shall give notice of such withdrawal to the Depositary. Such notice shall include a statement of the extraordinary events that it regards as having jeopardized its supreme interests.

3. Such withdrawal shall only take effect 12 months after the date of the receipt of the notification of withdrawal by the Depositary. If, however, on the expiry of that 12-month period, the withdrawing State Party is a party to an armed conflict, the State Party shall continue to be bound by the obligations of this Treaty and of any additional protocols until it is no longer party to an armed conflict.

Article 18: Relationship with other agreements

The implementation of this Treaty shall not prejudice obligations undertaken by States Parties with regard to existing international agreements, to which they are party, where those obligations are consistent with the Treaty.

Article 19: Depositary

The Secretary-General of the United Nations is hereby designated as the Depositary of this Treaty.

Article 20: Authentic texts

The Arabic, Chinese, English, French, Russian and Spanish texts of this Treaty shall be equally authentic.

DONE at New York, this seventh day of July, two thousand and seventeen.

Gar Pardy

Summary of United States – Soviet Union/Russia Nuclear Arms Control Agreements inclusive of 2010 Strategic Arms Reduction Treaty [United States Arms Control Association]

SALT I

Begun in November 1969, by May 1972, the Strategic Arms Limitation Talks (SALT) had produced both the <u>Anti-Ballistic Missile (ABM) Treaty</u>, which limited strategic missile defenses to 200 (later 100) interceptors each, and the Interim Agreement, an executive agreement that capped U.S. and Soviet intercontinental ballistic missiles (ICBM) and submarine-launched ballistic missile (SLBM) forces. Under the Interim Agreement, both sides pledged not to construct new ICBM silos, not to increase the size of existing ICBM silos "significantly," and capped the number of SLBM launch tubes and SLBM-carrying submarines. The agreement ignored strategic bombers and did not address warhead numbers, leaving both sides free to enlarge their forces by deploying multiple warheads (MIRVs) onto their ICBMs and SLBMs and increasing their bomber-based forces. The agreement limited the United States to 1,054 ICBM silos and 656 SLBM launch tubes. The Soviet Union was limited to 1,607 ICBM silos and 740 SLBM launch tubes. In June 2002, the United States unilaterally withdrew from the ABM treaty.

SALT II

In November 1972, Washington and Moscow agreed to pursue a follow-on treaty to SALT I. SALT II, signed in June 1979, limited U.S. and Soviet ICBM, SLBM, and strategic bomber-based nuclear forces to 2,250 delivery vehicles (defined as an ICBM silo, a SLBM launch tube, or a heavy bomber) and placed a variety of other restrictions on deployed strategic nuclear forces. The agreement would have required the Soviets to reduce their forces by roughly 270 delivery vehicles, but U.S. forces were below the limits and could actually have been increased. However, President Jimmy Carter asked the Senate not to consider SALT II for its advice and consent after the Soviet Union invaded Afghanistan in December 1979, and the treaty was not taken up again. Both Washington and Moscow subsequently pledged to adhere to the agreement's terms despite its failure to enter into force. However, on May 26, 1986, President Ronald Reagan said that future decisions on strategic nuclear forces would be based on the threat posed by Soviet forces and not on "a flawed SALT II Treaty."

START I

The Strategic Arms Reduction Treaty (START I), first proposed in the early 1980s by President Ronald Reagan and finally signed in July 1991, required the United States and the Soviet Union to reduce their deployed strategic arsenals to 1,600 delivery vehicles, carrying no more than 6,000 warheads as counted using the agreement's rules. The agreement required the destruction of excess delivery vehicles which was verified using an intrusive verification regime that involved on-site inspections, the regular exchange of information (including telemetry), and the use of national technical means (i.e., satellites). The agreement's entry into force was delayed for several years because of the collapse of the Soviet Union and ensuing efforts to denuclearize Ukraine, Kazakhstan, and Belarus by returning their nuclear weapons to Russia and making them parties to the nuclear Nonproliferation Treaty (NPT) and START I agreements. START I reductions were completed in December 2001, and the treaty expired on Dec. 5, 2009.

START II

In June 1992, Presidents George H. W. Bush and Boris Yeltsin agreed to pursue a follow-on accord to START I. START II, signed in January 1993, called for reducing deployed strategic arsenals to 3,000-3,500 warheads and banned the deployment of destabilizing multiple-warhead land-based missiles. START II would have counted warheads in roughly the same fashion as START I and, also like its predecessor, would have required the destruction of delivery vehicles but not warheads. The agreement's original implementation deadline was January 2003, ten years after signature, but a 1997 protocol moved this deadline to December 2007 because of the extended delay in ratification. Both the Senate and the Duma approved START II, but the treaty did not take effect because the Senate did not ratify the 1997 protocol and several ABM Treaty amendments, whose passage the Duma established as a condition for START II's entry into force. START II was effectively shelved as a result of the 2002 U.S. withdrawal from the ABM treaty.

START III Framework

In March 1997, Presidents Bill Clinton and Boris Yeltsin agreed to a framework for START III negotiations that included a reduction in deployed strategic warheads to 2,000-2,500. Significantly, in addition to requiring the destruction of delivery vehicles, START III negotiations were to address "the destruction of strategic nuclear warheads… to promote the irreversibility of deep reductions including prevention of a rapid increase in the number of warheads." Negotiations were supposed to begin after START II entered into force, which never happened.

SORT (Moscow Treaty)

On May 24, 2002, Presidents George W. Bush and Vladimir Putin signed the Strategic Offensive Reductions Treaty (SORT or Moscow Treaty) under which the United States and Russia reduced their strategic arsenals to 1,700-2,200 warheads each. The warhead limit took effect and expired on the same day, Dec. 31, 2012. Although the two sides did not agree on specific counting rules, the Bush administration asserted that the United States would reduce only warheads deployed on strategic delivery vehicles in active service (i.e., "operationally deployed" warheads) and would not count warheads removed from service and placed in storage or warheads on delivery vehicles undergoing overhaul or repair. The agreement's limits are similar to those envisioned for START III, but the treaty did not require the destruction of delivery vehicles, as START I and II did, or the destruction of warheads, as had been envisioned for START III. The treaty was approved by the Senate and Duma and entered into force on June 1, 2003. SORT was replaced by New START on Feb. 5, 2011.

New START

On April 8, 2010, the United States and Russia signed New START, a legally binding, verifiable agreement that limits each side to 1,550 strategic nuclear warheads deployed on 700 strategic delivery systems (ICBMs, SLBMs and heavy bombers) and limits deployed and non-deployed launchers to 800. The treaty-accountable warhead limit is 30 percent lower than the 2,200 upper limit of SORT, and the delivery vehicle limit is 50 percent lower than the 1,600 allowed in START I. The treaty has a verification regime that combines elements of START I with new elements tailored to New START. Measures under the treaty include on-site inspections and exhibitions, data exchanges and notifications related to strategic offensive arms and facilities covered by the treaty, and provisions to facilitate the use of national technical means for treaty monitoring. The treaty also provides for the continued exchange of telemetry (missile flight-test data on up to five tests per year) and does not meaningfully limit missile defenses or long-range conventional strike capabilities. The U.S. Senate approved New START on Dec. 22, 2010. The approval process of the Russian parliament (passage by both the State Duma and Federation Council) was completed Jan. 26, 2011. The treaty entered into force on Feb. 5, 2011, and both parties met the treaty's central limits by the Feb. 5, 2018, deadline for implementation. The United States and Russia agreed on Feb. 3, 2021, to extend New START by five years, as allowed by the treaty text, until Feb. 5, 2026.

Strategic Nuclear Arms Control Agreements

	SALT I	SALT II	INF Treaty	START I	START II	START III	SORT	New START
Status	Expired	Never Entered Into Force	Terminated	Expired	Never Entered Into Force	Never Negotiated	Replaced by New START	In Force
Deployed Warhead Limit	N/A	N/A	N/A	6,000	3,000-3,500	2,000-2,500	1,700-2,200	1,550
Deployed Delivery Vehicle Limit	US: 1,710 ICBMs & SLBMs USSR: 2,34	2,250	Prohibits ground-based missiles of 500-5,500 km range	1,600	N/A	N/A	N/A	700
Date Signed	May 26, 1972	June 18, 1979	Dec. 8, 1987	July 31, 1991	Jan. 3, 1993	N/A	May 24, 2002	April 8, 2010
Date Ratified, U.S.	Aug. 3, 1972	N/A	May 28, 1988	Oct. 1, 1992	Jan. 26, 1996	N/A	March 6, 2003	Dec. 22, 2010
Ratification Vote, U.S.	88-2	N/A	93-6	93-6	87-4	N/A	95-0	71-26
Date Entered Into Force	Oct. 3, 1972	N/A	June 1, 1988	Dec. 5, 1994	N/A	N/A	June 1, 2003	Feb. 5, 2011
Implementation Deadline	N/A	N/A	June 1, 1991	Dec. 5, 2001	N/A	N/A	N/A	Feb. 5, 2018
Expiration Date	Oct. 3, 1977	N/A	Aug. 2, 2019	Dec. 5, 2009	N/A	N/A	Feb. 5, 2011	Feb. 5, 2026*

*Initially set to expire Feb. 5, 2021, New START was extended by five years until 2026 as allowed by the treaty text.

Nonstrategic Nuclear Arms Control Measures

Intermediate-Range Nuclear Forces (INF) Treaty

Signed Dec. 8, 1987, the INF Treaty required the United States and the Soviet Union to verifiably eliminate all ground-launched ballistic and cruise missiles with ranges between 500 and 5,500 kilometers. Distinguished by its unprecedented, intrusive inspection regime, including on-site inspections, the INF Treaty laid the groundwork for verification of the subsequent START I. The INF Treaty entered into force June 1, 1988, and the two sides completed their reductions by June 1, 1991, destroying a total of 2,692 missiles. The agreement was multilateralized after the breakup of the Soviet Union, and current active participants in the agreement include the United States, Russia, Belarus, Kazakhstan, and Ukraine. Turkmenistan and Uzbekistan are also parties to the agreement but do not participate in treaty meetings or on-site inspections. The ban on intermediate-range missiles is of unlimited duration.

Both the United States and Russia have raised concerns about the other side's compliance with the INF Treaty. The United States first publicly charged Russia in 2014 with developing and testing a ground-launched cruise missile—the 9M729 missile—with a range that exceeds the INF Treaty limits.

Russia denies that it breached the agreement and has raised its own concerns about Washington's compliance. Moscow has charged that the United States is placing a missile defense launch system in Europe that could also be used to fire cruise missiles, using targets for missile defense tests with similar characteristics to INF Treaty-prohibited intermediate-range missiles, and is making armed drones that are equivalent to ground-launched cruise missiles. On Oct. 20, 2018 President Donald Trump announced his intention to "terminate" the agreement citing Russian noncompliance and concerns about China's missiles, and on Dec. 4, Secretary of State Mike Pompeo declared

Russia in "material breach" of the treaty. The Trump administration provided official notice to the other treaty states-parties on Feb. 2 that it would both suspend its obligations to the treaty and withdraw from the agreement in six months—per the treaty's terms—and "terminate" the agreement unless Russia returned to compliance by eliminating its ground-launched 9M729 missiles.

On Aug. 2, 2019, the United States formally withdrew from the INF Treaty.

Presidential Nuclear Initiatives

On Sept. 27, 1991, President George H. W. Bush announced that the United States would remove almost all U.S. tactical (nonstrategic) nuclear forces from deployment so that Russia could undertake similar actions, reducing the risk of nuclear proliferation as the Soviet Union dissolved. Specifically, Bush said the United States would eliminate all its nuclear artillery shells and short-range nuclear ballistic missile warheads and remove all nonstrategic nuclear warheads from surface ships, attack submarines, and land-based naval aircraft. Soviet leader Mikhail Gorbachev reciprocated on Oct. 5, pledging to eliminate all nuclear artillery munitions, nuclear warheads for tactical missiles, and nuclear landmines. He also pledged to withdraw all Soviet tactical naval nuclear weapons from deployment. Under these initiatives, the United States and Russia reduced their deployed nonstrategic stockpiles by an estimated 5,000 and 13,000 warheads, respectively. However, significant questions remain about Russian implementation of its pledges, and there is considerable uncertainty about the current state of Russia's tactical nuclear forces. The Defense Department estimates that Russia possesses roughly 2,000 non-strategic nuclear weapons and the numbers are expanding. The United States maintains several hundred nonstrategic B61 gravity bombs for delivery by short-range fighter aircraft.

Treaty for the Prohibition of Nuclear Weapons in Latin America and the Caribbean

Date in Force April 25, 1969

There are seven treaties for nuclear weapon free zones. These include 114 countries in Latin America and the Caribbean, the South Pacific, ASEAN, Central Asia, and Africa. There are also treaties covering Antarctica, Outer Space, and the Seabed. Such treaties ban the development, manufacturing, control, possession, testing, stationing, or transporting of nuclear weapons in a specified location. Such treaties also include mechanisms for verification and control in order to enforce obligations. The treaties cover 39% of the global population, while the nine nuclear weapon states have 47% of the world's people. There are 74 countries with 14% of the global population which are neither nuclear weapon states nor part of a nuclear weapons free zone. The treaty covering Latin America and the Caribbean is typical of all such treaties.

****

The Treaty

Preamble

In the name of their peoples and faithfully interpreting their desires and aspirations, the Governments of the States which sign the Treaty for the Prohibition of Nuclear Weapons in Latin America,

Desiring to contribute, so far as lies in their power, towards ending the armaments race, especially in the field of nuclear weapons, and towards strengthening a world at peace, based on the sovereign equality of States, mutual respect and good neighborliness,

Recalling that the United Nations General Assembly, in its Resolution 808 (IX), adopted unanimously as one of the three points of a coordinated programme of disarmament "the total prohibition of the use and manufacture of nuclear weapons and weapons of mass destruction of every type,"

Recalling that militarily denuclearized zones are not an end in themselves but rather a means for achieving general and complete disarmament at a later stage,

Recalling United Nations General Assembly Resolution 1911 (XVIII), which established that the measures that should be agreed upon for the denuclearization of Latin America should be taken "in the light of the principles of the Charter of the United Nations and of regional agreements,"

Recalling United Nations General Assembly Resolution 2028 (XX), which established the principle of an acceptable balance of mutual responsibilities and duties for the nuclear and non-nuclear powers, and

Recalling that the Charter of the Organization of American States proclaims that it is an essential purpose of the Organization to strengthen the peace and security of the hemisphere,

Convinced:

That the incalculable destructive power of nuclear weapons has made it imperative that the legal prohibition of war should be strictly observed in practice if the survival of civilization and of mankind itself is to be assured,

That nuclear weapon, whose terrible effects are suffered, indiscriminately and inexorably, by military forces and civilian population alike, constitute, through the persistence of the radioactivity they release, an attack on the integrity of the human species and ultimately may even render the whole earth uninhabitable,

That general and complete disarmament under effective international control is a vital matter which all the peoples of the world equally demand,

That the proliferation of nuclear weapons, which seems inevitable unless States, in the exercise of their sovereign rights, impose restrictions on themselves in order to prevent it, would make any agreement on disarmament enormously difficult and would increase the danger of the outbreak of a nuclear conflagration,

That the establishment of militarily denuclearized zones is closely linked with the maintenance of peace and security in the respective regions,

That the military denuclearization of vast geographical zones, adopted by the sovereign decision of the States comprised therein, will exercise a beneficial influence on other regions where similar conditions exist,

That the privileged situation of the signatory States, whose territories are wholly free from nuclear weapons, imposes upon them the inescapable duty of preserving that situation both in their own interest and for the good of mankind,

That the existence of nuclear weapons in any country of Latin America would make it a target for possible nuclear attacks and would inevitably set off, throughout the region, a ruinous race in nuclear weapons which would involve the unjustifiable diversion, for warlike purposes, of the limited resources required for economic and social development,

That the foregoing reasons, together with the traditional peace-loving outlook of Latin America, give rise to an inescapable necessity that nuclear energy should be used in that region exclusively for peaceful purposes, and that the Latin American countries should use their right to the greatest and most equitable possible access to this new source of energy in order to expedite the economic and social development of their peoples,

Convinced finally:

That the military denuclearization of Latin America — being understood to mean the undertaking entered into internationally in this Treaty to keep their territories forever free from nuclear weapons — will constitute a measure which will spare their peoples from the squandering of their limited resources on nuclear armaments and will protect them against possible nuclear attacks on their territories, and will also constitute a significant contribution towards preventing the proliferation of nuclear weapons and a powerful factor for general and complete disarmament, and

That Latin America, faithful to its tradition of universality, must not only endeavour to banish from its homelands the scourge of a nuclear war, but must also strive to promote the well-being and advancement of its peoples, at the same time co-operating in the fulfillment of the ideals of mankind, that is to say, in the consolidation of a permanent peace based on equal rights, economic fairness and social justice for all, in accordance with the principles and purposes set forth in the Charter of the United Nations and in the Charter of the Organization of American States.

Have agreed as follows:

Obligations

Article 1

1. The Contracting Parties hereby undertake to use exclusively for peaceful purposes the nuclear material and facilities which are under their jurisdiction, and to prohibit and prevent in their respective territories:

(a) The testing, use, manufacture, production or acquisition by any means whatsoever of any nuclear weapons, by the Parties themselves, directly or indirectly, on behalf of anyone else or in any other way, and

(b) The receipt, storage, installation, deployment and any form of possession of any nuclear weapons, directly or indirectly, by the Parties themselves, by anyone on their behalf or in any other way.

2. The Contracting Parties also undertake to refrain from engaging in, encouraging or authorizing, directly or indirectly, or in any way participating in the testing, use, manufacture, production, possession or control of any nuclear weapon.

Definition of the Contracting Parties

Article 2

For the purposes of this Treaty, the Contracting Parties are those for whom the Treaty is in force.

Definition of territory

Article 3

For the purposes of this Treaty, the term "territory" shall include the territorial sea, air space and any other space over which the State exercises sovereignty in accordance with its own legislation.

Zone of application

Article 4

1. The zone of application of this Treaty is the whole of the territories for which the Treaty is in force.

2. Upon fulfillment of the requirements of article 28, paragraph 1, the zone of application of this Treaty shall also be that which is situated in the western hemisphere within the following limits (except the continental part of the territory of the United States of America and its territorial waters): starting at a point located at 35o north latitude, 75° west longitude; from this point directly southward to a point at 30° north latitude, 75° west longitude; from there, directly eastward to a point at 30° north latitude, 50° west longitude; from there, along a loxodromic line to a point at 5° north latitude, 20° west longitude; from there directly southward to a point 60° south latitude, 20° west longitude; from there, directly westward to a point at 60° south latitude, 115° west longitude; from there, directly northward to a point at 0 latitude, 115° west longitude; from there, along a loxodromic line to a point at 35° north latitude, 150° west longitude; from there, directly eastward to a point at 35° north latitude, 75° west longitude.

Definition of nuclear weapons

Article 5

For the purposes of this Treaty, a nuclear weapon is any device which is capable of releasing nuclear energy in an uncontrolled manner and which has a group of characteristics that are appropriate for use for warlike purposes. An instrument that may be used for the transport or propulsion of the device is not included in this definition if it is separable from the device and not an indivisible part thereof.

Meeting of signatories

Article 6

At the request of any of the signatory States or if the Agency established by article 7 should so decide, a meeting of all the signatories may be convoked to consider in common questions which may affect the very essence of this instrument, including possible amendments to it. In either case, the meeting will be convoked by the General Secretary.

Organization

Article 7

1. In order to ensure compliance with the obligations of this Treaty, the Contracting Parties hereby establish an international organization to be known as the "Agency for the Prohibition of Nuclear Weapons in Latin America and the Caribbean," hereinafter referred to as "the Agency." Only the Contracting Parties shall be affected by its decisions.

2. The Agency shall be responsible for the holding of periodic or extraordinary consultations among Member States on matters relating to the purposes, measures and procedures set forth in this Treaty and to the supervision of compliance with the obligations arising therefrom.

3. The Contracting Parties agree to extend to the Agency full and prompt cooperation in accordance with the provisions of this Treaty, of any agreements they may conclude with the Agency and of any agreements the Agency may conclude with any other international organization or body.

4. The headquarters of the Agency shall be in Mexico City.

Organs

Article 8

1. There are hereby established as principal organs of the Agency a General Conference, a Council and a Secretariat.

2. Such subsidiary organs as are considered necessary by the General Conference may be established within the purview of this Treaty.

The General Conference

Article 9

1. The General Conference, the supreme organ of the Agency, shall be composed of all the Contracting Parties; it shall hold regular sessions every two years, and may also hold special sessions whenever this Treaty so provides or, in the opinion of the Council, the circumstances so require.

2. The General Conference:

(a) May consider and decide on any matters or questions covered by this Treaty, within the limits thereof, including those referring to powers and functions of any organ provided for in this Treaty.

(b) Shall establish procedures for the control system to ensure observance of this Treaty in accordance with its provisions.

(c) Shall elect the Members of the Council and the General Secretary.

(d) May remove the General Secretary from office if the proper functioning of the Agency so requires.

(e) Shall receive and consider the biennial and special reports submitted by the Council and the General Secretary.

(f) Shall initiate and consider studies designed to facilitate the optimum fulfillment of the aims of this Treaty, without prejudice to the power of the General Secretary independently to carry out similar studies for submission to and consideration by the Conference.

(g) Shall be the organ competent to authorize the conclusion of agreements with Governments and other international organizations and bodies.

3. The General Conference shall adopt the Agency's budget and fix the scale of financial contributions to be paid by Member States, taking into account the systems and criteria used for the same purpose by the United Nations.

4. The General Conference shall elect its officers for each session and may establish such subsidiary organs as it deems necessary for the performance of its functions.

5. Each Member of the Agency shall have one vote. The decisions of the General Conference shall be taken by a two-thirds majority of the Members present and voting in the case of matters relating to the control system and measures referred to in article 20, the admission of new Members, the election or removal of the General Secretary, adoption of the budget and matters related thereto. Decisions on other matters, as well as procedural questions and also determination of which questions must be decided by a two-thirds majority, shall be taken by a simple majority of the Members present and voting.

6. The General Conference shall adopt its own rules of procedure.

The Council

Article 10

1. The Council shall be composed of five Members of the Agency elected by the General Conference from among the Contracting Parties, due account being taken of equitable geographic distribution.

2. The Members of the Council shall be elected for a term of four years. However, in the first election three will be elected for two years. Outgoing Members may not be reelected for the following period unless the limited number of States for which the Treaty is in force so requires.

3. Each Member of the Council shall have one representative.

4. The Council shall be so organized as to be able to function continuously.

5. In addition to the functions conferred upon it by this Treaty and to those which may be assigned to it by the General Conference, the Council shall, through the General Secretary, ensure the proper operation of the control system in accordance with the provisions of this Treaty and with the decisions adopted by the General Conference.

6. The Council shall submit an annual report on its work to the General Conference as well as such special reports as it deems necessary or which the General Conference requests of it.

7. The Council shall elect its officers for each session.

8. The decisions of the Council shall be taken by a simple majority of its Members present and voting.

9. The Council shall adopt its own rules of procedure.

The Secretariat

Article 11

1. The Secretariat shall consist of a General Secretary, who shall be the chief administrative officer of the Agency, and of such staff as the Agency may require. The term of office of the General Secretary shall be four years and he may be re-elected for a single additional term. The General Secretary may not be a national of the country in which the Agency has its headquarters. In case the office of General Secretary becomes vacant, a new election shall be held to fill the office for the remainder of the term.

2. The staff of the Secretariat shall be appointed by the General Secretary, in accordance with rules laid down by the General Conference.

3. In addition to the functions conferred upon him by this Treaty and to those which may be assigned to him by the General Conference, the General Secretary shall ensure, as provided by article 10, paragraph 5, the proper operation of the control system established by

this Treaty, in accordance with the provisions of the Treaty and the decisions taken by the General Conference.

4. The General Secretary shall act in that capacity in all meetings of the General Conference and of the Council and shall make an annual report to both bodies on the work of the Agency and any special reports requested by the General Conference or the Council or which the General Secretary may deem desirable.

5. The General Secretary shall establish the procedures for distributing to all Contracting Parties information received by the Agency from governmental sources and such information from non-governmental sources as may be of interest to the Agency.

6. In the performance of their duties the General Secretary and the staff shall not seek or receive instructions from any Government or from any other authority external to the Agency and shall refrain from any action which might reflect on their position as international officials responsible only to the Agency; subject to their responsibility to the Agency, they shall not disclose any industrial secrets or other confidential information coming to their knowledge by reason of their official duties in the Agency.

7. Each of the Contracting Parties undertakes to respect the exclusively international character of the responsibilities of the General Secretary and the staff and not to seek to influence them in the discharge of their responsibilities.

Control system

Article 12

1. For the purpose of verifying compliance with the obligations entered into by the Contracting Parties in accordance with article 1, a control system shall be established which shall be put into effect in accordance with the provisions of articles 13-18 of this Treaty.

2. The control system shall be used in particular for the purpose of verifying:

(a) That devices, services and facilities intended for peaceful uses of nuclear energy are not used in the testing or manufacture of nuclear weapons,

(b) That none of the activities prohibited in article 1 of this Treaty are carried out in the territory of the Contracting Parties with nuclear materials or weapons introduced from abroad, and

(c) That explosions for peaceful purposes are compatible with article 18 of this Treaty.

IAEA safeguards

Article 13

Each Contracting Party shall negotiate multilateral or bilateral agreements with the International Atomic Energy Agency for the application of its safeguards to its nuclear activities. Each Contracting Party shall initiate negotiations within a period of 180 days after the date of the deposit of its instrument of ratification of this Treaty. These agreements shall enter into force, for each Party, not later than eighteen months after the date of the initiation of such negotiations except in case of unforeseen circumstances or force majeure.

Reports of the Parties

Article 14

1. The Contracting Parties shall submit to the Agency and to the International Atomic Energy Agency, for their information, semi-annual reports stating that no activity prohibited under this Treaty has occurred in their respective territories.

2. The Contracting Parties shall simultaneously transmit to the Agency a copy of any report they may submit to the International Atomic Energy Agency which relates to matters that are the subject of this Treaty and to the application of safeguards.

3. The Contracting Parties shall also transmit to the Organization of American States, for its information, any reports that may be of

interest to it, in accordance with the obligations established by the Inter-American System.

Special reports requested by the General Secretary

Article 15

1. With the authorization of the Council, the General Secretary may request any of the Contracting Parties to provide the Agency with complementary or supplementary information regarding any event or circumstance connected with compliance with this Treaty, explaining his reasons. The Contracting Parties undertake to co-operate promptly and fully with the General Secretary.

2. The General Secretary shall inform the Council and the Contracting Parties forthwith of such requests and of the respective replies.

Special inspections

Article 16

1. The International Atomic Energy Agency and the Council established by this Treaty have the power of carrying out special inspections in the following cases:

(a) In the case of the International Atomic Energy Agency, in accordance with the agreements referred to in article 13 of this Treaty;

(b) In the case of the Council:

(i) When so requested, the reasons for the request being stated, by any Party which suspects that some activity prohibited by this Treaty has been carried out or is about to be carried out, either in the territory of any other Party or in any other place on such latter Party's behalf, the Council shall immediately arrange for such an inspection in accordance with article 10, paragraph 5.

(ii) When requested by any Party which has been suspected of or charged with having violated this Treaty, the Council shall immediately arrange for the special inspection requested in accordance with article 10, paragraph 5.

The above requests will be made to the Council through the General Secretary.

2. The costs and expenses of any special inspection carried out under paragraph 1, sub-paragraph (b), sections (i) and (ii) of this article shall be borne by the requesting Party or Parties, except where the Council concludes on the basis of the report on the special inspection that, in view of the circumstances existing in the case, such costs and expenses should be borne by the agency.

3. The General Conference shall formulate the procedures for the organization and execution of the special inspections carried out in accordance with paragraph 1, sub-paragraph (b), sections (i) and (ii) of this article.

4. The Contracting Parties undertake to grant the inspectors carrying out such special inspections full and free access to all places and all information which may be necessary for the performance of their duties and which are directly and intimately connected with the suspicion of violation of this Treaty. If so requested by the authorities of the Contracting Party in whose territory the inspection is carried out, the inspectors designated by the General Conference shall be accompanied by representatives of said authorities, provided that this does not in any way delay or hinder the work of the inspectors.

5. The Council shall immediately transmit to all the Parties, through the General Secretary, a copy of any report resulting from special inspections.

6. Similarly, the Council shall send through the General Secretary to the Secretary-General of the United Nations, for transmission to the United Nations Security Council and General Assembly, and to the Council of the Organization of American States, for its information, a copy of any report resulting from any special inspection carried out in accordance with paragraph 1, sub-paragraph (b), sections (i) and (ii) of this article.

7. The Council may decide, or any Contracting Party may request, the convening of a special session of the General Conference for the purpose of considering the reports resulting from any special inspection. In such a case, the General Secretary shall take immediate steps to convene the special session requested.

8. The General Conference, convened in special session under this article, may make recommendations to the Contracting Parties and submit reports to the Secretary-General of the United Nations to be transmitted to the United Nations Security Council and the General Assembly.

Use of nuclear energy for peaceful purposes

Article 17

Nothing in the provisions of this Treaty shall prejudice the rights of the Contracting Parties, in conformity with this Treaty, to use nuclear energy for peaceful purposes, in particular for their economic development and social progress.

Explosions for peaceful purposes

Article 18

1. The Contracting Parties may carry out explosions of nuclear devices for peaceful purposes — including explosions which involve devices similar to those used in nuclear weapons — or collaborate with third parties for the same purpose, provided that they do so in accordance with the provisions of this article and the other articles of the Treaty, particularly articles 1 and 5.

2. Contracting Parties intending to carry out, or to cooperate in carrying out, such an explosion shall notify the Agency and the International Atomic Energy Agency, as far in advance as the circumstances require, of the date of the explosion and shall at the same time provide the following information:

(a) The nature of the nuclear device and the source from which it was obtained,

(b) The place and purpose of the planned explosion,

(c) The procedures which will be followed in order to comply with paragraph 3 of this article,

(d) The expected force of the device, and

(e) The fullest possible information on any possible radioactive fall-out that may result from the explosion or explosions, and measures which will be taken to avoid danger to the population, flora, fauna and territories of any other Party or Parties.

3. The General Secretary and the technical personnel designated by the Council and the International Atomic Energy Agency may observe all the preparations, including the explosion of the device, and shall have unrestricted access to any area in the vicinity of the site of the explosion in order to ascertain whether the device and the procedures followed during the explosion are in conformity with the information supplied under paragraph 2 of this article and the other provisions of this Treaty.

4. The Contracting Parties may accept the collaboration of third parties for the purposes set forth in paragraph 1 of the present article, in accordance with paragraphs 2 and 3 thereof.

Relations with other international organizations

Article 19

1. The Agency may conclude such agreements with the International Atomic Energy Agency as are authorized by the General Conference and as it considers likely to facilitate the efficient operation of the control system established by this Treaty.

2. The Agency may also enter into relations with any international organization or body, especially any which may be established in the future to supervise disarmament or measures for the control of armaments in any part of the world.

3. The Contracting Parties may, if they see fit, request the advice of the Inter-American Nuclear Energy Commission on all technical

matters connected with the application of this Treaty with which the Commission is competent to deal under its Statute.

Measures in the event of violation of the Treaty

Article 20

1. The General Conference shall take note of all cases in which, in its opinion, any Contracting Party is not complying fully with its obligations under this Treaty and shall draw the matter to the attention of the Party concerned, making such recommendations as it deems appropriate.

2. If, in its opinion, such non-compliance constitutes a violation of this Treaty which might endanger peace and security, the General Conference shall report thereon simultaneously to the United Nations Security Council and the General Assembly through the Secretary-General of the United Nations, and to the Council of the Organization of American States. The General Conference shall likewise report to the International Atomic Energy Agency for such purposes as are relevant in accordance with its Statute.

United Nations and Organization of American States

Article 21

None of the provisions of this Treaty shall be construed as impairing the rights and obligations of the Parties under the Charter of the United Nations or, in the case of States Members of the Organization of American States, under existing regional treaties.

Privileges and immunities

Article 22

1. The Agency shall enjoy in the territory of each of the Contracting Parties such legal capacity and such privileges and immunities as may be necessary for the exercise of its functions and the fulfillment of its purposes.

2. Representatives of the Contracting Parties accredited to the Agency and officials of the Agency shall similarly enjoy such privileges and immunities as are necessary for the performance of their functions.

3. The Agency may conclude agreements with the Contracting Parties with a view to determining the details of the application of paragraphs 1 and 2 of this article.

Notification of other agreements

Article 23

Once this Treaty has entered into force, the Secretariat shall be notified immediately of any international agreement concluded by any of the Contracting Parties on matters with which this Treaty is concerned; the Secretariat shall register it and notify the other Contracting Parties.

Settlement of disputes

Article 24

Unless the Parties concerned agree on another mode of peaceful settlement, any question or dispute concerning the interpretation or application of this Treaty which is not settled shall be referred to the International Court of Justice with the prior consent of the Parties to the controversy.

Signature

Article 25

1. This Treaty shall be open indefinitely for signature by:
(a) All the Latin American Republics, and
(b) All other sovereign States situated in their entirety south of latitude 35° north in the western hemisphere; and, except as provided

in paragraph 2 of this article, all such States which become sovereign, when they have been admitted by the General Conference.

2. The General Conference shall not take any decision regarding the admission of a political entity part or all of whose territory is the subject, prior to the date when this Treaty is opened for signature, of a dispute or claim between an extra-continental country and one or more Latin American States, so long as the dispute has not been settled by peaceful means.

Ratification and deposit

Article 26

1. This Treaty shall be subject to ratification by signatory States in accordance with their respective constitutional procedures.

2. This Treaty and the instruments of ratification shall be deposited with the Government of the Mexican United States, which is hereby designated the Depositary Government.

3. The Depositary Government shall send certified copies of this Treaty to the Governments of signatory States and shall notify them of the deposit of each instrument of ratification.

Reservations

Article 27

This Treaty shall not be subject to reservations.

Entry into force

Article 28

1. Subject to the provisions of paragraph 2 of this article, this Treaty shall enter into force among the States that have ratified it as soon as the following requirements have been met:

(a) Deposit of the instruments of ratification of this Treaty with the Depositary Government by the Governments of the States mentioned in article 25 which are in existence on the date when this Treaty is opened for signature and which are not affected by the provisions of article 25, paragraph 2;

(b) Signature and ratification of Additional Protocol I annexed to this Treaty by all extra-continental or continental States having de jure or de facto international responsibility for territories situated in the zone of application of the Treaty;

(c) Signature and ratification of the Additional Protocol II annexed to this Treaty by all powers possessing nuclear weapons;

(d) Conclusion of bilateral or multilateral agreements on the application of Safeguards System of the International Atomic Energy Agency in accordance with article 13 of this Treaty.

2. All signatory States shall have the imprescriptible right to waive, wholly or in part, the requirements laid down in the preceding paragraph. They may do so by means of a declaration which shall be annexed to their respective instrument of ratification and which may be formulated at the time of deposit of the instrument or subsequently. For those States which exercise this right, this Treaty shall enter into force upon deposit of the declaration, or as soon as those requirements have been met which have not been expressly waived.

3. As soon as this Treaty has entered into force in accordance with the provisions of paragraph 2 for eleven States, the Depositary Government shall convene a preliminary meeting of those States in order that the Agency may be set up and commence its work.

4. After the entry into force of this Treaty for all the countries of the zone, the rise of a new power possessing nuclear weapons shall have the effect of suspending the execution of this Treaty for those countries which have ratified it without waiving requirements of paragraph 1, sub-paragraph (c) of this article, and which request such suspension; the Treaty shall remain suspended until the new power, on its own initiative or upon request by the General Conference, ratifies the annexed Additional Protocol II.

Amendments

Article 29

1. Any Contracting Party may propose amendments to this Treaty and shall submit its proposals to the Council through the General Secretary, who shall transmit them to all the other Contracting Parties and, in addition, to all other signatories in accordance with article 6. The Council, through the General Secretary, shall immediately following the meeting of signatories convene a special session of the General Conference to examine the proposals made, for the adoption of which a two-thirds majority of the Contracting Parties present and voting shall be required.

2. Amendments adopted shall enter into force as soon as the requirements set forth in article 28 of this Treaty have been complied with.

Duration and denunciation

Article 30

1. This Treaty shall be of a permanent nature and shall remain in force indefinitely, but any Party may denounce it by notifying the General Secretary of the Agency if, in the opinion of the denouncing State, there have arisen or may arise circumstances connected with the content of this Treaty or of the annexed Additional Protocols I and II which affect its supreme interests or the peace and security of one or more Contracting Parties.

2. The denunciation shall take effect three months after the delivery to the General Secretary of the Agency of the notification by the Government of the signatory State concerned. The General Secretary shall immediately communicate such notification to the other Contracting Parties and to the Secretary-General of the United Nations for the information of the United Nations Security Council and the General Assembly. He shall also communicate it to the Secretary-General of the Organization of American States.

Authentic texts and registration

Article 31

This Treaty, of which the Spanish, Chinese, English, French, Portuguese and Russian texts are equally authentic, shall be registered by the Depositary Government in accordance with article 102 of the United Nations Charter. The Depositary Government shall notify the Secretary-General of the United Nations of the signatures, ratification and amendments relating to this Treaty and shall communicate them to the Secretary-General of the Organization of American States for its information.

Transitional Article

Denunciation of the declaration referred to article 28, paragraph 2, shall be subject to the same procedures as the denunciation of this Treaty, except that it will take effect on the date of delivery of the respective notification.

Gar Pardy

India and Pakistan–Agreement on the Prohibition of Attacks against Nuclear Installations and Facilities

Effective 1991, First Exchange of Information, January 1, 1992

The agreement provides for India and Pakistan to annually exchange information on their nuclear installations. The exchanges are in accordance with Article-II of the Agreement on Prohibition of Attacks against Nuclear Installations and Facilities between Pakistan and India.

According to the agreement, both countries have to inform each other of their nuclear facilities. The agreement was signed in 1988 and ratified in 1991. There have been 31 consecutive exchanges. The first exchange was on January 1, 1992.

The agreement covers nuclear power and research reactors, fuel fabrication, uranium enrichment, isotopes separation, and reprocessing facilities, as well as any other installations with fresh or irradiated nuclear fuel and materials in any form and establishments storing significant quantities of radioactive materials. All are included under the umbrella term "nuclear installations and facilities".

Index

A

acute radiation syndrome (ARS), 132–133
African National Union (ANU), 74
Akizuki, Tatsuichiro, 131
Alamogordo Trinity Test Site, 101
Algeria, 38–42, 71, 162–164, 188
Amendments, 232–233
American Agreements on Nuclear Weapons, 152, 155
American nuclear systems, 30
Anami, Korechika, 134
annihilation, 28, 87
Anti-Ballistic Missile Treaty (ABM), 153, 236, 238
anti-Russian, 38
application, Zone of, 247, 261
Argentina, 17, 29, 62, 71, 73, 150, 185, 196
Articles of the Treaty, 221
    Article IV, 221
    Article IX, 221
    Article V, 221
    Article VI, 221
    Article VII, 221
    Article VIII, 221
    Article X, 221
    Article XI, 221
    Article XIII, 221
    Article XIV, 221
    Article XV, 221
    Article XVI, 221
    Article XVII, 221
Atom, Nucleus, Sub Atomic Particles, 201
Atomic Age, 14, 19, 25, 111, 144, 190
atomic energy, 19, 23–24, 38, 40–41, 210–214, 227–228, 253–258
Atomic Energy Act, 21, 38, 108
Atomic Heritage Foundation, 123
Authentic texts, 235, 263

B

Banbridge, Kenneth, 34, 115
On the Beach, 182
Becquerel, Henri, 84
Begin, Menachem, 64
Bergmann, Ernst David, 172
Betts, Richard, 75
Bhabha Atomic Research Centre, 50, 195
Bhabha, Homi, 50

265

Bhabha's death, 50
Biden, Joe, 59
Biological Weapons Convention of 1975, 181
Bleu, Gerboise, 41
Bonner, Yelena, 36
Brazil, 29, 183
Bush, George H. W., 237, 242

C

Canada, 16–17, 19–23, 140–141, 158–159, 184–188, 194–197
Canada India Reactor Utility Services (CIRUS), 50, 52
Caron, Robert, 124
Carter, Jimmy, 176–177, 237
catastrophic humanitarian consequences, 223
Chain and Nuclear Chain Reactions, 201
Chalk River, 22, 38, 41, 102, 176
Charter of the United Nations, 65, 209, 212, 217, 222, 224, 234, 244, 246, 258
Chernobyl, Ukraine, 132, 177
Chiang Kai-shek, 134
China, 15–17, 24–33, 38, 44–52, 148–150
China's National Nuclear Corporation (CNNC), 174
Chirac, Jacques, 43
Clinton, Bill, 238
Clinton Engineering Works, 100
Cockcroft, John, 85
Cognizant, 223
Cold War, 24, 29–30, 122, 182–183

Comprehensive Nuclear Test Ban Treaty (CNTBT), 31, 37, 43, 149–150, 155, 195, 200, 220–221
Comprehensive Nuclear-Test-Ban Treaty Organization (CTBTO), 220
Conflicts with, 29
  China/Taiwan, 29
  Korea/China, 29
  Soviet Union/Cuba, 29
  Vietnam/China, 29
Contracting Parties, definition of the, 246
Control system, 121, 249–252, 257
Crozet Islands, 56
Cuban Missile Crisis, 27, 152

D

de Gaulle, Charle, 41, 188
Declarations, 68, 226–227, 232
Deeply concerned, 223
demonstration, 36, 46, 87, 110, 120
denunciation, 262–263
Depleted uranium (DU), 167, 202–204
deposit, 197–198, 208, 216–217, 233–234, 253, 260–261
Depositary, 208–209, 216–218, 221, 260–261, 263
Devastation, 124, 211
disputes, Settlement of, 221, 233, 259
Donne, John, 101, 114
Dulles, John Foster, 25
Duration, 107, 178, 209, 221, 235, 241, 262

E

East Asia, 46–47, 138
Egypt, 61–62, 74, 150–151, 189, 220
Einstein, Albert, 19, 82, 88, 92–93, 120
Eisenhower, Dwight, 144
Enola Gay, 122–123, 128
environmental remediation, 230–231
escalation, 26, 87
Eshkol, Levi, 55

F

Fantappie, Maria, 61
Farrell, Thomas, 111, 115
Fermi, Enrico, 19, 86, 93, 95, 98, 119
Feynman, Richard, 82
First Atomic Bomb, 20, 101, 116, 123, 161
First Exchange of Information, 264
Force de Frappe, 39, 41
France, 15, 26, 28, 38–43, 55–56, 69–71, 162–163, 167–168
Frisch, Otto, 87, 96, 109
frustration, 71, 87
Fukushima Daiichi Nuclear Power Plant, 178
Full Fuzing Option (FUFO) weapon, 168
Full Life: Reflections at Ninety book, 176

G

the Gadget, 111–112, 116
Gamow, George, 85, 109
Gandhi, Indira, 50
General Conference, 249–252, 255–262
Germany, 19, 22, 94–97, 100, 103–107, 109, 113, 119–120, 165–166
Ghaddafi, Muammar, President, 66–67, 70
global inventory, 15, 171
global non-proliferation regime, 31
Goldschmidt, Bertrand, 41
Great Bear Lake, 197–198
Groves, Leslie R., 106
Guéron, Jules, 41

H

Hahn, Otto, 35, 85, 87, 109, 203
Ham, Paul, 143
Hanford Engineer Works Reactor, 101
Harry S. Truman, 90
Heavy Water, 22, 41, 50, 55, 97, 99, 102–105, 202
Heavy Water Production Plants, 102
highly enriched uranium (HEU), 62–63, 205
Hirohito, Emperor, 128, 134, 136–137, 139
Hiroshima, 14, 18–19, 121–124, 128–136
Hiroshima and Nagasaki Bombings, Aftermath of, 133
historic mistake, 58

I

IAEA, 52, 58, 62–68, 73–74, 77–78, 147–148
IAEA safeguards, 52, 62–63, 67, 73, 148, 196, 253
immunities, 258–259
imperial rescript, 137
implosion methods, 166
India, 15–17, 50–52, 148–150, 153, 162–163, 170–171, 191–192, 195–196
India-Pakistan Agreement, 200
Indian program, 51, 171
Indo-China empire, 26
Institute for Defense Analyses (IDA), 55
intercontinental ballistic missiles (ICBM), 30, 45, 153, 161–162, 166, 169, 239–240
Interim Committee, 119–120
Intermediate-Range Nuclear Forces (INF) Treaty, 154, 157, 240–242
International Atomic Energy Agency (IAEA), 62–68, 73–74, 77–78, 227–228, 253–258
international humanitarian law, 223–224
international organizations, 215, 232, 250, 257
International Red Cross and Red Crescent Movement, 226
Iran, 30–32, 58–61, 72–74, 149–151, 189–191, 220
Iraq, 29–30, 58, 61–64, 69, 73
Iraqi nuclear activities, 63
Islamic Revolutionary Guards Corps (IRGC), 59
Isotopes, 74, 88, 96, 167, 201–205, 264
Israel, 15–16, 28–29, 53–66, 72–75, 148–151, 170–171, 188–191
Israeli and North Korean programs, 28
Israeli Atomic Energy, 56, 76, 172
Israeli nuclear weapons program, 61

J

Japanese Army, 90, 141
Japan's self-preservation, 138
JCPOA process, 190
Joint Comprehensive Plan of Action (JCPOA), 58–61, 189–191
Joliot-Curie, Frédéric, 103, 107
Joliot-Curie, Irène, 40, 103, 107
Joly, Melanie, 196

K

Kamysh, Markiyan, 178
Karachi Nuclear Power Plant (KANUPP), 52
Kazakh Soviet Socialist Republic, 35
Kazakhstan, 87, 163–164, 183, 186–187, 196, 237, 241
Kelly, Harry, 126
Kennedy, President, 27
Khamenei, Ayatollah Ali, 60
Khan Research Laboratories (KRL), 51

Kim Il-Sung, 142
Kim Jong-un, 47, 49
Kissinger, Henry, 56
Kowalski, Lew, 41
Kramer, Stanley, 183
Kurchatov, Igor V., 35
Kuwait, 73

L

Lawrence, Ernest, 96, 119
Lehrer, Tom, 18, 25
Libya, 29–30, 51, 61, 66–71, 149
Linde, Ann, 186
Little Boy, 18, 114, 116, 121–123, 126, 129
Los Alamos Laboratory, 100, 102, 116

M

MacArthur, Douglas, 132, 140–141
Manhattan Project, 90–111
Marianas Islands, 116
Marshall, George C, 95
material breach, 242
McArthur River, 198
Meir, Golda, 56
Meitner, Lise, 87, 109
Military Balance 2010, 45
Mindful, 139, 223
Mining, Eldorado, 198
modernize Canadian diplomacy, 196
Monte Bello Islands, 39, 188
Moscow, 16, 26, 76, 127, 134–135, 218, 236–238, 241
Moskva, 79

mutually assured destruction (MAD), 166, 182

N

Nagasaki, 14, 18–19, 122, 128–133, 136, 143, 161, 166, 168
Naka, Midori, 133
National implementation, 230
National Research Council (NRC), 20–22, 98–99
Natural Uranium, 66, 95–97, 99, 102, 107, 202–205
Nazis, 19
New Mexico, 18, 35, 54, 100–101, 111, 116, 163
New Strategic Arms Reduction Treaty, 192
nine nuclear weapons states, 14–15, 158, 180–181
1945 nuclear explosion, 19
1996 Comprehensive Test Ban Treaty (CTBT), 31, 33, 43, 164, 191, 220–221
1970 Non-Proliferation Treaty, 16, 62, 73, 157, 184
1963 Limited Test Ban Treaty, 163
Nobel Peace Prize non-proliferation, 36
Non-Proliferation of Nuclear Weapons Treaty (NPT), 62, 147–150, 157–160, 172, 179–180, 182, 184, 186, 189–191
Non-Proliferation Efforts, 65, 147
North Atlantic Treaty Organization (NATO), 17, 69–70, 76, 79, 158–159, 169, 183–187

269

North Korea, 15–16, 24–25, 28–30, 47–49, 51, 65–67, 86, 170–171
Nuclear Age, 19, 173, 179
Nuclear Critical Event, 204
Nuclear Disarmament, 16, 157, 179–186, 212, 215, 223–225
nuclear fission, The discovery of, 87
Nuclear Nonproliferation Treaty (NPT), 15–16, 66–67, 148–150, 158–160, 172, 179–180, 190–191
Nuclear Power Reactor, 41, 46, 52, 77, 195, 204
Nuclear Reactors, 41, 64, 173–175, 178, 194, 204
Nuclear Suppliers Group (NSG), 17, 149, 174, 191–192, 196
Nuclear Test Ban Treaty, 43, 148–149, 152–153, 155, 195, 200
Nuclear Testing of 1998, 16
Nuclear Umbrellas, 159
nuclear weapons
  catastrophic consequences of, 223
  definition of, 223
  the Elimination of, 179–194
  Free Zones, 45, 158, 200, 225, 243
U.S. Nuclear Weapons: The Secret History, 166–167
nuclear weapons (hibakusha), 179–207, 209–213
nuclear weapons states, 14–15, 149–150, 158–162, 173–174, 180–183

O

Obama, President, 31–32
Obligations, 62, 66, 180, 196, 213, 227–230, 235, 242–243
Olivi, Fred J., 130
Oman, 73
Oppenheimer, J Robert, 179
Oppenheimer, Robert, 34, 36, 114, 119, 143, 179
Organs, 249–250
Ota River Delta, 123
Ottawa, 17, 23, 98, 103, 108, 176–177, 181

P

Pacific Proving Grounds, 162
Pakistan, 15–17, 44–45, 50–52, 66–68, 72–73, 148–150, 162–163, 191–192, 195–196
Pakistan's nuclear weapons program, 50, 67
Parsons, William, 123
Partial Nuclear Test Ban Treaty of 1963, 148
Partial Test Ban Treaty (PTBT), 163, 166, 206
peaceful purposes, Explosions for, 172, 200, 219, 253, 256
Peierls, Rudolf, 96
Perry, William, 31
Plutonium-239, 204
Polsby, Nelson W, 197
pre-emptive military operation, 79
Preamble, 207, 212, 214, 216, 220, 243
prejudice the prerogatives, 136
Prince Edward Islands, 56
Privileges, 258–259

Prohibitions, 226
public conscience, 224–225
Putin, President, 37, 75, 79–81

Q

Qahafi regime, 70
Quebec Conference, 99

R

radiation implosion, 36
Rajasthan Atomic Power Project, 52
Ratification, 75, 214, 216–217, 220–221, 233–234, 260–261, 263
Regan, Ronald, 61
registration, 263
Rescript term, 137
Reservations, 195, 221, 234, 260
retaliation, 87, 105, 145
Revolution of Libya, 66
Roosevelt, Franklin D., 19, 82, 88, 90, 92, 95, 118, 120
Russia, 15–16, 75–81, 127, 135–136, 154–159, 167–174
Russia-Ukraine War, 75
Russian invasion of Ukraine, 33, 37, 76, 187, 192
Russophobia, 79

S

Safeguards, 24, 52, 62–63, 67–68, 148–149, 175, 196–197, 210–211
SALT II, 153, 236–237, 240
Sato, Naotake, 134
Saudi Arabia, 72–74, 183
Scandia National Laboratories, 102

Seaborg, Glenn, 96
The Secretariat, 251, 259
Segre, Emilio, 96
self-determination, 14, 76, 184
self-injuring syndrome, 80
Settlement of disputes, 221, 233, 259
Shute, Nevil, 182
signatories, Meeting of, 248, 262
Signature, 234
Six Day War of 1967, 54
small modular reactors (SMR), 175
South Africa, 15, 27, 56–57, 74–75, 162, 183, 185
South China Sea, 33, 46
Soviet explosion, 35
Soviet/Russian, 152, 170
Soviet Socialist Republics, 207–209, 217
Soviet Union/Russia, 15, 23–30, 34–37, 150, 190, 200, 206, 219, 236–237, 241–242
Soviet Union/Russia Nuclear Arms Control Agreements, 200, 236
Special inspections, 254–255
stabilization of East Asia, 138
Stalin, Joseph, 35
Stanley, Anna, 198
START I, 153–154, 237, 239–241
START III Framework, 238
States Parties, Meeting of, 228–234
Stimson, Henry L, 118
Stockholm Initiative for Nuclear Disarmament (SIND), 185–186
Strangelove, Dr, 14, 152, 183
Strassman, Fritz, 87, 109, 203

271

Strategic Arms Limitation Talks (SALT), 153, 236–237, 240
Strategic Arms Reduction Treaty (START), 16, 19, 21, 34, 63, 79, 152–154, 187, 192, 234, 236–241
Strategic Nuclear Arms Control Agreements, 153, 240
Strategic Offensive Reductions Treaty (SORT), 70, 142, 154, 238–240
submarine launched ballistic missile (SLBM), 45, 153, 162, 169–170, 236, 239–240
Suez crisis, 188
Suez war of 1956, 54
Sullivan, Jake, 79
Suzuki, Kantaro, 134
Symptoms of ARS, 133
　bleeding, 133
　confusion, 133
　dehydration, 133
　infections, 133
　loss of appetite, 133
　nausea, 133
　vomiting, 133
Syria, 29–30, 51, 58, 61, 63–66
Szilard, Leo, 19, 88, 92–93, 120

T

Taiwan, 17, 25, 44, 46–47, 52, 74–75, 140, 175, 195
Tannenwald, Nina, 26
Teller, Edward, 36, 88, 95 territory, definition of, 247
Test-Ban Treaty, 172, 182, 220
Three Mile Island, 177
Threshold Test Ban Treaty (TTBT), 219
Tibbets, Paul, 122–123, 128
Tinian Island, 116, 161
Tizard Mission, 98
Toyoda, Soemu, 126, 134
Transitional Article, 263
Treaty on the Prohibition of Nuclear Weapons (TPNW), 16–17, 62, 75, 183–184, 186, 195, 200, 222
Treaty Banning Nuclear Weapons Testing, 200
the Treaty, Summary of
　Annex 1, 220
　Annex 2, 220–221
　Protocol Part I, 220
　Protocol Part II, 220
　Protocol Part III, 220
Treaty, violation of the, 258
Truman, Harry, 143
Truman, President, 23, 25, 113, 135, 140, 144
Trump, President, 33, 189, 191, 193
Tsar Bomba, 36
Tube Alloy, 20–21, 41, 98–99, 205
Turkmenistan, 154, 163, 241
Tuwaitha Nuclear Research Centre, 63
2018 Nuclear Posture Review (NPR), 32–33
2001 attacks, 30

U

Ukraine, 16, 154–155, 159, 163, 174, 177, 182–183

Umezu, Yoshijiro, 134
United Arab Emirates, 61, 73, 189
United Kingdom, 15, 17, 162–165, 205–209, 217, 222
United Kingdom's first nuclear test explosion, 38
United Nations Trust Territory, 117
United States, 14–22, 24–30, 117–118, 122, 142, 144–148
universal bereavement, 18, 26, 87
Universality, 83, 234, 246
Uranium and Enriched Uranium U-235, 205
Urchin, 111
Uzbekistan, 154, 163, 241

V

Van Kirk, Theodore, 124
Victim assistance, 230–231

W

Wallace, Henry A, 95
Walton, Ernest, 85
Western Australia, 38–39, 108, 188
Wigner, Eugene, 88, 92
Windscale, 177
withdrawal, 48, 189, 209, 218, 235, 238
Witness Whereof, 209, 218
World War I, 141
World War II, 14, 17–18, 79, 84, 103, 121, 141, 145, 165, 179, 182, 196, 202

Z

Zangger Committee, 17, 148–149, 196
Zaporizhzhia, 77–78
Zedong, Mao, 24
zone of alienation, 178

Biographical Note

Gar Pardy was born in Bishop's Falls, Newfoundland and Labrador, on November 10, 1939. He was educated first in Norris Arm on the edge of the North Atlantic and then in Gander in the days immediately after the ending of the war. Gar worked with the Meteorological Service of Canada in Gander, Goose Bay and Frobisher Bay, now Iqaluit in Nunavut. The latter two were, at the time, bases for the Strategic Air Command of the United States. After graduating from Acadia and MacMaster universities, Gar became a member of Canada's Foreign Service in 1967. During his career, Gar held assignments in India; Kenya; Washington, D.C.; Costa Rica; El Salvador; Honduras; Nicaragua; and Panama, where he was ambassador. These experiences contributed to a keen and continuing interest in and understanding of world affairs and cultures. He retired in 2003 and continues to write on international and domestic affairs from Ottawa. He is married to author Laurel Balsor Pardy.

www.ingramcontent.com/pod-product-compliance
Lightning Source LLC
Chambersburg PA
CBHW070648120526
44590CB00013BA/872